STOP THE
NEXT WAR
NOW

P9-DDR-092

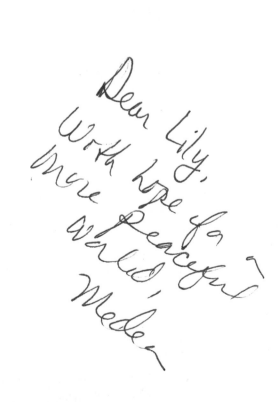

Dear Lily,
With hope for a
more peaceful
world,
Medea

STOP THE
NEXT WAR
NOW

EFFECTIVE RESPONSES
TO VIOLENCE AND TERRORISM

Edited by

Medea Benjamin and **Jodie Evans**

Inner Ocean Publishing, Inc.
Maui, Hawai'i • San Francisco, California

Inner Ocean Publishing, Inc.
P.O. Box 1239
Makawao, Maui, HI 96768-1239
www.innerocean.com

© 2005 by Medea Benjamin and Jodie Evans
All rights reserved. No part of this book may be reproduced by any means or in any form
whatsoever without written permission from the publisher.

Cover design by Innosanto Nagara/Design Action Collective
Book design by Maxine Ressler

PUBLISHER CATALOGING-IN-PUBLICATION DATA
    Stop the next war now / edited by Medea Benjamin and Jodie Evans. — 1st ed. —
    Makawao, HI : Inner Ocean, 2005.
        p. ; cm.
        Includes essays, photography, letters, questions and answers, and resources
            on the peace movement.
        ISBN: 1-930722-49-4
        1. Peace movements. 2. World politics. 3. Pacifism. I. Benjamin, Medea, 1952–
    II. Evans, Jodie.
JZ5574 .S76 2005
303.6/6—dc22   0505

Printed in the United States of America on recycled paper

05 06 07 08 09 10 DATA 10 9 8 7 6 5 4 3 2 1

_____

DISTRIBUTED BY PUBLISHER'S GROUP WEST

For information on promotions, bulk purchases, premiums, or educational use, please
contact: 866.731.2216 or sales@innerocean.com.

Dedicated to all the peacemakers of the world

CONTENTS

PART II: A CHALLENGE TO THE SUPPORT STRUCTURE OF WAR AND VIOLENCE

FOREWORD:
TO BE LED BY HAPPINESS

ALICE WALKER

Not buying
War
Grief remains
Unsold.

It started with Einstein. I had written a poem about his hair. It wasn't just about his hair: I was thinking about his statement that World War III might be fought with nuclear weapons but World War IV would be fought with sticks and stones. I was walking down a gray, chilly street near my home in Berkeley, thinking about the sadness of his eyes, the sadness of our situation: about to invade and massively bomb Iraq, a country inhabited by old people, orphans, women and children. Boys and men. The children, half the country's population, under fifteen years of age. I was thinking about my impending journey to Washington, D.C., to join a demonstration against the war; a city whose streets, during slavery, were laid out by Benjamin Bennaker, a free African American (father African, mother Irish African) tobacco planter from Maryland. I thought of the ancestors who, enslaved, built (eyes lowered, muscles straining) the imposing symbols of freedom in Washington, including the White House.

Though I did want to join the women of CODEPINK who had been holding a vigil in front of the White House for four months, dressed in pink to signify the feminine concern for the safety, especially, of children, I was dreading the long lines at the airport, and the flight. I stopped at a light, thinking of how our experience now at airports, being searched and sometimes seized, bears a resemblance worth scrutinizing to what Palestinians, attempting to enter and leave their Israeli-restricted areas, go through. Reflecting on this I rested my hand on a telephone pole before rather wearily crossing the street. A piece of paper near my hand fluttered in the wind. There, just above my head, was another famous quotation from Einstein someone had stapled to the pole: "The problems we face today cannot be solved by the minds that created them."

It was a pretty grim message, perhaps grimmer than the earlier one; still, I found myself beginning to smile. Here he was: an ancestor who knew, and said out loud, that if we keep going in the direction we're headed, the jig is up. By the time I reached the other side of the street I was thinking, "Whose mind has not been heard at all on this question?" The Mind of the Grandmothers of the World. But that's another story.

Ten thousand women dressed in hot pink, cool pink, all shades of pink, marched and rallied in Washington to celebrate March 8, International Women's Day 2003. There were rousing speeches; there was music and dance. Enormous and magical puppets. There was laughter and solemnity. The march was led by several rows of small children chanting, "One Two Three Four, We Don't Want Your Crummy War. Five Six Seven Eight, We Will Not Participate." They were followed by writers and artists and activists, including Rachel Bagby, Medea Benjamin, Susan Griffin, Maxine Hong Kingston, Nina Utne, Terry Tempest Williams, and me. Behind us the sea of pink stretched as far as the eye could see.

At the edge of Lafayette Park, across from the White House, we paused. We chose twenty-five of us to enter the park (the number of demonstrators that had been allowed to enter the park for months before) only to find we were denied admittance. After a brief huddle, squatting at the knees of a line of police, we moved past the barricade. We were arrested several hours later, having sung "Peace Salaam Shalom" and "All We Are Saying . . ." the entire time. And it is of that time, those several hours because it took a long time to be arrested, put in holding cells, and then booked, that I wish to speak.

I had been arrested before. While protesting apartheid in South Africa; while attempting to block the shipment of weapons, by train, to Central America. Those were serious times too, but this time felt different. This time felt like: All the information is in. If our species does not outgrow its tendency to fight wars, we can kiss all we have created, and ourselves, good-bye. To bring children into the world at all, given the state of things, seems not only self-indulgent but cruel. And it was of the children I thought, partly because there, right across from us, as we sang in front of the White House, were huge photographs of dismembered fetuses held by an antiabortion group whose leader began to harangue us through a bullhorn. He called us traitors and murderers and accused us of nagging.

Nagging. "What century is he from?" I asked myself. That he could not make the connection between the gruesomely dismembered bodies in his photographs and those of children bombed in Iraq seemed unbelievable to all of us. As he shouted at us we sang, "Protect the women and the children of Iraq," until eventually, scowling and looking extremely churlish, he left.

Standing between my Irish American sister (Susan Griffin) and my Chinese American one (Maxine Hong Kingston), and with twenty-two other courageous women all around us—as Amy Goodman of *Democracy Now!* interviewed us for our communities across the world, and Kristin Michaels made a videotape—I felt the sweetest of all feelings: peace. The police began to gather their horses, their paddy wagons, their plastic handcuffs. We sang. Being women, we noticed and made much of the fact that a rainbow appeared suddenly in the sky.

Amy (who within minutes would be arrested herself) asked each of us how we felt about being arrested. Maxine said she felt it was the least she could do. I said I felt happier than I'd felt in years. Susan said her happiness went beyond happiness to joy. None of us could live with ourselves if we sat by and did nothing while a country filled with children, a lot of them disabled, homeless, hungry, was blown to bits using money we need in the United States to build hospitals, housing, and schools.

The arrest went smoothly. I thought the police were considerate, humane. Some of us tried to help them do their job by sticking our arms out in front of us, but the handcuffs go behind, not in front. We sang in the paddy wagons, we sang later in the holding cells. We recited poetry to each other and told stories from our lives. And all the while, there was this sweetness. Even though the floor of the cell was cold, where some of us had to sit, and even though the toilet wouldn't flush. I found Fannie Lou Hamer's voice coming out of my throat and led our cell in singing "This Little Light of Mine."

I realized that at the root of the peace cradling me were not only Einstein and other ancestors who told us the truth, but especially Martin Luther King. I had followed him faithfully since I was in my teens; his fearless, persistent struggle against injustice mesmerized me. Perfect love casts out fear. That is what he had. And that is, ultimately, what the sea of pink symbolized. We were women and children who loved ourselves in the form of Iraqi women and children because we knew that to love ourselves as humans means to love ourselves as all humans. We understood that whatever we did to stop war, we did it not for the "other" but for a collective us.

The heart enjoys experiencing the liberating feeling of compassion; it actually expands and glows, as if beaming its own sun upon the world. That is the warmth our cooling emotional world so desperately needs to preserve its humanity. It is this savoring of the ecstatic nature of impersonal love that lets the peacemakers of the world do our job. It is this love whose inevitable companion is not only peace, but happiness and, as Susan said, joy.

Author's note: I wrote this essay as a thank-you to Medea Benjamin, who asked if I would write an op-ed piece about a CODEPINK-led protest on March 8, 2003. It was submitted to numerous newspapers, including the *New York Times*, but it was never published until now.

PREFACE

CODEPINK started around a picnic table when a group of wild, passionate, and peace-loving women began laughing uncontrollably at George Bush's color-coded security system—code yellow, code orange, code red. We knew that the terrorist attack of 9/11 was no laughing matter. Many of us had had friends killed in the attack. But the government's advice to buy duct tape and plastic sheeting in the event of a code orange alert had us in stitches. Should we put the duct tape over our mouths or the mouths of the terrorists? And who gets wrapped in plastic sheeting—us or them?

When the laughter subsided, we grew somber. We agreed that the terrorist attack of 9/11 should be treated as a crime against humanity, not a call for war. We grieved over the innocent Afghans killed in the post-9/11 invasion. We talked with dread about a possible war in Iraq. And then we started dreaming and scheming about what we, as women, could do to stop the spiral of violence.

Gentle Nina Utne from *Utne* magazine imagined thousands of circles of ordinary women gathering around kitchen tables, defining for themselves what real security meant. Radical Texas fisherwoman Diane Wilson saw anarchic clusters of unreasonable women hurling their naked bodies into the war machine. Medea envisioned a global uprising of women—Americans and Saudis, Muslims and Jews—linking arms and demanding that men stop the killing. Visionary astrologer Caroline Casey imagined a gathering of wise women calling for a code hot pink alert to save the earth. Jodie, picking up on the pink, dreamed of a pink tent city outside the White House, with women singing and dancing and growing so powerful that George Bush could no longer take us to war.

The imagination and creativity of many women, woven together, became CODEPINK: Women for Peace. Determined to stop the invasion of Iraq, we threw our hearts and souls into that effort. We held a four-month peace vigil outside the White House during the coldest winter in Washington in many years; we organized massive rallies; we staged sit-ins in congressional offices and "wake-up calls" at their homes; we lobbied members of the UN Security Council. We draped forty-foot pink slips (in the shape of women's lingerie) off rooftops to call for the firing of the armchair warriors. We brought pink badges of courage to the lonely truth tellers who advocated peace. And in February 2003, before the invasion was a certainty, we organized a fifteen-person delegation to Iraq.

Our experience in Iraq was overwhelming. We found intelligent, gracious, hospitable people eager to invite us into their homes to share their food, their lives, their dreams, and their fears. While the U.S. press was churning out stories about the Iraqi threat, we saw a regime economically and militarily crippled by sanctions and a people terrified by the most powerful country in the world—our own.

On one of our last nights in Baghdad, secretary of state Colin Powell addressed the United Nations. We were at the Ministry of Information in a room packed with journalists from around the world. Many of them had been in Iraq for months, closely following the efforts of the weapons inspectors. They scoffed at Powell's unsubstantiated claims about Iraq's weapons. "With such thin evidence," a BBC reporter reassured us, "the U.S. can't possibly go to war." We went to bed relieved.

The next morning we awoke to the news that after Powell's speech, George Bush had addressed the nation. He said Saddam Hussein posed a danger that "reaches across the world" and that it was time to take action. "The game is over," he declared. Everyone in Iraq knew exactly what that meant: war.

The woman taking care of our room buried her head in our chests, crying, and then looked to the sky. "How do I protect my children?" she asked. As we walked to the hotel lobby, the fear was palpable. The workers were grimly taping up the windows. Outside we heard the soldering of metal as other workers installed a generator. In the markets, people were stocking up on supplies.

Jodie began to sob, her head swimming with thoughts of bombs falling on these people we had come to love. "Nothing we've done has worked. What do we do now?" Jodie asked. "We expose the truth to the American public," Medea replied, "and we build a movement capable of stopping the next war."

That's how we kept going, 24/7, through the insanity of the war and the occupation of Iraq. The educating and organizing and mobilizing are weaving a network strong enough to stop the next war. We caught a glimpse of that network on February 15, 2003, when an estimated twelve million people poured into the streets of more than six hundred cities and small towns, from the United States to Brazil, from South Africa to Moscow. For one shining moment, the liberal and the conservative, the religious and the agnostic, the young and the old, raised their voices together to declare: The World Says No to War.

The Bush administration ignored what the *New York Times* called the second superpower—world opinion—and the 2004 presidential election marked another setback to the global call for peace. But in our efforts to prevent war and defeat Bush, we initiated a new era of civic engagement on a scale never seen before. People began to feel part of a massive, powerful, and profound movement. Rather than succumb to despair at our failure to stop the war machine or overthrow the administration that so callously took us to war, now is the time to absorb the lessons learned, gather new insights, refortify ourselves, and move forward.

This book is our attempt to do just that. In it, you will find an amazing bouquet of voices—activists, journalists, soldiers, scholars, elected officials. Part 1, "A Passion for Peace," starts with the self, the singular voice of dissent, and continues from there to contemplate the humanity we share with others and the movement we must build and the culture we must shape to reflect peace.

Barbara Ehrenreich suggests supporting feminism as a strategy to counter fundamentalist terrorism, while playwright-actress Eve Ensler extols the "vagina warriors" for pioneering a paradigm that is not about conquering but collaborating, not about invading but inviting. Lifelong activist Leslie Cagan offers firsthand insights into building an effective peace movement. And writers such as Nobel Prize winner Shirin Ebadi offer insights from a global perspective.

In part 2, "A Challenge to the Support Structure of War and Violence," the essayists examine the constructs that keep us in a perpetual warlike state of mind and economy—these include the media, our use of natural resources, the way we elect our leaders, and the weapons we build—and explore how we can reshape a world based on a peaceful community model. Veteran reporter Helen Thomas reflects on how we might transform the media so that they truly educate the public. U.S. representative Cynthia McKinney paints our movement as a continuum in the successful battles our ancestors waged to free the slaves and gain women's rights. Nobel laureate Jody Williams lays out the components of a successful international campaign. Arianna Huffington offers ideas for overcoming our nation's addiction to oil. And inspiring us for the long road ahead, muralist Juana Alicia encourages us to bring art and beauty into our peace work.

While most of our authors are from the United States, since we are primarily focusing on violence inflicted on and by our nation, you will also hear peacemakers from Colombia, Ireland, Iran, Israel, Pakistan, Palestine, Serbia, Sri

Lanka, and Uganda. What comes across so strikingly in their reflections is the need to humanize "the other," to reach out to "the enemy," to find common ground.

That is a lesson we learned from an Iraqi border guard during the regime of Saddam Hussein. When our group was passing through customs at the Jordanian-Iraqi border, a guard took Medea's passport and looked at her last name. "Benjamin," he muttered. "Isn't that Jewish?" Medea turned ashen, knowing the enmity between Iraq and Israel. The guard kept her passport and disappeared, leaving Medea to conjure up thoughts of being kidnapped and beheaded by Saddam's henchmen.

A half hour later he returned, huffing and puffing. "Here," he said, putting a dog-eared notebook in her hand. "I've been teaching myself Hebrew and I just ran home to get my notebook. I'd appreciate it if you'd check my grammar." Relieved and amazed, we asked why he was studying Hebrew. "During the war with Iran, I taught myself Farsi and now that Jews and Muslims are at war, I've been teaching myself Hebrew. We should learn to communicate with those we are taught to see as enemies," he said, smiling.

It is, indeed, our responsibility as global citizens to learn to communicate with those we are taught to see as enemies. For it is only when we understand each other, love each other, and think of every man and woman as our brother and sister that we will finally be on our way to ending war.

—MEDEA BENJAMIN AND JODIE EVANS

INTRODUCTION

ARUNDHATI ROY

In January 2003, thousands of us from across the world gathered in Porto Alegre in Brazil and declared—reiterated—that "Another World Is Possible." A few thousand miles north, in Washington, George W. Bush and his aides were thinking the same thing.

Our project was the World Social Forum. Theirs—to further what many call the Project for the New American Century.

In the great cities of Europe and America, where a few years ago these things would only have been whispered, now people are openly talking about the good side of imperialism and the need for a strong empire to police an unruly world. The new missionaries want order at the cost of justice. Discipline at the cost of dignity. And ascendancy at any price. Occasionally some of us are invited to "debate" the issue on "neutral" platforms provided by the corporate media. Debating imperialism is a bit like debating the pros and cons of rape. What can we say? That we really miss it?

In any case, New Imperialism is already upon us. It's a remodeled, streamlined version of what we once knew. For the first time in history, a single empire with an arsenal of weapons that could obliterate the world in an afternoon has complete, unipolar, economic and military hegemony. It uses different weapons to break open different markets. There isn't a country on God's earth that is not caught in the crosshairs of the American cruise missile and the IMF checkbook. Argentina's the model if you want to be the poster boy of neoliberal capitalism, Iraq if you're the black sheep.

Poor countries that are geopolitically of strategic value to the empire, or that have a "market" of any size, or infrastructure that can be privatized, or, God forbid, natural resources of value—oil, gold, diamonds, cobalt, coal— must do as they're told, or become military targets. Those with the greatest reserves of natural wealth are most at risk. Unless they surrender their resources willingly to the corporate machine, civil unrest will be fomented, or war will be waged. In this new Age of Empire, when nothing is as it appears to be, executives of concerned companies are allowed to influence foreign-policy decisions. The Center for Public Integrity in Washington found that nine out of the thirty members of the Defense Policy Board of the U.S. government were connected to companies that were awarded defense contracts for $76 billion between 2001 and 2002. George Shultz, former U.S. secretary of state, was chairman of the Committee for the Liberation of Iraq. He is also on the board of directors of the Bechtel Group. When asked about a conflict of interest in the case of a war in Iraq, he said, "I don't know that Bechtel would particularly benefit from it. But if there's work to be done, Bechtel is the type of company that could do it. But nobody looks at it as something you benefit from." After the war, Bechtel signed a $680 million contract for reconstruction in Iraq.

This brutal blueprint has been used over and over again, across Latin America, Africa, and Central and Southeast Asia. It has cost millions of lives. It goes without saying that every war the empire wages becomes a Just War. This, in large part, is due to the role of the corporate media. It's important to understand that the corporate media doesn't just support the neoliberal project. It *is* the neoliberal project. This is not a moral position it has chosen to take; it's structural. It's intrinsic to the economics of how the mass media works.

Most nations have adequately hideous family secrets. So it isn't often necessary for the media to lie. It's what's emphasized and what's ignored. Say, for example, India was chosen as the target for a righteous war. The fact that about 80,000 people have been killed in Kashmir since 1989, most of them Muslim, most of them by Indian security forces (making the average death toll about 6,000 a year); the fact that in March 2003, more than 2,000 Muslims were murdered on the streets of Gujarat, that women were gang-raped and children were burned alive and 150,000 people driven from their homes while the police and administration watched, and sometimes actively participated; the fact that no one has been punished for these crimes and the government that oversaw them was reelected—all of this would make perfect headlines in international newspapers in the run-up to war.

Next we know, our cities will be leveled by cruise missiles, our villages fenced in with razor wire; U.S. soldiers will patrol our streets, and Narendra Modi, Pravin Togadia, or any of our other popular bigots could, like Saddam Hussein, be in U.S. custody, having their hair checked for lice and the fillings in their teeth examined on prime-time TV.

But as long as our "markets" are open, as long as corporations like Enron, Bechtel, Halliburton, Arthur Andersen are given a free hand, our "democratically elected" leaders can fearlessly blur the lines between democracy, majoritarianism, and fascism.

No individual nation can stand up to the project of Corporate Globalization on its own. Time and again we have seen that when it comes to the neoliberal project, the heroes of our time are suddenly diminished. Extraordinary, charismatic men, giants in opposition, when they seize power and become heads of state, become powerless on the global stage. I'm thinking here of President Lula of Brazil. Lula was the hero of the World Social Forum last year. This year he's busy implementing IMF guidelines, reducing pension benefits, and purging radicals from the Workers' Party. I'm thinking also of the former president of South Africa, Nelson Mandela. Within two years of taking office in 1994, his government genuflected with hardly a caveat to the Market God. It instituted a massive program of privatization and structural adjustment, which has left millions of people homeless, jobless, and without water and electricity.

Why does this happen? There's little point in beating our breasts and feeling betrayed. Lula and Mandela are, by any reckoning, magnificent men. But the moment they cross the floor from the Opposition into Government they become hostage to a spectrum of threats—most malevolent among them the threat of capital flight, which can destroy any government overnight. To imagine that a leader's personal charisma and a CV of struggle will dent the corporate cartel is to have no understanding of how capitalism works, or for that matter, how power works. Radical change will not be negotiated by governments; it can only be enforced by people.

It was wonderful that on February 15 last year, in a spectacular display of public morality, ten million people in five continents marched against the war on Iraq. It was wonderful, but it was not enough. February 15 was a weekend. Nobody had to so much as miss a day of work. Holiday protests don't stop wars. George W. Bush knows that. The confidence with which he disregarded overwhelming public opinion should be a lesson to us all. Bush believes that Iraq can be occupied and colonized—as Afghanistan has been, as Tibet has been, as Chechnya is being, as East Timor once was and Palestine still is. He thinks that all he has to do is hunker down and wait until a crisis-driven media, having picked this crisis to the bone, drops it and moves on. Soon the carcass will slip off the bestseller charts, and all of us outraged folks will lose interest. Or so he hopes.

So if we are against imperialism, shall we agree that we are against the U.S. occupation and that we believe that the United States must withdraw from Iraq and pay reparations to the Iraqi people for the damage that the war has inflicted?

How do we begin to mount our resistance? Let's start with something really small. The issue is not about *supporting* the resistance in Iraq against the occupation or discussing who exactly constitutes the resistance. (Are they old killer Ba'athists? Are they Islamic fundamentalists?)

We have to *become* the global resistance to the occupation.

Our resistance has to begin with a refusal to accept the legitimacy of the U.S. occupation of Iraq. It means acting to make it materially impossible for the empire to achieve its aims. It means soldiers should refuse to fight, reservists should refuse to serve, workers should refuse to load ships and aircraft with weapons. It certainly means that in countries like India and Pakistan we must block the U.S. government's plans to have Indian and Pakistani soldiers sent to Iraq to clean up after it.

The Project for the New American Century seeks to perpetuate inequity and establish American hegemony at any price, even if it's apocalyptic. The World Social Forum demands justice and survival.

For these reasons, we must consider ourselves at war.

Note: This piece is an excerpt of a speech delivered at the World Social Forum in Mumbai, India, January 16, 2004, and published as "Do Turkeys Enjoy Thanksgiving?" in Arundhati Roy's *An Ordinary Person's Guide to Empire.*

PART I:

A PASSION FOR PEACE

Chapter 1

IT STARTS WITH WITH **ONE VOICE**

REGAINING MY **HUMANITY**

CAMILO MEJIA

Camilo Mejia was the first American veteran of the Iraq war to publicly refuse further service in Iraq. His application for discharge as a conscientious objector was rejected by the military. He was found guilty of desertion and was sentenced to a one-year prison term in Fort Sill, Oklahoma. He was released February 15, 2005.

I was deployed to Iraq in April 2003 and returned home for a two-week leave in October. Going home gave me the opportunity to put my thoughts in order and to listen to what my conscience had to say. People would ask me about my war experiences, and answering them took me back to all the horrors—the firefights, the ambushes, the time I saw a young Iraqi dragged by his shoulders through a pool of his own blood, or an innocent man decapitated by our machine-gun fire. The time I saw a soldier broken down inside because he had killed a child, or an old man on his knees, crying with his arms raised to the sky, perhaps asking God why we had taken his son's life.

I thought of the suffering of a people whose country was in ruins and who were further humiliated by the raids and curfews of an occupying army.

And I realized that none of the reasons we were given about why we were in Iraq turned out to be true. There were no weapons of mass destruction. There was no link between Saddam Hussein and Al-Qaeda. We weren't helping the Iraqi people, and the Iraqi people didn't want us there. We weren't preventing terrorism or making Americans safer. I couldn't find one reason for my having been in Iraq, for having shot at people and having been shot at.

Coming home gave me the clarity to see the line between military duty and moral obligation. I realized that I was part of a war that I believed was immoral and criminal, a war of aggression, a war of imperial domination. I realized that acting on my principles was incompatible with my role in the military, and I decided that I could not return to Iraq.

By putting my weapon down, I chose to reassert myself as a human being. I have not deserted the military or been disloyal to the men and women of the military. I have not been disloyal to a country. I have only been loyal to my principles.

When I turned myself in, with all my fears and doubts, I did it not only for myself. I did it for the people of Iraq, even for those who fired upon me— they were just on the other side of a battleground where war itself was the only enemy. I did it for the Iraqi children, who are victims of mines and depleted uranium. I did it for the thousands of unknown civilians killed in war. My time in prison is a small price compared with the price paid by Iraqis and Americans who have given their lives. Mine is a small price compared with the price humanity has paid for war.

Many have called me a coward, while others have called me a hero. I believe I can be found somewhere in the middle. To those who have called me a hero, I say that I don't believe in heroes, but that ordinary people can do extraordinary things. To those who have called me a coward, I say that they arc wrong but that without knowing it, they are also right. They are wrong when they think that I left the war for fear of being killed. I admit that fear was there, but there was also the fear of killing innocent people; the fear of putting myself in a position where to survive means to kill; the fear of losing my soul in the process of saving my body; the fear of abandoning my daughter, the people who love me, the man I used to be, and the man I wanted to be. I was afraid of waking up one morning to realize my humanity had abandoned me.

I say without any pride that I did my job as a soldier. I commanded an infantry squad in combat, and we never failed to accomplish our mission. But those who call me a coward are also right. I was a coward, not for leaving the war, but for having been a part of it in the first place. Resisting this war was my moral duty, a moral duty that called me to take a principled action. I failed to fulfill my moral duty as a human being, and instead I chose to fulfill my duty as a soldier. All because I was afraid. I was terrified. I did not want to stand up to the government and the army; I feared punishment and humiliation. I went to war because at that moment I was a coward, and I apologize to my soldiers for not being the type of leader I should have been.

I also apologize to the Iraqi people. To them, I say I am sorry for the curfews, for the raids, for the killings. May they find it in their hearts to forgive me.

One of the reasons I did not refuse the war from the beginning was that I was afraid of losing my freedom. Today, as I sit behind bars, I realize that there are many types of freedom, and that in spite of my confinement I remain free in many important ways. What good is freedom if we are afraid to follow our conscience? What good is freedom if we are not able to live with our own actions? I am confined to a prison, but I feel, today more than ever, connected to all humanity. Behind these bars I sit a free man because I listened to a higher power, the voice of my conscience.

During my confinement, I've come across a poem written by a man who refused and resisted the government of Nazi Germany. For doing so he was executed. His name was Albrecht Haushofer, and he wrote the following poem as he awaited execution.

GUILT

The burden of my guilt before the law
weighs light upon my shoulders; to plot
and to conspire was my duty to the people;
I would have been a criminal had I not.

I am guilty, though not the way you think,
I should have done my duty sooner, I was wrong,
I should have called evil more clearly by its name
I hesitated to condemn it for far too long.

I now accuse myself within my heart:
I have betrayed my conscience far too long
I have deceived myself and fellow man.

I knew the course of evil from the start
My warning was not loud nor clear enough!
Today I know what I was guilty of . . .

To those who are still quiet, to those who continue to betray their consciences, to those who are not calling evil more clearly by its name, to those of us who are still not doing enough to refuse and resist, I say, "Come forward." I say, "Free your minds."

Let us, collectively, free our minds, soften our hearts, comfort the wounded, put down our weapons, and reassert ourselves as human beings by putting an end to war.

BREAKING THE
CODE OF SILENCE

NANCY LESSIN

Nancy Lessin is a cofounder of Military Families Speak Out, an organization of over two thousand families who oppose the U.S.-led invasion and occupation of Iraq. Nancy's stepson Joe served with the marines in Iraq in spring 2003.

In the U.S. military there is a code of silence that extends to the families of servicemen and servicewomen and beyond. The troops must obey the Uniform Code of Military Justice, the congressional code of military criminal law that, in part, puts limits on free speech. Soldiers can be punished, for example, if they engage in speech or conduct that is "to the prejudice of good order and discipline in the armed forces, or conduct of a nature to bring discredit upon the armed forces." The Supreme Court has often reinforced the limits on service members' rights to free speech. And the court of public opinion has been harsher: many in the United States—both within and outside the military—believe that speaking out against actions taken by the military is a betrayal of the troops, especially in times of war.

Civilian families of service members are just that—civilians who are legally free to criticize the government and the military. But the vast majority of military families have never spoken out, even when they have strongly disagreed with decisions that affect their loved ones. An unwritten policy as strong as any force of law keeps them silent—much as it keeps the rest of the nation silent too. In the fall of 2002, my family decided to break that code of silence.

My stepson Joe, a marine, was deployed with the Twenty-fourth Marine Expeditionary Unit in August 2002. He was headed for Kosovo. He told us he would be ending up in Iraq, and indeed he did. In September 2002, when the drumbeats for war were getting deafening, my husband, Charley Richardson, and I saw no good reason for the United States to be invading Iraq. We weren't convinced that mystery weapons of mass destruction, supposedly hidden somewhere in Iraq, were imminent threats to the United States. We saw no links between Saddam Hussein and Al-Qaeda. We didn't see how invading Iraq would address the terrible tragedy of 9/11 or solve the problem of terrorism. In fact, we believed that if the United States invaded Iraq, we were likely to see more, not less, terrorism.

We saw that all those who were saying, "We've got to go to war!" weren't going anywhere. Nor were their loved ones. It was our loved ones who would be used as cannon fodder. We made our first poster in September 2002. It had Joe's picture on it, and it said, "Our son is a Marine. Don't send him to war for oil."

At an antiwar demonstration in Washington, D.C., in October 2002, we met Jeffrey McKenzie, a father whose son would be deployed in January. The next month, Jeff's family and ours formed an organization called Military Families Speak Out (www.mfso.org). We wanted to break the code of silence, to use our special need to speak out—and the special voice with which we speak—to prevent an invasion of Iraq.

Through word of mouth, and via the Internet, MFSO began to grow. We met with members of Congress. We wrote letters to George W. Bush and to editors of our local papers. We participated in vigils and antiwar marches.

On March 27, 2003, Fernando Suarez del Solar lost his son Jesus, who stepped on a U.S. cluster bomb while fighting in Iraq. Since then, Jesus's father has been traveling around the country speaking out against the invasion and occupation of Iraq. Here he is in New York City's Union Square in September 2004. See www.guerreroazteca.org for more information. © Fred Askew

We spoke at teach-ins at community centers, universities, union halls, and churches. A group of fifteen parents of soldiers and marines, my husband and I included, brought a lawsuit against President Bush and secretary of defense Donald Rumsfeld, seeking to prevent an invasion of Iraq without a congressional declaration of war.

Despite our efforts and those of the global antiwar community, on the night of March 19, 2003, the "shock and awe" bombing of Iraq began. Within two weeks, MFSO had doubled its membership, and four hundred military families were fighting to end a war that we'd hoped would never happen. We spoke about low morale among the troops, about the lack of adequate equipment, about suicide attempts and psychological trauma. We called attention to the toll of this war, a toll the Bush administration was trying hard to hide. Families who had suffered the ultimate tragedy—the deaths of their loved ones—began joining our group; their powerful voices moved all who would listen.

In July 2003, from his well-guarded room in the White House, President Bush responded to a reporter's question about the armed Iraqi resistance by saying, "Bring 'em on!" Outraged by this statement, MFSO, together with Veterans for Peace, Vietnam Veterans Against the War, and several other groups, began a campaign of our own. While George Bush was saying, "Bring 'em on," we said, "Bring them home! NOW!" The Bring Them Home Now campaign (www.bringthemhomenow.org), launched at press conferences in Washington, D.C., and Fayetteville, North Carolina, reached out to troops in Iraq, to families and veterans, to politicians, and to peace activists across the United States and around the world. Our message created an important dialogue. While many Americans, including many who were against the war, cautioned that withdrawing U.S. troops would promote chaos in Iraq, we've maintained that chaos is now the order of the day in Iraq, chaos that the U.S. military occupation is perpetuating and worsening.

As their loved ones return from Iraq, more and more families must welcome back haggard, hollow-eyed strangers. Kevin and Joyce Lucey's son Jeffrey served in the marine reserves in the battle of Nasariyah in the spring of 2003. He came home broken, but the full extent of the psychological damage didn't really manifest itself until six months after he returned. Jeffrey spoke of being a killer, a murderer. He wore the dog tags of two unarmed Iraqi soldiers whose lives he took under orders from his command. He wore the tags to remember and honor them. He began drinking heavily and was briefly committed to a Veterans Administration hospital, but was released four days later. On June 22, 2004, this young marine went into the cellar of his parents' home in western Massachusetts and hanged himself.

Our hearts cry out for Jeffrey and for all who were killed on the battlefield or in its cross fire—both our troops and the people of Iraq—and for the many more who will die in their souls because of what they saw or did in this war. By the end of 2004, two years after its founding, MFSO included almost two thousand military families. We are of African, Latino, Asian, Arab, American Indian, European descent. We are the parents, spouses, brothers, sisters, aunts, uncles, grandparents, cousins, fiancés, and partners of service members. We are families who opposed this war from the beginning and families who supported the invasion of Iraq, only to find out that it was a war based on lies. We are Democrats, Republicans, Independents, and people who never before voted.

Together we challenge the powers that be—the military, the Bush administration, and Congress—to face the same truths that we military families hear from loved ones on a daily basis, about the lack of protective equipment and the shortage of armored Humvees. We expose painful and personal stories of loved ones who have been diagnosed with severe post-traumatic stress disorder yet are declared "fit for duty" and redeployed to the front; of loved ones kept in Iraq despite severe physical or psychological problems. We expose the lack of care that many of our troops receive when they do come home. And we emphasize that all these failures are taking place within the biggest failure of all—the fact that our troops were taken into a war based on lies; an illegal, immoral wa; a war that should never have happened.

Never before have so many military families broken the code of silence and spoken out to support the troops and end a war. Together with Veterans for Peace, Vietnam Veterans Against the War, and the new Iraq Veterans Against the War, we say:

> Not one more day!
> Not one more dime!
> Not one more life!
> Not one more lie!
>
> End the occupation!
> Bring the troops home now!
> And take care of them when they get here!

FROM CINDY TO GEORGE

Angered that her son, Casey Sheehan, was sent to fight and die in an unjust war for reasons that have proven to be lies, Cindy is speaking out about the Iraq invasion. Cindy has joined other moms and families who have lost loved ones in the conflict to tell Americans about the true costs of the war. They have started an organization called Gold Star Families for Peace (www.gsfp.org).

Dear George,

You don't mind if I call you George, do you? When you sent me this letter offering your condolences on the death of my son, Spc. Casey Austin Sheehan, you called me Cindy, so I naturally assume we are on a first-name basis.

George, it has been seven months today since your reckless and wanton foreign policies killed my son in the illegal and unjust war on Iraq. Casey, my big boy, my hero, my best friend.

Casey was always a good boy. He could play for hours by himself. He loved Nintendo, GI Joes, the World Wrestling Federation, baseball (especially the Dodgers), his church, and God. He joined the Cub Scouts when he was in the first grade, and he eventually earned the rank of Eagle Scout. He became an altar boy when he was eight, and he continued serving his church for the rest of his life. He never talked back to his dad or me. He rarely fought with his brother and sisters. He loved our animals and he loved little children.

Everyone assumed Casey was going to be a priest because he was so faithful to God and to the church. He never missed Mass even when he went into the Army. If he was on post, he went to Mass. Casey was such a good Christian that after he died, his chapel on Fort Hood started a new Knights of Columbus Council, and the members voted unanimously to name it the Spc. Casey Austin Sheehan Council. They said that Casey embodied everything that they want to stand for: love of God, country, family, church, and service. We are honored that Casey's name and what he stood for will always be remembered on Fort Hood.

Back in 2000 when Casey was still alive, after you stole the election, I had the most ironic thought of my life: "Oh well, how much damage can he do in four years?" Now I know too well how much you have damaged my family, this country, and this world. The 2004 election has come and gone. But if you think I am going to allow you another four years to do even more damage, then you are truly mistaken. I will fight your lies and your agenda every step of the way. The only thing is, I'm not politically savvy, and I don't have a Karl Rove to plan my strategy. But I do have a big mouth and a righteous cause, which still mean something in this country, I hope.

During the presidential debates, you kept talking about "hard work." You said you know how hard the war is because you watch it on TV and get the casualty reports every day. George, let me tell you what "hard work" really is. Hard work is seeing your oldest son, your brave and honorable man-child, go off to a war that had, and still has, no basis in reality. Hard work is worrying yourself gray and not being able to sleep because you don't know whether your child is safe. Hard work is seeing your son's murder on CNN one Sunday evening while you're enjoying the last supper you'll ever truly enjoy again. Hard work is having three military officers come to your house a few hours later to confirm the aforementioned murder of your son . . . your firstborn . . . your kind and gentle sweet baby. Hard work is burying your child forty-six days before his twenty-fifth birthday. Hard work is holding your other three children as they lower the body of their big "baba" into the ground. Hard work is not jumping in the grave with him and having the earth cover you both.

But, George, do you know what the hardest work of all is? Trying to digest the fact that the leader of the country that your family has fought for and died for, for generations, lied to you and betrayed your dear boy's sense of honor and exploited his courage and exploited his loyalty to his buddies. Hard work is having your country abandon you after it killed your son. Hard work is coming to the realization that your son had his future robbed from him and that you have had your son's future and future grandchildren stolen from you. Hard work is knowing that there are so many people in this world that have prospered handsomely from your son's death.

George, I must confess that my family and I worked very hard to redefeat you this time, but you refuse to stay defeated. Well, we are watching you very carefully. We are going to do everything in our power to have you impeached for misleading the American people into a disastrous war and for misusing and abusing your power as commander in chief. We are going to scream until our last breath to bring the rest of our babies home from this quagmire of a war that you have gotten our country into: before too many more families learn the true meaning of hard work. It is going to be an uphill battle, knowing how Republican the Congress is. But thanks to you, we know the meaning of hard work and we're not afraid of it.

The fifty-six million citizens who voted against you and your agenda have given me a mandate to move forward with my agenda. Also, thanks to you and your careless domestic policies, I am unemployed, so this will be my full-time job. Helping to bring about your political downfall will be the most noble accomplishment of my life, and it will bring justice for my son and the hundreds of other brave Americans and tens of thousands of innocent Iraqis your lies have killed.

Thank you for that, George. Have a nice day and God bless America. We surely need it!

Cindy Sheehan

꙰

"Individuals have international duties which transcend the national obligations of obedience. Therefore [individual citizens] have the duty to violate domestic laws to prevent crimes against peace and humanity from occurring."

—Nuremberg War Crime Tribunal, 1950

❧ A NATION ROCKED TO SLEEP ❧

CARLY SHEEHAN, FOR HER BROTHER CASEY

Carly Sheehan wrote this poem after her
brother Casey died in Iraq on April 4, 2004.

Have you ever heard the sound of a mother screaming for her son?
The torrential rains of a mother's weeping will never be done
They call him a hero, you should be glad that he's one, but
Have you ever heard the sound of a mother screaming for her son?

Have you ever heard the sound of a father holding back his cries?
He must be brave because his boy died for another man's lies
The only grief he allows himself are long, deep sighs
Have you ever heard the sound of a father holding back his cries?

Have you ever heard the sound of taps played at your brother's grave?
They say that he died so that the flag will continue to wave
But I believe he died because they had oil to save
Have you ever heard the sound of taps played at your brother's grave?

Have you ever heard the sound of a nation being rocked to sleep?
The leaders want to keep you numb so the pain won't be so deep
But if we the people let them continue, another mother will weep
Have you ever heard the sound of a nation being rocked to sleep?

Veterans for Peace erects over 1,000 crosses every Sunday on the beaches of Southern California to honor our fallen U.S. military in a temporary "cemetery" called Arlington West. The documentary of the same name features interviews with soldiers coming from and going to Baghdad, military families, and veterans.
© Arlington West/www.arlingtonwestfilm.org

UNDERSTANDING THE U.S. MILITARY

MARTI HIKEN

Marti Hiken is the cochair of the Military Law Task Force of the National Lawyers Guild.

If we're going to stop war, we need to understand how the U.S. military operates and strengthen our ties with the soldiers themselves. Right now many GIs are angry. They don't want to be in Iraq, but they're not sure what to do. The kind of resistance they form will determine how long this war lasts.

When we work with soldiers, we encourage them to realize not only that they have options, but that they also have strength. They control the war:

they're the ones who can throw their shoes into the machinery; they're the ones who can put down the guns.

During the Vietnam War, the antiwar movement initially turned against the GIs. It took many years for activists to help GIs by starting coffee houses—a space near existing U.S. military bases where GIs, veterans, military counselors, and activists could talk and relax together in a comfortable setting. Coffee houses were an oasis for GIs coming back from Vietnam and a resource center for those going to learn firsthand the realities of war. It's time to form coffee houses around military bases again and step up the other kinds of support such as counseling.

Here are some ways you can help:

SUPPORT THE GI RIGHTS HOTLINE. In the mid-1990s, several groups came together to create a hotline to provide ongoing counseling to GIs. Women and men in the military can call 1-800-394-9544 to talk to a counselor, and they can read about the GI Rights Network online (www.nlg.org/mltf). If you're interested in helping with the hotline, please call the number above.

ORGANIZE ON THE BASES THEMSELVES. Go to places where GIs hang out in their own communities, and learn what it's like to serve in the U.S. military. Spend time listening, understanding, making contact.

STEP UP THE COUNTER-RECRUITMENT PROJECTS IN HIGH SCHOOLS AND COLLEGE CAMPUSES. The American Friends Service Committee and the Committee Opposed to Militarism and the Draft have both organized good efforts in this vein, but more are needed. See www.objector.org, the Web site of the Central Commitee for Conscientious Objectors, for a list of groups doing counter-recruitment. Download the literature, go to your local high schools, and pass it out.

‹∘›

"War will exist until that distant day when the conscientious objector
enjoys the same reputation and prestige that the warrior does today."

— John F. Kennedy

ESSENTIAL **DISSENT**

MARY ANN WRIGHT

Mary Ann Wright was the deputy chief of mission in the U.S. embassies of Sierra Leone, Micronesia, Afghanistan, and Mongolia. She received the State Department's award for heroism as chargé d'affaires during the evacuation of Sierra Leone in 1997. She has also been a U.S. Army colonel, with twenty-six years of military experience.

As a diplomat and a member of the U.S. military, I served my country for almost thirty-five years in some of the most isolated and dangerous parts of the world, such as Somalia, Sierra Leone, and Afghanistan. Although I wanted to continue to serve America, in March 2003 I resigned from my position as a foreign-service officer and senior diplomat because I didn't believe in many of the policies of the Bush administration and I couldn't defend or implement them. Two other senior diplomats, John Brady Kiesling and John H. Brown, also resigned in opposition to the Iraq war.

I disagreed with the Bush administration's policies on Iraq, the Israeli-Palestinian conflict, North Korea, and curtailment of civil liberties in the United States—these policies, I believed, were making the world a more dangerous, not a safer, place.

For example, U.S. military action in Iraq created deep chasms in important international organizations and in the international community, alienating many of our allies. I strongly disagreed with the use of a "preemptive attack" against Iraq, a move that seemed destined to be used against us—with the United States setting the precedent, what was to stop our enemies from "preemptively attacking" America and American citizens? We gave extremist Muslims a further cause to hate America and handed moderate Muslims a reason to join the extremists.

Likewise, I could not support the Bush administration's lack of effort to resurrect the Israeli-Palestinian peace process. As Palestinian suicide bombers killed Israelis and Israeli military operations killed Palestinians and destroyed Palestinian towns and cities, the administration did little to end the violence, when in fact we could exert our considerable financial influence to pressure the Israelis to stop destroying cities and the Palestinians to curb the young suicide bombers.

Additionally, I disagreed with the administration's position on North Korea—the president's lack of substantive discussion, dialogue, and engagement with North Korea during the first two years of his tenure jeopardized security on the peninsula and the region.

But one of my strongest concerns about U.S. policy was the unnecessary curtailment of civil rights following 9/11. While the investigation of those who might have ties to terrorist organizations is a critical matter, some of the investigative methods that the government has employed (including placing suspects in solitary confinement without access to legal counsel) seriously undermine the legal foundation on which our country has stood for more than two hundred years. Meanwhile the administration's secrecy about the judicial process made many Americans afraid to speak out.

After I resigned, I felt it was important to speak directly to the American public about my concerns. During the past eighteen months I have spoken all over the country—to classes in high schools, colleges, and universities; to civic groups, to activists groups, and to church groups—about U.S. foreign policy, America's standing in the world, and the role of disagreement and dissent in a democracy. I have been overwhelmed by the outpouring of good wishes from thousands of Americans who appreciate a person giving up, on principle, a career she dearly loved. In fact, several months ago, when Brady, John, and I spoke together in a number of cities, the standing ovations we received showed us that many, many Americans were deeply impressed by our decision to sacrifice our careers in order to underscore our opposition to the war in Iraq.

I encourage all Americans to look critically at what our government is doing in our name. If we do not agree with an administration's policies, it is our responsibility as citizens to let our voices be heard. But you don't have to give up your job to try to influence U.S. policies—letters and e-mails to the administration and to our congresspeople are also important, as are actions by social justice, peace, and religious groups. Attend public demonstrations, marches, and rallies in large numbers, which will force the media to cover them. In particular, we cannot stand by and let our Congress be hoodwinked into giving the president wide-ranging powers, including the power of waging war. We have the responsibility to make our concerns known, especially when an administration does not want to listen to alternative viewpoints.

Above all, when our own government takes actions that put us all in jeopardy, we cannot sit back.

∞

"You don't have to have fought in a war to love peace."

—Geraldine Ferraro

PROTECT YOUR RIGHT TO DISSENT

KIT GAGE

Kit Gage has directed the First Amendment Foundation and the National Committee Against Repressive Legislation (NCARL) since April 2001. She is president and a founder of the National Coalition to Protect Political Freedom (NCPPF).

We'll never be able to stop war if we don't have the right to speak freely, organize demonstrations, and meet without government interference. Since 9/11, with the passage of the USA Patriot Act and other regulatory changes, we have lost many of our basic freedoms enshrined in the Bill of Rights.

Remember, we will retain our rights only if we demand them. Here are some ways you can stand up to protect our rights:

REACQUAINT YOURSELF WITH YOUR RIGHTS. Go back to the source—read the Constitution and the Bill of Rights. They are amazing documents.

GATHER SUPPORT FOR OUR CIVIL LIBERTIES. The Bill of Rights Defense Committee (www.bordc.org) raises awareness about provisions of the USA Patriot Act that are a dangerous intrusion on our rights. By the end of 2004, more than 350 cities and counties—and 4 states—had passed resolutions to protect their residents' civil liberties. Help get a similar resolution passed in your city, and if that has already been done, get one passed in your church, school, labor union, and business association!

CHECK OUT THE WEB SITES OF NATIONAL GROUPS. The National Committee against Repressive Legislation (www.ncarl.org) has a site with links to about fifty groups, including the American Civil Liberties Union (www.aclu.org) and the Center for Constitutional Rights (www.ccr-ny.org).

WE MUST SEPARATE
THE WARRIOR
FROM THE WAR

PATRICIA FOULKROD

Patricia Foulkrod is a filmmaker and has produced and directed *They're Doing My Time*, a documentary regarding children of women in prison, and various features, including *American Rhapsody*. Patricia also teaches meditation to juveniles in prison, and is now helping Operation Truth to create a network and healing center for soldiers with PTSD (post-traumatic stress disorder.) She is currently filming *The Ground Truth*.

On the first anniversary of the U.S. invasion into Iraq, I began a documentary film, *The Ground Truth: The Human Cost of War*, which focuses on injured and mentally wounded men and women coming home from Afghanistan and Iraq. I believe that the trauma of war creates a lifelong isolation for these soldiers that is compounded by society's indifference. It also feeds into a profound sense of betrayal that is underneath the actions of many soldiers who perpetrate more violence, commit suicide, become homeless, become alcoholic, and go deeper into this isolation.

Kevin Lucey lost his son to suicide after Jeff returned from Iraq. Recently, he said to me, "We would do things so differently if we knew what we know now. We would never treat him like he was just having a bad day." Our commitment to peace must also be a commitment to being proactive with this new generation of soldiers—to engage in dialogue that allows all of us to truly separate the warrior from the war.

As women, mothers, daughters, and sister activists and organizers, we can be there for them as they try to find their voices.

CALL TO ACTION: SUPPORT VETERANS

CONTACT A VETERANS GROUP, A VA HOSPITAL COUNSELOR, NURSE, OR DOCTOR, AND ASK FOR GUIDANCE. Facilitate a small forum or dinner where soldiers can share their experiences, show their pictures, be allowed to talk, or just come to dinner. They want to be relieved of their isolation, and they have the best knowledge about what happens in a war.

We do not have to talk only of war—we do not have to be their doctors, or therapists, or the ones who pay their benefits, fix their marriages, or stop their nightmares. They have been away for a long time and their lives are shattered—a household repair that we can help facilitate, a divorce that we can help them get through, a job that we can help make happen could be just as healing.

FIND A SOLDIER AND HIS OR HER FAMILY AND ASK THEM TO DINNER. Many feel alone living in military communities, unable to be with their buddies away in combat, and unable to feel safe talking or connecting with civilians. I have seen firsthand many soldiers drop their assumptions about activists and antiwar protesters—and many activists begin to separate the warrior from the war.

The following are a few groups to contact for advice on (a) contacting soldiers who can speak publicly, (b) facilitating a discussion group, (c) hosting a potluck dinner, or (d) assisting soldiers who are physically or mentally challenged and need help at home:

Iraq Veterans Against War, www.ivaw.net

The Ground Truth, www.thegroundtruth.org

Operation Truth, www.optruth.org

Veterans for Common Sense, www.veteransforcommonsense.org

Veterans for Peace, www.veteransforpeace.org

Chapter 2

FROM
A CULTURE
OF VIOLENCE
TO
A CULTURE
OF PEACE

THE NEW PARADIGM
WE HOLD WITHIN

EVE ENSLER

Eve Ensler is the Obie Award–winning author of *The Vagina Monologues*, translated into more than thirty-five languages and running in theaters all over the world. Her newest play, *The Good Body* examines how women from Mumbai to Beverly Hills view their bodies. She is the founder of V-Day, a global movement to stop violence against women and girls.

I recently got an e-mail from one of my sisters in Iraq, Yanar Mohammed. When the occupation of Iraq occurred, there was the promise, as there was a promise in Afghanistan, that women would be liberated. Well, in occupied Iraq, women are worse off today than they were under Saddam Hussein, and it was pretty terrible then. In the name of occupation, with the lawlessness and the rise of fundamentalism, roughly seventy women a month are being abducted and sold and raped. Women are not leaving their houses. Those who were once doctors and lawyers are too frightened to go to work.

I am obsessed with the notion of occupation. I think about it every day. The word means "to invade or enter a country by force or as an army, especially in order to conquer it." I am obsessed with this because I am obsessed with women and violence and rape. And rape is, of course, the ultimate invasion, the ultimate occupation. Women's bodies around the world are being invaded and occupied at a terrifying rate. The earth, our mother, is being invaded and occupied and devastated. In the name of silencing women and the earth, in the name of undermining the power of life, of birth, of mystery, of passion and ambiguity, there is this occupation and invasion.

The concept of empire, the concept of corporations determining reality, and the concept of invasion, occupation, domination are central to those in power today. But millions of us know in our bodies, in our minds, in our spirits and that another paradigm is desperate to emerge on this planet. I believe we can feel it in every fiber of our beings. And with a little courage, with a lot of unity, and with faith that paradigm is going to emerge.

I believe that women and vagina-friendly men will be at the center of this new paradigm. They will be the carriers of it, the provokers of it, and the healers and the heart of it. Not because all women are kind and just and incapable of cruelty. We have seen women become easily absorbed into the patriarchal, capitalist structure and become heartless and devastating. But there are many if not millions of women on this planet who hold this new paradigm in their bodies, in their beings. And because we have been so far outside the current power structure, this paradigm has been allowed to grow in us.

What does the paradigm look like? How does it taste? What is its shape? Well, let's begin by saying that you cannot bomb people into trust and democracy and hope. This paradigm knows that terrorists are made, not born. It knows that violence and humiliation take many forms—the occupation of people's homelands, putting your troops in people's holy lands, stripping people naked in prison and forcing them to masturbate, or allowing millions of the world to starve while you eat steak. And shame, as we know, becomes violence. This is not to justify terrorism, state or individual. It is more a desire to look at the reasons. Why are there terrorists? Why are people flying planes through buildings? In the new paradigm, the why of things will be more crucial than vengeance.

The new paradigm will not be about conquering people, but about collaborating with people. It will not be invading people, it will be inviting people. Not occupying, but offering, inspiring, and serving people. In the new paradigm, there will be time to feel, to heal, to grieve. Unexpressed grief often becomes violence. Experienced grief becomes wisdom. As a nation, instead of grieving over September 11, we retaliated. We bombed.

We bombed Afghanistan, killing innocent people. And the Taliban? From everything I understand from the women there, I think it is still running wild throughout the country. We did not free the Afghan people. We did not invite their trust. We did not form alliances with them. On a recent trip there I discovered among the Afghan people an incredible sense of having been used and then abandoned. I believe if we had had our grief, if we had taken time to feel the center of the pain, what we felt for the loss of the people in those buildings, for the horror that people would be driven to such mind-numbing rage that they would fly planes through buildings, would have been expressed as compassion and an understanding that to drop more bombs would cure nothing.

Real power is about generosity. Real power is about being bigger than revenge. And it requires every part of our being to say, I'm not going to hit you back. I'm going to take a breath and find what within me is larger and has the power to enlighten.

Over the last six years I've had the great privilege of traveling all around the world. I've seen this country from the perspective of many other countries. But what I've also seen around the world is the emerging of this paradigm. I

Drake's Beach, Marin County, California, December 29, 2002: Baring Witness uses the power of beauty and naked-ness to awaken the public and heighten the awareness of human vulnerability. See www.baringwitness.org for more information.
© Jan Watson

have seen amazing women and vagina-friendly men all over this planet. We have come to call them vagina warriors.

Vagina warriors are men or women who have witnessed violence, experienced violence, and responded not by reaching for AK-47s, weapons of mass destruction, or machetes. Instead they hold the violence in their bodies, they grieve over the violence, they experience the violence, and they transform the violence into social justice. They devote their lives to making sure that what happened to them doesn't happen to anybody else.

Yanar Mohammed is a vagina warrior. She and her colleagues are building safe houses all over Iraq to protect the women, who are being killed and raped. She is organizing women, calling public demonstrations. She has round-the-clock bodyguards, as there have been many threats to her life.

Medea Benjamin is a vagina warrior. Medea Benjamin saw the war beginning in Iraq and she said, "I'm going to put my life and my heart and my spirit on the line, and I'm going to form CODEPINK." And with Jodie Evans she went out and started to transform that rage and that sorrow to make the world better.

Arundhati Roy is a vagina warrior. She wrote a gorgeous novel and became well known throughout the world. And instead of taking her money and her

fame and disappearing, she stood up against empire, she stood up for workers, she stood up to stop the desecration of the planet.

Charmaine Means is a vagina warrior. She was a major in the U.S. Army
stationed in Iraq in the town of Mosul. And when she was told by her supe-
rior to shut down the local TV station and muzzle the press, she said, "No,
I didn't join the U.S. Army to shut down freedom of speech."

Malalai Joya is a twenty-five-year-old social worker in Afghanistan. You may
have heard of her, but you probably haven't, because the media rarely report
on vagina warriors. Malalai Joya was at the Loya Jirga, the body writing
Afghanistan's new constitution. But the Loya Jirga was essentially populated
by warlords and members of the Taliban. So Malalai Joya, at twenty-five
years of age, stood up and said: "All or most of the people in power here are
warlords. We can't continue with them in power. They need to be held accountable for their actions. There needs to be justice." Subsequently, there have
been three assassination attempts on her life. And you know what? She is still
speaking out. That's a vagina warrior.

Every single person working for peace is a vagina warrior. We don't need
any more violence on this planet. The possibility of violence as a solution to
anything is no longer tolerable, permissible, or sane. Women hold the key in
our bodies, in our hearts, in our spirits. Every single one of us knows what needs
to be done. We need to see what we see, we need to know what we know,
and we need to stand up and talk about it everywhere we go and not be afraid
anymore.

I dedicate this to vagina warriors throughout the world:

❧ THIS WILL BE OUR REVOLUTION ❧

When I think how long it has taken
to remember,
to allow myself to remember.
When I think how hard it is
to believe what I remember,
to remember what I remember,
to make what I remember matter,
to not hurt my family with what I remember

When I think how hard it is to not go underground again,
to keep remembering that what happened,
did happen.

When I think that what I remember makes
Everyone uneasy
And that being a person who remembers
makes me a person
many people would like to forget.

But I already remember too much
There is no going back
The memories
break through like bleeding
and one memory leads to all memories,
all arteries,
one violence to all violence.

It did happen
my father whipped me with belts
and bloodied my nose in restaurants
with white linen.
Homeless woman on Fourteenth and Seventh
eating the cold and bug-infested remains of pizza.
She has cigarette burns on her inner thighs.
She doesn't remember the burning.
Woman in prison
who woke up one day
learned she had stabbed her John twenty-two times.
She only remembered the first three.
This happened because she had stopped
remembering everything
after she was raped
and raped before she was nine.

You are forgetting as I am speaking
You are wiping off the blood,
spraying air fresheners
to cover the smell of rotting corpses
They are holding invisible unidentified people
in filthy pens
in Guantánamo Bay
You don't remember them
or why they are there

or the leash around the naked crawling
hooded Iraqi man's neck
or the Iraqi boy lying on a cot
with no sheets, no arms, no legs
and these are the images of what was only
momentarily remembered.
The images of the rest—
melted children
screaming fathers
abducted daughters
collapsing grandmothers
sodomized little boys.
There was a war on Iraq
There was a war on Iraq
Thousands are dead,
the rest are drugged
or wrestling in their beds.
It doesn't matter if you remember it,
it remembers you.

You who can no longer look her in the eyes
or get wet between your legs
You who are listless
who can't remember how you got there
or why you bought the gun
or where these babies came from
or how you made yourself bleed.
It haunts you
It remembers you

We all knew it would happen like this.
We tried to remember
the terrible stupid wars
that had come before
with our bodies
in the streets of the world
but the ones in power had
forgotten us a long time ago.

Eventually we will forget each other
That's how the memory works
It must erase all paths that lead back
and so we will be here
but we will not be here
for each other.

I want to remember
with you.
This will be our revolution
Retrieving
Who we were
What we desired
What we knew
Before it happened
Before we were broken
Censored and bruised.

I want to remember
We can do this together
Slowly at first,
Lying down with each other
Then biting and licking
Remembering
Refusing
Refusing
Remembering

I'll do that
I will
With you.

❧

"Democracy and Freedom cannot be force fed
at the point of an occupier's gun."

—U.S. senator Robert Byrd

COLOMBIAN WOMEN CREATE A PATH TO PEACE

Excerpted from *Building from the Inside Out: Peace Initiatives in War-Torn Colombia*, produced by the American Friends Service Committee and the Fellowship of Reconciliation.

During a regional security council meeting in late 1996, a nun revealed that 95 percent of the women in one community of Urabá had been raped. This ignited something deep within a few women activists in the city of Medellín. They called for an act of solidarity: a thousand Colombian women from women's groups around the country to go to Urabá and put their arms around those who had suffered the humiliation of war.

Across Colombia, busloads of women departed for Urabá. Many traveled for several days. Some left their communities for the first time. Many did not have permission from their husbands or fathers, but went anyway. And when fifteen hundred Colombian women arrived in Urabá on November 25—the International Day for the Elimination of Violence against Women—they hugged their sisters. Thus was born La Ruta Pácifica de las Mujeres, or Ruta (Path).

After the first mobilization, women set out for other regions that were under the assault of war. They launched nationwide marches to Bolívar, Cartagena, Barrancabermeja, and Bogotá. On November 25, 2003, Ruta led three thousand women in a caravan of a hundred buses to the southern jungle department of Putumayo, the heart of joint U.S.-Colombian drug-eradication efforts that include the aerial fumigation of coca fields. Ruta denounced the "militarist policy of the current government, which favors the use of weapons and force to treat problems that are rooted in poverty," and demanded that the "women and men of Putumayo be allowed to influence the decisions that affect their lives and health and those of their children, and the land which sustains them."

In 2001, the UN Development Fund for Women (UNIFEM) and the British organization International Alert awarded the Millennium Peace Prize to Ruta. Ruta accepted the award with the following words:

"We have told the warring men that we do not deliver children for war, and that we will not allow our hands and wombs to contribute to war. Our

> bodies will not serve as war booty. We demand that the arms race supported by the developed countries stop. We demand that not one more dollar be spent on war."
>
> It is Ruta's unique solidarity—indeed, its sisterhood—that gives women the strength to march in the face of war and violence and authoritarianism. And it is their efforts to be coherent in word and action from a feminist perspective that make Ruta an unconventional movement so full of hope.

∽⚭∼

"There never was a good war, or a bad peace."
—Benjamin Franklin

THE OPEN SPACE OF
DEMOCRACY

TERRY TEMPEST WILLIAMS

Terry Tempest Williams is a writer who focuses on social issues and their relationship to the natural world. She is the author of *Refuge, Leap,* and *Red: Passion and Patience in the Desert.* Her most recent book is *The Open Space of Democracy.* A recipient of a Lannan Literary Fellowship, she lives in Castle Valley, Utah.

My brother Steve was diagnosed one year ago with lymphoma. I see him sitting at the family dinner table after he has gone through an intensive cycle of chemotherapy that leaves his body ravaged and weak. I see him sitting next to his wife, Ann, in their living room with daughters Callie, Sarah, and Diane, and with Brook and me there at their side. My other brother, Hank. And our father. Gathered together to hear what Steve has to say. He speaks of healing, not cure. He speaks of gratitude for his life and his desire to be true to the integrity of his own voice. He has brought back a stone for each of us and passes a bowl of stones around the dinner table. And he talks about how, when he was walking at Point Reyes, he picked up only stones that had a hole in them. And he says, "I know we have had a hole in our hearts. We can look at this hole in our hearts as a wound or we can see it as a window. May we vow tonight as a family to see it as a window."

In June 2003, I was invited to deliver the commencement address at the University of Utah, my alma mater. My niece Callie was graduating. You'll remember George W. Bush stepping onto the aircraft carrier Abraham Lincoln, announcing, "Mission accomplished!" This was the following day. And I thought, if I don't have the courage to speak my own thoughts at this point in time to my own people, my own family, in my own community, at my own school, then I have no business being there. And I gave a very short talk, for fifteen minutes, about the open space of democracy. I said that in the open space of democracy there is room for dissent. In the open space of democracy, community is defined as the well-being of all species, not just our own. I was thinking about Thoreau when he said, "Cast not your whole vote, but your whole influence." And I urged the students to question, stand, speak, and act. My talk was met with equal boos and applause. And what I saw was the split within our own country. How do we have civil dialogue when we are not even civil to each other?

After the talk, my senator, Bob Bennett, came up to me and said, "Terry, I just want to register my extreme dissent to what you said today. You've inspired me to write you a letter."

I would like to share an excerpt of his letter and my response, because I think it has everything to do with how we bypass this political rhetoric that has diminished all of us in this country and find that point of humanity, our deeper selves. "Dear Terry," Senator Bennett wrote, "as I listened to you outline things that are important to you, an interesting question popped into my mind. What would she be willing to die for?" And then he goes on to outline his concerns and thoughts. It was an incredibly thoughtful, provocative letter.

I'm embarrassed to tell you I was not able to answer his letter for months. I was haunted by what he had asked me. What am I willing to die for? And I realized for me, that wasn't the question. It's not what I'm willing to die for, but what I am willing to give my life to.

"Dear Senator Bennett: You asked me a critical question in your letter, one I have pondered for months. What am I willing to die for? After much thought, what I would be willing to die for and give my life to, is the freedom of speech. It is the open door to all other freedoms. We are a nation at war with ourselves until we can turn to one another and offer our sincere words as to why we feel the way we do, with an honest commitment to hear what others have to say. We will continue to project our anger on the world in true unconscious acts of terror. Democracy invites us to take risks. It asks that we vacate the comfortable seat of certitude, remain pliable, and act ultimately on behalf of the common good. Democracy's only agenda is that we participate. If we cannot engage in respectful listening, there can be no civil dialogue. And without civil dialogue, we the people will simply become bullies in boots, deaf to the truth that we are standing on the edge of a political chasm that is beginning to crumble. We all stand to lose ground. Democracy is an insecure landscape."

Democracy felt a bit more insecure when I received a call from Florida Gulf Coast University. I was to learn that the freshman convocation, at which I had been invited to speak, was being postponed until after the election. This decision was made by the university president, William Merwin (not to be confused with the poet), because of criticisms I had made against George W. Bush in print. He felt my partisan views would be threatening to the university and could be harmful to his students. He said, "If a hurricane is threatening my university, then I'm going to shut it down." And I said, "But what if it's only a tempest?" With all due respect, he didn't think it was funny. We had a long conversation and he was very candid, to his credit. He said, "Let me be very clear. The Board of Regents of the state of Florida, my board of trustees at this university, are all appointees of Governor Jeb Bush. And my donors are supporters of the Bush brothers. In the name of political balance, I cannot allow you on this campus before the election."

That same night, our family gathered in Salt Lake City to learn that my brother Steve's tests revealed metastatic disease, that his lymphoma was progressing. He was no longer eligible for the stem-cell transplant we had all been praying for. With silence and with stillness, with sorrow and with love, we embraced the moment and each other and stood in the center of sacred time. Life. As T. S. Elliot said, "Turning shadow into transient beauty."

The experience at the Florida Gulf Coast University was a painful one. But it has taught me that this is not personal. This story is not about me. It's a shadow play where we are characters in an ongoing drama, a theater of democracy. The students rose. The faculties rose. And finally, the president and I joined the students and the faculty in a discussion of how to keep this open space exactly that.

I think together we've realized that what is most threatening to the status quo is dialogue. Because honest dialogue and deep listening require us to change, to give up the rigidity of our opinions for the sacred heart of stories, where we remember who we are and who we are not.

My brother has shared with us that his cancer is teaching him to act and speak from a place of honesty. To follow what he loves, not to be simply responsible for what he does. If you had told me one year ago that my brother, who's a pipeline contractor, would be advocating for a labyrinth to be placed in the center of a new health care facility for cancer patients, I would not have believed you. If you had told me that his focus on pipeline had shifted to sculpture, to making a sculpture out of granite, cut and pulled and stretched, that he would call *Lymphoma Leaving*, if you had told me that alongside his Mormon scriptures he would be reading Emerson and Thoreau and Rachel Remin, I would not have believed it. The other day he said to me, "Terry, we are all terminal. How do you want to spend your one beautiful life?"

The human heart is the first home of democracy. It is where we embrace our questions. Can we be equitable? Can we be generous? Can we listen with our whole being, not just our mind, and offer our attention rather than our opinion? And do we have enough resolve in our heart to act courageously, relentlessly, without giving up, ever—trusting our fellow citizens to join us in a determined pursuit of a living democracy? The heart is the house of empathy, whose door opens when we receive the pain of others. This is where bravery lives, where we'll find our mettle to give and receive, to love and be loved, to stand in the center of uncertainty with strength, not fear, understanding this is all there is. The heart is the path to wisdom because it dares to be vulnerable in the presence of power.

∽◦∾

"I dream of giving birth to a child who will ask, 'Mother, what was war?'"

—Eve Merriam

WARRIORS FOR PEACE

ROSE KABUYE

Rose Kabuye was raised in a Ugandan refugee camp following her parents' flight from Rwanda because of Hutu-Tutsi violence. She later joined the Rwandan Patriotic Front, an opposition movement and guerrilla army. She was the mayor of Kigali after the 1994 genocide, was a member of Parliament for two years, and is a lieutenant colonel in the Rwandan army.

Rwandans throughout the country have been trying to bridge the divide between Hutus and Tutsis. Telling the truth. Healing. The government's Unity and Reconciliation Commission sets up regular meetings for people of all ethnic groups where we learn about each other's history, about the experiences of the other side.

Rwanda is coping not only with internal Hutu-Tutsi friction; there are also tensions between our country and the Democratic Republic of the Congo. In 2000, I was part of a group of Rwandan and Congolese women who went through conflict-resolution training at Mennonite University in Virginia. At first, the Congolese women didn't want to talk to us. When they did talk to us, they said, "You are aggressors. What are you doing in our country?" And of course, we said, "Why are you supporting the militias? These people, who killed our innocent people, are regrouped in the Congo. You are arming them. You are sending them back to kill us. Why do you support them?" In the beginning we listened to one another with a mediator. Later, we learned how to listen on our own. We also learned that each one of us had a point. We were already in a better place. And we tried to figure out a solution together: they couldn't arrest the militia members in the Congo, but they could lobby the Congolese government to stop supporting them. And we could lobby the Rwandan government to pull out of their territory. When we went back home, I was able to talk to my leaders about what the Congolese and Rwandan women, together, thought might work.

In March 2003, CODEPINK marched to Congress highlighting the casualties of war.
Photo by Medea Benjamin

Some people think it's strange that I work for peace, because I'm in the army. But others are glad. They say to me, "You waged war, and now you are waging peace!" I know how terrible wars can be. That's why I want to leave behind a safer world for our children.

∽๑∾

"Darkness cannot drive out darkness; only light can do that. Hate cannot drive out hate; only love can do that. Hate multiplies hate, violence multiplies violence, and toughness multiplies toughness in a descending spiral of destruction.... The chain reaction of evil— hate begetting hate, wars producing more wars— must be broken, or we shall be plunged into the dark abyss of annihilation."

—Martin Luther King Jr.

CHOOSING **PEACE**

ELISE BOULDING

Dr. Elise Boulding is a pioneer in the peace movement. Professor emerita of sociology at Dartmouth College and a founder of the International Peace Research Association, she has written extensively on strategies for peace, focusing on indigenous cultures, the workings and possibilities of the United Nations, and family structure.

A peace culture maintains a creative balance among bonding, community closeness, and the need for separate spaces. It can be defined as a mosaic of identities, attitudes, values, beliefs, and patterns that leads people to live nurturingly with one another and the earth itself without the aid of structured power differentials, to deal creatively with their differences, and to share their resources. Usually, we find coexisting clusters of peaceableness and aggression. Each society develops its own pattern of balancing the needs for bonding and autonomy.

The balance may change over time, with periods of more peaceable behavior following periods of more violent behavior. It cannot be said that humans are innately peaceful or aggressive. Both capacities are there. It is socialization, the process by which society rears its children and shapes the attitudes and behaviors of its members of all ages, that determines how peacefully or violently individuals and institutions handle the problems that every human community faces in the daily work of maintaining itself.

It seems that in spite of the visibility of violence and war, many are able to see past that violence to a different future world. People who cannot imagine peace will not know how to work for it. Those who can imagine it are using that same imagination to devise practices and strategies that will render war obsolete. The importance of the imagination cannot be overestimated.

Peace cultures, however, are not just a figment of the imagination. They exist in daily life and habitual interaction as people get on with their lives and work, negotiating differences rather than engaging in interminable battles over just how to solve each problem as it comes up. Aggressive posturing slows down problem solving. Violence is more visible and gets more attention in our history books and in our media than peace does. But a peace culture will take us where we want to go.

Kenneth Boulding always used to say, "What exists is possible." Since peace cultures exist, they are possible. If we want the world to be one planetary zone of peace, full of adventure and the excitement of dealing with diversity and difference, without violence, humans can make it so.

BUILDING A JUST AND CARING WORLD:
FOUR CORNERSTONES

RIANE EISLER

Dr. Riane Eisler, a scholar and an activist, is the author of the international best seller *The Chalice and the Blade*, as well as the award-winning *Tomorrow's Children* and *The Power of Partnership*. She is the president of the Center for Partnership Studies and cofounder of the Spiritual Alliance to Stop Intimate Violence. A different version of this essay first appeared in *Tikkun*, May-June 1998.

Throughout our history, human beings have experimented with almost every kind of society imaginable, from pacifist communities to totalitarian states, with a thousand variations in between. For all their unique peculiarities, though, most of our attempts at civilization have taken on one of two shapes; I call these configurations the "dominator model" and the "partnership model."

In societies ruled by the dominator model, we often find top-down authoritarianism (strongman rule), the subordination of a large portion of the population to another portion, and a high degree of institutionalized (or built-in) violence, whether in the form of wife and child beating or warfare and terrorism. At the partnership side of the spectrum—and it is always a matter of degree—societies are organized in a more democratic way, economically as well as politically, with everyone equally valued. Stereotypically feminine values such as caring and nonviolence (considered "unmanly" in the dominator model) are highly regarded , whether they are embodied in women or men. And partnership-based societies are less violent. (For examples, see Sweden, Finland, and Norway.)

Given their markedly different qualities, can one model ever hope to become its opposite? you might wonder. If we find ourselves in a dominator-style society, how do we transform it into a culture that prioritizes partnership? We can begin to build this new structure by putting into place four cornerstones.

THE FIRST CORNERSTONE: CHILDHOOD RELATIONS

We are learning that the physical structure of the brain—including the neural pathways that determine not only intelligence but also creativity, predisposition to violent or nonviolent behaviors, empathy or insensitivity, venturesomeness or overconformity—is not set at birth but is largely determined while we're young children. We are also learning that coercive, inequitable, and violent child rearing—what I call dominator child rearing—is fundamental to the imposition and maintenance of a coercive, inequitable, and chronically violent social and cultural organization.

This knowledge has enormous implications for social policy. It is through our intimate relations that we learn how to feel, think, and behave in all human relations, be they personal or political. If these relations are violent, children learn early on that violence committed by those who are more powerful against those who are less powerful is acceptable as a means of dealing with conflicts and problems.

What's needed is no less than a global campaign against intimate violence and the abuse of children. We must educate an international audience about the consequences of violence at an early age, and we must provide both women and men with the knowledge and skills necessary for empathic, nonviolent, and equitable child rearing. We must enact and enforce laws criminalizing child abuse, as well as legislation funding education for better child rearing. We must change the mass media, first by raising awareness about routine representations of violence in movies and television shows. And we must persuade spiritual and religious leaders to take a moral stand on this pivotal issue of intimate violence—the violence that every year blights, and all too often takes, the lives of millions of children and women and perpetuates cycles of violence in all relations. This is the mission of the Spiritual Alliance to Stop Intimate Violence (www.saiv.net).

THE SECOND CORNERSTONE: GENDER RELATIONS

How a society understands the roles and relations of women and men is central to the construction of every social institution, from the family to organized religions to the government. Not only do gender relations underlie a society's fundamental value system, but they can also have a profound impact on the nation's general quality of life. For example, *Women, Men, and the Global Quality of Life*—a study by the Center for Partnership Studies (www.part nershipway.org), based on statistics from eighty-nine nations—found that the status of women can predict the general quality of life in any given state better than GDP or GNP, the conventional measures of economic health.

When societies with institutionalized gender discrimination claim that they prioritize caring, compassion, and nonviolence, their pronouncements are often only rhetoric; in practice, these kinds of partnership values, which tend to be associated with women, remain subordinate as long as women themselves are excluded from governing.

This is not to say that women possess fundamentally different qualities than men. Both women and men exhibit stereotypically feminine traits, such as caring and nonviolence, and both genders engage in so-called women's work, such as caring for a family's health and maintaining a clean environment. However, in societies adhering closely to the dominator model, these activities are considered appropriate only for women and inappropriate for "real men."

In recent decades we have seen a strong movement toward real partnership between men and women in all spheres of life, along with a blurring of rigid gender distinctions. Men are nurturing babies, and women are entering positions of leadership. But this movement is still slow and localized; in some cultures and subcultures it's fiercely, even violently, opposed (by certain fundamentalist leaders, for example).

To continue to make change, the world's progressive leaders must prioritize a global campaign for equitable and nonviolent gender relations. Valuing so-called women's issues has enormous implications for the environment, the peace process, economic equity, and political democracy. As long as boys and men are socialized to equate "real masculinity" with violence and control—be it through "heroic" epics or war toys or violent and brutal television shows—how can we realistically expect to end the arms buildups that are today bankrupting our world as well as the terrorism and aggressive warfare that threaten our species' survival?

THE THIRD CORNERSTONE: ECONOMIC RELATIONS

It makes no sense to talk of hunger and poverty in generalities when the mass of the world's poor and the poorest of the poor are women and children. Many studies show that in most regions of the developing world women allocate far more of their resources to their families than men do. Development policies need to shift their focus to women, and we must include the work of caring and caregiving—still performed primarily by women worldwide as part of the "informal" economy—in national and international systems of economic measurement and accounting (since they are not included in either GDP or GNP).

We should encourage and reward economic and social inventions that assign value to caring and caregiving work in both the market and nonmarket economic sectors. For example, we have national programs to train soldiers to kill people—and we offer these soldiers pensions. By contrast, we have no national programs to train women and men to effectively care for children—even though we have gained solid scientific knowledge about what is and is not effective and humane child care.

People need meaningful work. Is there any more important or meaningful work than caring for other humans, particularly our children, and for our natural environment? In the dominator model, work is motivated primarily by fear and the artificial creation of scarcities through wars and misallocations and misdistributions of resources. Redefining what productive work is allows us to imbue work with what it lacks in a dominator system: a spiritual dimension.

THE FOURTH CORNERSTONE: BELIEFS, STORIES, AND SPIRITUALITY

As more and more of us come to realize that partnership is a viable possibility for human society, our understanding of spirituality may change radically: not merely an escape to otherworldly realms, spirituality offers us the opportunity for active engagement in creating a better world right here on earth.

But to spread this consciousness will require what I have called spiritual courage: the courage of political, religious, educational, and business leaders to actively oppose injustice and cruelty in all spheres of life. We must summon great bravery to end domination and violence not only in international relations but also in intimate relations, not only in the so-called public sphere of politics and business but also in the so-called private sphere of parent-child, gender, and sexual relations. Domination and violence have been with many of us a long time—they may still be part of our most deeply ingrained traditions—and challenging this heritage will be unpopular at best, dangerous at worst.

But it must be done.

Only if we consciously and concertedly build these four foundations for a partnership way of living can we move from a violent dominator culture to a more equitable, peaceful, and sustainable future for ourselves, our children, and generations still to come.

⌒○⌒

"It isn't enough to talk about peace. One must believe in it.
And it isn't enough to believe in it. One must work at it."

—Eleanor Roosevelt

"If we despair over the way in which war seems such an ingrained habit of most of the human race, we can take comfort from the fact that a poor invention will usually give place to a better invention.

—Margaret Mead

THE CHALLENGE
OF EDUCATING FOR PEACE

JOAN ALMON

Joan Almon is the U.S. coordinator of the Alliance for Childhood. She is a Waldorf kindergarten master teacher and the chair of the Waldorf Kindergarten Association. The following is reprinted with permission of the Alliance for Childhood (www.allianceforchildhood.org).

American children, fed a nonstop toxic diet of electronic-media images, are increasingly fearful about the threats of war, terrorism, crime, and other forms of violence. The threats, in some cases, are real. In other ways, they are greatly exaggerated by our preoccupation with violence and gore, which inundates children daily on television, movie, and video-game screens.

Today, parents and teachers are asking for an antidote.

In the past few years, the United States has changed from a confident nation to one beset by fear. In times of fear we tend either to seek security and hide away or to rush forward and attack. But those are not the only options. Many parents and teachers are asking how we can help children face the world with courage and equanimity. How can we educate them for a life of caring and compassion when the news is so full of stories of hatred, revenge, and cruelty? How can we prepare them to work through conflicts in creative ways?

The answer is a new national commitment to peace education. Teaching about peace can touch the lives of children at every level—in the home and at school, in both local and global communities.

It is easy to teach children about war. It is much more challenging to teach them how to create peace. In war, we draw lines and barricade ourselves against the enemy. Educating for peace means building bridges between people across every divide, including ethnic, racial, religious, and national lines.

Since the 9/11 terrorist attacks—and amid ubiquitous talk of war—many new toys and games that glorify violence have appeared in stores. Examples include Forward Command Post, marketed by Ever Sparkle Industrial Toys, with a two-foot-tall dollhouse that looks like a typical American home—but one that's been bombed out and turned into battlefield headquarters. J.C. Penney, at its online site, recommends the $44.99 Command Post for children ages five and up, and notes that it's loaded with realistic toy weapons and other battlefield gear. J.C. Penney's site also promotes World Peace Keepers Battle Station, which includes "everything needed to stage a battle," including a cannon with battery-generated light and sound effects. That one is recommended for ages three and up.

These kinds of toys "focus children's play on violent themes, undermine lessons adults teach, and bring in scary real-world themes young children cannot fully understand," notes the *Toy Action Guide* recently published by Teachers Resisting Unhealthy Children's Entertainment (TRUCE), a national organization of educators concerned with how toys and entertainment affect children's play and behavior.

"Such toys may fulfill a need for adults to feel patriotic or support U.S. troops," says Diane Levin, a professor of education at Wheelock College and the author of *Teaching Young Children in Violent Times*. "But they often channel children into narrowly scripted play and convey a message that violent play is OK and exciting." Choosing toys wisely is one way to begin teaching peace to children.

Schools can teach peace as well. Research shows that well-designed violence-prevention and conflict-resolution programs can have a significant positive impact on students. For example, independent evaluations of the Resolving Conflict Creatively Program, an initiative of Educators for Social Responsibility (ESR), found that it successfully teaches young people the skills of negotiation, mediation, and peacemaking.

ESR offers its program in four hundred schools around the country. In those schools, educators were better prepared for the events of 9/11, says Linda Lantieri, founding director of the program. "The children in our programs have learned the healing power of love and respect and understanding," Lantieri says. "They see the connection between the way they treat one another and the way they will treat the world when they are in charge."

The Alliance for Childhood, a nonprofit partnership of educators, health care professionals, and other advocates for children, has prepared a brief guide for parents and educators outlining eight concrete steps they can take for peace education at home and at school:

Make room for peace at home. Outer peace begins with inner peace. Children and adults need special places that give them a sense of privacy and peace and that can serve as a quiet refuge for times when hurt or angry feelings might lead to violent words or actions. It could be a room or just a corner, decorated simply and lovingly, where any family member can go for quiet reflection or prayer, or to work through turbulent feelings.

Find peace in nature. Turn off the television and the computer and go outside. Take children for a walk or let them explore nature in their own way. The beauty of nature is a great balm to the soul. Children often seek out their own secret outdoor spaces, even if it's only a corner of the backyard.

Make time for creative play. Young children need plenty of time for unstructured, creative play. Research indicates that make-believe social play in particular reduces aggression and increases empathy in children. Children also use make-believe play with others to work through feelings of fear and sadness. Choose children's toys carefully, avoiding those that encourage or glorify violence. TRUCE (www.truceteachers.org) prepares an annual guide to help parents choose good toys. The Lion and Lamb Project (www.lionlamb.org) focuses on how to avoid violent toys.

Engage children's hands and hearts. Young children need a direct, hands-on experience of giving. They love to make things, small and large—their own cards, tree ornaments, cookies, or bread—for neighbors, family, or friends. They can learn to enjoy sorting through their own things and even giving away some treasured possessions to others in need if it is part of a family tradition.

Establish a "family foundation." Create a homemade bank for donations—a miniature family foundation. Parents, children, visitors, and friends can put money in the bank. Children can be introduced to tithing when they receive gifts, earnings, or allowance. Choose a charity together—one that has personal meaning for the children. When there is a flood, fire, or other disaster, the family can gather to decide whether to make a special donation from the family bank. As the children mature, talk to them more about the needs of the world and ways they can help.

Support peace education at school. Urge your early-childhood center or school to establish or strengthen peace education and conflict-resolution programs. Contact ESR (www.esrnational.org) or the National Peace Foundation (www.nationalpeace.org) for ideas, including advice on how to create "peace places" in schools, where students can go to negotiate and mediate conflicts and resolve disputes nonviolently.

Encourage older students to study a conflict-ridden area of the world, looking at it from two or more perspectives. When students read books and talk to people from each side, they learn that every conflict has many layers and that building peace requires working respectfully with all sides. For resources to help you with this kind of study, contact the Karuna Center for Peacebuilding (www.karunacenter.org); Facing History and Ourselves (www.facinghistory.org), which has resources for students to learn about the dangers of stereotyping, prejudice, and hatred; and the Public Conversations Project (www.publicconversations.org), which also offers resources for creating dialogues on divisive issues.

Face local needs. Help children become comfortable with the people in your community who need help—the elderly, the disabled, the poor. Starting in middle school, students benefit enormously from working in hospitals, soup kitchens, animal shelters, and the like. Make sure there is someone there to mentor the young person when such experiences become emotionally painful or confusing.

Make a difference in the world. Help young people find active ways of working for peace, the preservation of the natural world, the relief of human suffering, or other concerns through organizations like Jane Goodall's Roots and Shoots (www.janegoodall.org), Larry and Jane Levine's Kids Can Make a Difference (www.kidscanmakeadifference.org), Craig Kielburger's Free the Children (www.freethechildren.org), or PeaceJam (www.peacejam.org), in which students work directly with Nobel Peace Prize laureates.

DARK ENOUGH
TO SEE THE STARS

CATHERINE INGRAM

Catherine Ingram is an internationally known dharma teacher with communities serving several thousand students in a dozen cities in the United States and Europe. She is the author of *In the Footsteps of Gandhi* and *Passionate Presence*. She is a cofounder of Insight Meditation Society in Barre, Massachusetts, widely considered the most prestigious Buddhist meditation center in the West. She is also a cofounder of the Unrepresented Nations and Peoples Organization. This excerpt is adapted from *In the Footsteps of Gandhi*.

The history of war in both the ancient and modern world makes one wonder if war is an irresistible compulsion for human beings. Perhaps the pull toward violence or at least occasional bloodletting is a deep need in the human psyche, an evolutionary adaptation we struggle to understand. What is this love of war, of violence, of bloodshed? Is it ever possible to, as a species, love peace more than war?

To answer this we need only look at the lives of people who dedicated themselves to loving peace. The names we remember and celebrate in history—Gautama Buddha, Jesus Christ, Saint Teresa of Avila, Lao-tzu, and many others—were all beings of peace. We mostly do not know and certainly do not celebrate the names of the warriors of those times. In more recent history, Mahatma Gandhi, Martin Luther King Jr., Aung San Suu Kyi, and the Dalai Lama are spoken of with the reverence reserved for people whose presence on this troubled earth soothes the spirit. We celebrate their existence because there is an awareness in most of us that recognizes goodness, kindness, and fair play when we see it. In other words, those people who have most inspired us have always offered messages of love and nonviolence. This speaks to an inherent wisdom that exists in our hearts, despite our behavior.

We sometimes make the conceptual mistake of thinking that people whose message was love and peace belonged on the whole to former times. We think of those people as legends in a historical context, or we assume that they were from traditional cultures whose values accommodated such quaint views. But what if those lives were not so much an example of where we have historically been as of where we need to go? Not of how we once were but how we might become? What if humankind is being compelled to evolve into peaceful animals, or else face extinction?

Martin Luther King Jr. said, "I know somehow that only when it is dark enough can you see the stars." It is now our time to shine in the darkness, to honor the values for which we have worked over many years, and to keep our strength by remembering that love is the only power that lasts.

❧⦿❧

"Peace cannot be achieved through violence;
it can only be attained through understanding."

—Albert Einstein

THE MIND CAN BE
A PRISON OR A DOOR

SUSAN GRIFFIN

"Is not the change we have seen astonishing . . ."
—John Adams, 1776

War starts in the mind, not in the body.

Waging war is not a primary physical need.

Though war can cause anger and grief, or be fueled by those emotions, war is not a feeling. Nor, though war is aggressive, is it an impulse.

War must be carefully organized.

War is not designed by nature and it is not universal. It is instead the product of some but not all human cultures.

To become good soldiers, men must be trained, humiliated, and taught to obey orders automatically. They must learn to ignore their own intelligence, their natural physical reactions (such as fear) and basic emotions (such as compassion).

War arises from unfounded ideas and distorted perceptions aided by lies and silence.

Very few wars have been judged by history as necessary for self-defense.

To imagine peace is not nearly as sentimental as to think of war as glorious. In modern warfare, more civilians die than soldiers.

War is not inevitable. The only thing in the universe that is inevitable is change.

Chapter 3

BUILDING A
STRONGER
ANTIWAR
MOVEMENT

ACTIVISTS AS
AMBASSADORS

PHYLLIS BENNIS

Phyllis Bennis has been a writer, an analyst, and an activist for many years. Her publications include *Understanding the Palestinian-Israeli Conflict, Before and After*, which analyzes U.S. foreign policy after 9/11, and *Calling the Shots*, about the United States' role in the United Nations. Currently she is a fellow of the Institute for Policy Studies (www.ips-dc.org).

In late 2002, when American antiwar groups began working with groups in other countries to oppose the pending war on Iraq, something new happened: for the first time, masses of people showed an extraordinary understanding of the global consequences of the war and the need for the whole world to stand against it. I've been calling this phenomenon "the new internationalism."

For my generation, who came of age during the last years of the Vietnam War, the movement against the war in Iraq marked the first time we had seen such widespread global resistance, thanks partly to the presence of technology that allows for easy communication and a coordination of efforts around the world. The February 15, 2003, demonstrations in cities and towns across the planet were a triumph of mobilization: they made it impossible for governments to sign on to the Bush agenda, which in turn made it impossible for the Bush administration to claim that this was a war backed by the whole world. So even though the demonstrators were not able to prevent the war from being waged, they were able to prevent it from being legitimized. And this lack of international legitimacy helped broaden the movement at home to more mainstream organizations. Campaigns such as Cities for Peace, in which 165 American cities signed antiwar resolutions, would never have happened if this war had been authorized by the UN Security Council.

But looking back, I can see that I didn't understand early enough the significance of the global movement. I don't think American activists did enough to mobilize people around the world to pressure the United Nations. Unfortunately, there is a strong anti-UN streak in the global peace movement. In 1995, Madeleine Albright shocked many by bluntly stating Washington's view that the United Nations was a tool of American foreign policy. But the truth is that the UN is a tool of American foreign policy only sometimes.

There are also times when it stands up to U.S. pressure, and that happens when there's a global mobilization that compels governments to take difficult positions.

During the buildup to the war in Iraq, CODEPINK engaged in enormously creative actions, such as support rallies at the Washington embassies of several nations that opposed the war. Activists would have been wise to keep up the pressure on the recalcitrant countries and continue praising the countries that were doing the right thing, even if they were countries whose policies on other issues are found wanting. The South African government, for example, enters into terrible arms deals with countries around the continent, but in the international arena it is playing an extraordinarily important role in building international governmental support against empire.

We have to be sophisticated enough to understand that governments standing against war, even for the wrong reasons, can be tactical allies. France, Germany, and Russia had their own opportunistic motives for opposing the U.S. invasion—we can recognize that, yet welcome their position. We can't afford to be absolutist in our tactics and our strategies. Our principles are absolute, but our strategies have to be responsive to current conditions.

In the fall of 2002, a very small team of us from IPS tried to work some magic at the United Nations—we hoped the international body would invite Nelson Mandela to speak to the Security Council against the impending war. Mandela's impassioned words, we thought, might keep the Security Council from caving in to Bush's war. Despite ill health, Mandela seemed agreeable, but the process of wrangling an invitation was nightmarish, with late-night phone calls to government representatives on the other side of the world. While this plan ultimately fell through because of diplomatic challenges, it opened my eyes to the potential of enlisting the aid of the most influential individuals in the world in a moment of global crisis.

On the day of the massive global peace rallies, a small group—Archbishop Desmond Tutu from South Africa; Harry Belafonte and his wife, Julie; and I—had an extraordinary meeting with UN Secretary-General Kofi Annan. The secretary-general, Archbishop Tutu, and Harry Belafonte had all known each other for years, but they were sitting on opposite sides of the table, literally—Kofi Annan and his advisers on one side and our delegation on the other. When the meeting began, Archbishop Tutu said a prayer, and then he made the most extraordinary statement: "We are here today on behalf of the people that are marching in 665 cities around the world," he said. "We're here to tell you that those people marching in those cities all around the world claim the United Nations as our own, and we claim it in the name of the global mobilization for peace." I'll never forget the magnificent dignity with which he delivered those stirring words.

Kofi Annan's response could be seen in his face. Probably the last thing he wanted to hear that day from his close friends and allies was that we were holding him accountable, because the pressures on him to give in to the United States were intense. You could see that every fiber of him wanted to say, "Yes, I stand with you and the people outside. I'm going to come out with you and speak to the crowd." But he didn't say that. He couldn't say that—the pressure was just too great.

Then we each spoke in turn. I talked about the global nature of the mobilization; Julie Belafonte addressed the particular danger of the war for women; Harry spoke about the significance of this global movement. When it was over, we bundled up and went back outside to what was the coldest day of the year in New York, with a bitter wind blowing down First Avenue as we made our way through the huge crowd that had swelled to over five hundred thousand.

After we each addressed the crowd, we received a call backstage from someone who had seen an Associated Press story that had come over the wire. It was just two lines: "The U.S. and Britain, stunned by the outpouring of global criticism, today announced their intention to change their proposed resolution at the UN. The new resolution would not explicitly call on the UN to endorse the war." That was all it said.

If true, it was a huge victory. We huddled backstage to figure out whether we should announce it to the crowd, and several of us said, "We've got to say it. Even if it turns out not to be true, the fact that AP is running the story at this moment means there's enough of a buzz in Washington that these demonstrations around the world are having an effect." So I went out onstage again in front of half a million people and said, "If anyone believes that these kinds of demonstrations don't matter, listen up." I read the AP story and the crowd roared.

∞

"You can no more win a war than you can win an earthquake."

—Jeanette Rankin

A PERMANENT
PEOPLE'S MOVEMENT

LESLIE CAGAN

Leslie Cagan is the national coordinator of United for Peace and Justice, the nation's largest antiwar coalition. She has a lifelong history of activism on domestic issues such as lesbian/gay rights and foreign-policy issues such as the Cuba embargo. She was one of the coordinators of the massive February 15, 2003, rallies to protest the impending war on Iraq.

In the fall of 2002, when Congress was voting for the bill to authorize the invasion of Iraq, I started to sense that a resurgent antiwar movement was brewing. Those in Washington who follow Congress more closely than I do were hoping that 25 or 30 representatives would vote against the authorization for war being sought by the Bush administration. The bill passed by a wide margin, but to our amazement, 133 members of the House voted against it! We knew they must have been hearing from their constituents.

Dissent was bubbling up from below. Throughout the country, people felt they had to do something to stop the war. With a crucial vote coming up in Congress, they decided to contact their representatives—by telephone, e-mail, fax, or visits to their offices. At that time, there was really no national organization coordinating all of this work. Discussions amongst a dozen or so long-time peace activities led to the conclusion that it was time to form a national coalition that could strengthen the growing antiwar movement, and so United for Peace and Justice was created in October 2002.

In June 2003, United for Peace and Justice had its founding conference in Chicago, with representatives from hundreds of organizations. This was one of the most amazing moments in my long experience in the peace and social-justice movement—a rare example of individual groups understanding that they are stronger when acting as part of a larger collective and functioning as a movement.

With 550 attendees representing 325 organizations, we faced a difficult task as we tried to agree on a strategic framework for our work and a program for the coming eighteen months. In the end, virtually everyone embraced the goals that we hammered out, and many people expressed their appreciation for this experience in grassroots democracy. It demonstrated that local, community-based organizations want to be part of a federation that allows them

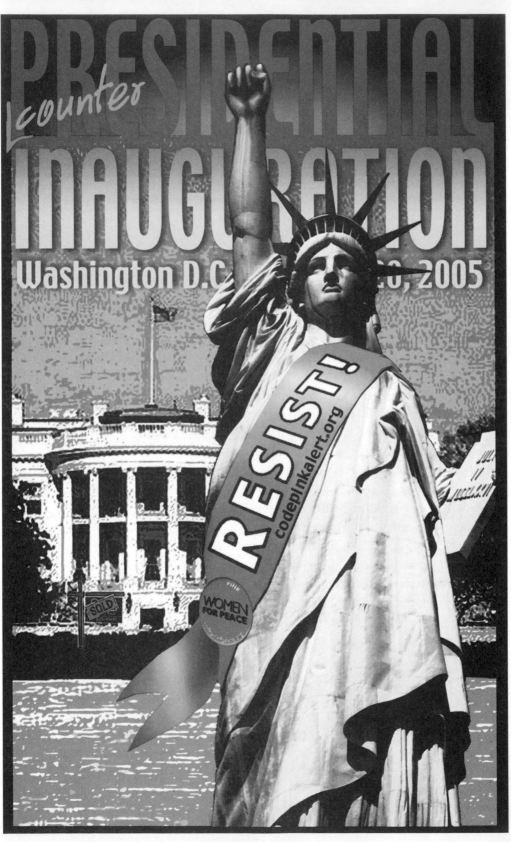

Presidential Counter Inauguration
Washington D.C. ...0, 2005

RESIST!
codepinkalert.org

PINK
WOMEN FOR PEACE

© 2005 by Sarah Rath

to keep control over their own plans and agendas but that also links them to other local and national groups that think about the world in similar ways. By the end of 2004, our coalition numbered more than 900 groups.

We encourage lots of local activism, and we've also organized mass national mobilizations. Our most phenomenal rally took place on February 15, 2003, right before the war began. In New York City, hundreds of thousands of people came out in the freezing cold, in spite of a concerted effort by the mayor and police department to block our demonstration. And on the same day millions of other people, in more than nine hundred places around the world (by our count), staged their own protests. Some were massive, some were tiny—but all were extraordinary. At a nursing home in lower Manhattan, for example, the residents who felt strongly against the war made signs and held a little demonstration of their own in the lobby of the nursing home.

There's no way to know how many people hit the streets or the lobbies of their nursing homes on that day. But millions of people around the world knew that what the Bush administration was doing was absolutely wrong. And by protesting together, we all knew we were part of something much bigger than ourselves; we were part of a historic global outcry against war.

The organizing of simultaneous demonstrations of millions of people gave us a glimpse of what it would be like to have a permanent global people's movement. The work of this burgeoning movement goes on every single day. People are holding educational forums, organizing vigils, lobbying their elected officials, writing letters to the editor, gathering shipments of humanitarian aid to Iraq—these day-to-day actions are the heart and soul of the movement. But one of the shortcomings of the movement is our lack of long-term planning. During the Bush administration, in particular, we have been jumping from crisis to crisis—trying to defeat the Bush agenda in the 2004 elections, trying to stop the war in Iraq, trying to deal with the ongoing crisis in Palestine and Israel, and so many other important issues.

When a building is burning down, you rush to hose it down. You don't immediately start analyzing what led to the fire and what could be done to prevent future fires. But while we respond to emergencies and the urgent needs of the moment, we must also engage in strategic planning. We have to do a better job challenging the corporate and political forces that drive us to war. We have to create a global people's movement that is firmly grounded at the local level and is coordinated at both the national and international levels. That's the only way we're going to stop present wars. And it's certainly the only way we're going to prevent future ones.

A LIFE IN THE MOVEMENT:
AN INTERVIEW WITH FRIDA BERRIGAN

MEDEA BENJAMIN

Frida Berrigan is a senior research associate with the World Policy Institute's Arms Trade Resource Center. The eldest daughter of peace activists Liz McAlister and Phillip Berrigan, she was raised in a Catholic peacemaking community. Here she is in conversation with CODEPINK cofounder Medea Benjamin.

Q: *What was it like growing up with a family and a community dedicated to trying to end war and rid the world of nuclear weapons?*

A: My parents founded the Jonah House Community in 1973, the year before I was born. Jonah House is an experiment in nonviolence by a radical Catholic community. Hundreds of people came through the house, many of whom spent time in prison for acts of civil disobedience, first against the war in Vietnam and then against nuclear weapons and militarism.

The Jonah House Community was located in a very poor neighborhood in Baltimore. We painted houses to make a living and lived way below the taxable income. I learned very early on about the monthly cycle that many Americans go through who depend on public assistance—with a little bit of money at the beginning of the month and none at the end. We organized weekly food drives and shared the food with about two hundred people in the neighborhood. For many of our neighbors, the fruits and vegetables that we scavenged often made up the core of their food.

As a child I learned how wasteful and unjust our society is, with so much money for the military and so little to help the poor. Now that I'm looking at the military budget as an analyst for the World Policy Institute, I see the full dimensions of this waste and maldistribution of resources. Lockheed Martin receives more each year from the Defense Department than is spent on the entire public-assistance program—Temporary Assistance for Needy Families—a program that tens of millions of Americans depend on.

Q: *Your parents and your uncle Daniel Berrigan became famous as a result of their acts of civil disobedience against the Vietnam War. Can you describe these?*

A: My dad, my uncle, and some friends started this new form of civil disobedience that consisted of destroying draft records. The Catonsville Nine is the best known of those actions. In 1968, they walked into the draft-board office in Catonsville, Maryland, carried about six hundred draftees' files out to the parking lot, and burned them with homemade napalm. As Catholics, they had a sense of reverence for the act as ritual, but it was also real and tangible. Afterward, guys used to come up to my dad and say, "Thank you for destroying my draft files. You saved my life, because I didn't have to go to Vietnam."

Q: *After the Vietnam War ended, the Jonah House Community turned its focus to abolishing nuclear weapons. This seems so much harder than struggling against a particular war, because the weapons industry is less visible to the public and has no "end." Tell us about the "plowshares actions."*

A: In 1980, my dad and seven others began what are now known as "plowshares actions." It comes from the idea that the biblical prophet Isaiah calls us to turn spears into pruning hooks, swords into plowshares. They went into a General Electric plant in Pennsylvania and did a symbolic disarmament of Mark 12A nose cones, which carry the nuclear material. They were convicted of felonies and spent about a year and a half in prison for that action. During his life, my dad did four more plowshares actions. My mom was involved in one at an air force base in upstate New York in 1983. My dad says he and my mother spent eleven years apart because of their periods of prison time.

Q: *Some people say that these kinds of actions require too much sacrifice, that they take our best activists out of commission for years, that they are too hard on families—especially families with children. Some also question whether these actions really make changes that are significant enough to warrant the sacrifice. How would your parents or your uncle respond to that type of criticism?*

A: They would probably say that you can never sacrifice enough for peace. More than thirty years ago my uncle Dan wrote: "We have assumed the name of peacemaker, but we have been, by and large, unwilling to pay any significant price. And because we want peace with half a heart and half a life and will, the war, of course, continues. Because the waging of war, by its nature, is total, but the waging of peace, by our own cowardice, is partial."

Q: *How would you evaluate the movement against war in Iraq? We managed to get lots of people out for some large demonstrations, but do we lack the kind of "put your body on the line" commitment that your parents had and still have?*

A: I think that twelve million people around the world coming out on February 15, 2003, was extraordinary and really powerful. Yet once the war started, the protesters went home. They felt demoralized and defeated, as if their efforts hadn't paid off. We didn't manage to hold the space that was created on that day when the world said no to war. Through the months of the war and occupation, we have had an opportunity and, really, a responsibility to continue to be in the streets and to be a visible opposition to the war, day after day.

The problem, of course, is that we all have this tension between our personal and political lives where we say, "OK, I've done that, but now I want to go home and get back to normal." We need to ask, "Can we go back to normal when our government is killing people in our name?" We need to think about how to create a lifestyle that is opposed to war in every way, so that there is no going home at the end of the march to our "normal lives."

Q: *It's so hard to do that.* CODEPINK *called for an ongoing vigil in front of the White House in opposition to the pending war in Iraq, and we kept it going for four months, in the dead of winter. We created this critical space right in front of the most important location in this country, and we thought people would give up their lives and join us en masse. They didn't—especially absent were women your age, women in their thirties and forties. We had younger women and middle-aged women. What accounts for that?*

A: I think it's a problem of our whole culture, and I'm guilty of it also. Even people who, on an intellectual level, know what's wrong and what needs to be done feel limited in what they can do. "I can vigil at the White House on my day off or be part of a protest on a Saturday, but I couldn't commit a week because I have rent to pay, I have student loans to pay off," and so on. We need to figure out how to create cultures that support more than weekend opposition to war.

My parents and the Jonah House Community created a communal structure that sustained them. They didn't own a house or anything worth confiscating; they didn't have salaries or worry about where their next meal was coming from. That freed them to act at any hour on any day, to go to prison for long periods of time, to have their whole lives be about resisting war, whether it was an active war in Vietnam or the preparations for the next war.

Q: *So, forgive me, but I have to ask: Given that you grew up learning how to create that amazing kind of activist life, with such intense dedication and personal sacrifice, why aren't you living like that now?*

A: I guess I wanted to put on the suit of a professional and see what that felt like. Once you do that, it's hard to move out of that again. I'm still in touch with communities that resist, but I personally live in real tension and contradiction, and that's very uncomfortable.

Q: *It's not like you became a corporate CEO. You do important research on militarism, building on the connections that you first made as a young child. You and your institute put out critical information about war profiteering and the impact of militarism.*

A: A lot of people say that research is very important and we need more people who can provide good information. People are very kind in validating the work I do, but having this conversation about the shortcomings of our movement is uncomfortable, because I know I could be doing so much more.

Q: *Me, too. After our four-month vigil in front of the White House, after leaving my kids, my husband, and spending time in cold, lonely jail cells when we got arrested, I couldn't wait to go back to my comfortable life. And I see so many people who think they are good activists because they respond to an e-mail alert or sign an online petition. Do you think the computer age and e-activism have given people an easy out?*

A: Yes. That stuff is not bad, but it's not going to change anything all by itself. Every time you press a button on your computer to respond to some action alert, you feel you've done something and perhaps it relieves you of the need to do more. The other problem is that everyone is giving money to MoveOn and other groups that run ads in newspapers and on TV, but that money is moving in the wrong direction. The idea that we would spend $800,000 of people's hard-earned $15 and $20 donations for a thirty-second spot during the Super Bowl—as MoveOn was planning to do—is just nuts. The money should be moving the other way, to community organizers. If large numbers of people started supporting organizers in local communities, people who are actually working full time as peace and justice activists, then we would have a real impact.

Let's remember, human connections and relationships are what make change happen. At the end of the day, it's who we are and how we educate, treat, help, and inspire each other that will put an end to war.

Q: *Speaking of education, would you say that educating the public about militarism and the scourge of nuclear weapons is one of the most critical things we can do?*

A: We certainly need to do a better job educating people about this massive military machine that doesn't sleep and is churning out weapons constantly, whether the nation is in active conflict or not. When you have all these weapons, you will find opportunities to use them. When Bush went to war in Afghanistan in October of 2001, everything was basically in place, including a huge standing army. The United States spends more than $1 billion a day just on maintaining this military complex, excluding the "extra costs" of military ventures in Afghanistan, Iraq, and elsewhere.

We could cut at least $100 billion from the military budget without jeopardizing our security. For example, there are three new fighter-plane programs that are redundancies of the existing fighter-plane programs—the F-16s and F-18s—that will cost U.S. taxpayers about $200 billion. We need to demand that funds earmarked for unnecessary weapons programs go to vital human services instead.

As a movement, we should also do a better job working with members of Congress when the military budget comes up every year and some congresspeople start questioning particular weapons systems. And, of course, we need to get better at talking to Middle America about the bread-and-butter issues, about how all this wasted money is coming out of their pockets—and is not making them more secure. We have people in this country working two or three jobs to make $25,000 or $30,000 a year to support their families. We have to show them that one of the reasons they're struggling is that so much of the wealth of this country is going into this cult of militarism.

Q: *Do you have any concrete examples of campaigns that have done a good job making these connections?*

A: We have this tendency to think only about national campaigns or programs. I think we need to take our lead from local initiatives. There is a group in Brooklyn called Families United for Racial and Economic Equality, FUREE.

They are mostly women on public assistance who have organized poor people in Brooklyn to get access to the types of assistance that are available. They lobby state officials like Hillary Clinton. In 2003, they took a bus to Bush's ranch in Crawford on this poor people's march. The idea was to bring Bush a manifesto about what he should be doing for poor people in this country instead of making wars overseas. Of course, they got stopped miles from Bush's ranch, but they came back making these connections between their daily lives and U.S. foreign policy.

Antiwar activists need to be involved in those sorts of local initiatives. We don't need to lead those efforts, but we need to be participants. It keeps you going between crises, because you're connected to real communities. These people live near each other; they know each other's families; they are involved with each other as friends and neighbors. Being part of that for me, as a single person, has been incredibly important.

Q: *When you are out speaking on campuses, what's the most important message you try to convey to students?*

A: I tell them that there is no reason for Americans to be poor. There is no reason for students to incur tens of thousands of dollars in debt to go to college. There is no reason that a whole class of Americans should be homeless. We have the resources, and we have the obligation to share them with each other and the rest of the world. But we can't do that if we continue to spend over $400 billion a year on the military.

I also encourage them to become activists. I let them know that although our efforts may not bring instant success, there are still rewards: a meaningful life, the community and friendship we find on the vigil lines, in the paddy wagons, and even in the long meetings. The communities we build among ourselves are an antidote to despair and selfishness. They hold us accountable and challenge us to be more radical. And, surely, at this time in our history, we have to nurture more radical activism.

∾o∾

"Activism is my rent for living on this planet."
—Alice Walker

THE PATIENCE **TO WIN**

EISHA MASON

Eisha Mason is the executive director of the Center for the Advancement of Nonviolence. She has worked with teens for more than twenty years and coauthored the *64 Ways to Practice Nonviolence* curriculum and resource guide. She is also the cofounder and director of the community outreach ministries of the Agape International Center of Truth.

If we listen uncritically to the mass media, we may believe that we in the peace movement have endured one defeat after another in the past few years. That is, however, far from the truth! A successful movement is so much more than a series of protests. It is more than a single campaign. Our individual and collective efforts to stop the war in Iraq became a catalyst for building the necessary framework of a movement capable of winning true peace and justice for our society and the world. We have much to celebrate and much to build upon as we face the challenges ahead of us.

In his reflections on the civil rights movement, Dr. Martin Luther King Jr. said, "The ultimate tragedy of Birmingham was not the brutality of the bad people, but the silence of the good people." Let us, therefore, celebrate that we were not silent. At a time when it was so easy to be cowed by media hysteria and an administration that called us "traitors" and "collaborators with the enemy," we dared to question authority and think for ourselves. When it was easier to keep silent in family gatherings or in the lunchroom at work, when neighbors may have turned away from us, when we sometimes thought we were all alone, we chose to stand in truth. When we were pumped an intravenous diet of fear each day, we chose to be true to our own consciences.

We created public debate. Even though we were all but shut out of the mainstream media, we created forums in which other voices representing intelligence communities, the government, progressive media, and peace and justice organizations could share information that corporate media could not or would not report. We countered the myth that this war was justified and that it would make us safer.

We united globally. Just as our spirits soared when we learned of the millions of people worldwide demonstrating for peace, for justice, and for international law, so did our global brothers and sisters take heart when they learned of our efforts in the United States. Our voices and actions might not have been covered effectively at home, but we were accurately reported abroad. Never before have ten million voices made a single cry: "Peace Now!"

We organized an infrastructure. In neighborhood peace and justice groups, we established our local communication networks and agreed on the principles by which we would operate. We came up with a process for decision making and conflict resolution, with methods of outreach, and with effective ways of working together and raising funds.

We connected the dots. We began to grasp the relationships between global trade policies and civil and economic policies in America. We came together with other populations in our communities, populations we did not previously take the time to know—and because of this, our movement broadened and deepened in numbers, in diversity, in resources, and in strength. Today, our togetherness continues, and many of us are supporting striking or locked-out workers, immigrants, and marginalized children and families in our communities.

We chose love. We have grown in love and compassion, because we learned that our anger alone would not sustain us. We have grown in our capacity to take responsibility for our own lives and for creating the world we want. We have grown in courage: the courage to occupy street corners with placards, the courage to march, the courage to say, "Peace and justice for all," and the courage not to retaliate when others call us names. We have discovered that our passion for what we love is so much greater than our fear.

We became leaders. Many of us never talked politics before, never spoke to our neighbors before, never organized a committee, never called an elected official, never sought out alternative news sources, never took action. Yet today we can assert that we have stepped into leadership.

We made peace the way. We have succeeded in maintaining our movement as a nonviolent one. In our marches, we are demonstrating what democracy and peace look like, and our movement is growing because of it.

We have succeeded in all of these ways, but we must do more. The victory we seek will not come today or tomorrow. Cesar Chavez knew all about that when he spoke of the "patience to win." It was sixteen years after the Gandhi Salt March that India finally won its independence. The civil rights movement did not begin with Rosa Parks's refusal to give up her bus seat—it had evolved through the sacrifices of community leaders and ordinary people who had worked for years to create the right conditions for Parks's historic moment. Our success will rest on no one campaign but on our cumulative, ongoing efforts—and we must be prepared for the ebb and flow that is a natural part of this work.

One of the signature moments in the long, hard struggle of the civil rights movement was the five-day march from Selma to Montgomery, Alabama, in 1965. Having arrived with twenty-five thousand other marchers, Dr. Martin Luther King Jr. spoke to the frustrations of so many dedicated activists:

> I know you are asking today, "How long will it take?" Somebody's asking, "How long will prejudice blind the visions of men, darken their understanding, and drive bright-eyed wisdom from her sacred throne?" Somebody's asking, "When will wounded justice, lying prostrate on the streets of Selma and Birmingham, be lifted from this dust of shame to reign supreme among the children of men?" Somebody's asking, "How long will justice be crucified?"
>
> I come to say to you: however difficult the moment, however frustrating the hour, it will not be long, because truth crushed to earth will rise again. How long? Not long, because no lie can live forever. How long? Not long, because you shall reap what you sow. How long? Not long, because the arc of the moral universe is long, but it bends toward justice.

King said, "The battle is in our hands." This is why we are here, on earth, at this time, in this nation. This is not the first time nor the last time that people will struggle for peace, but this is *our* time. We are the ones we've been waiting for: housewives, students, bus drivers, schoolteachers, librarians, welfare mothers, the unemployed, artists, and activists. Let us all look ahead: resolved, reenergized, and rededicated to creating a world that is just, and a world that thrives in peace.

CODEPINK marches at the Republican National Convention in New York City, August 2004.

A NEW COALITION

REBECCA SOLNIT

Rebecca Solnit is a writer whose work focuses on issues of environment, landscape, and place. Her books include *As Eve Said to the Serpent*, which was nominated for the National Book Critics Circle Award in criticism, and the recent *River of Shadows*, about Eadweard Muybridge and the impact of technology on the Wild West.

So many people felt, after 9/11, not only grief and fear but a huge upwelling of openness, of a readiness to question and to learn, and to understand our connections to each other. That desire is still out there. It's the force behind a huge new movement we don't have a name for yet, a movement that's not a left opposed to a right, but perhaps a below against an above, little against big, local and decentralized against consolidated—it's a vast aquifer of passion now stored up to feed the river of change.

In the spring of 2003, several hundred peace activists gathered at dawn at the port of Oakland, California, to picket the gates of a company shipping arms to Iraq. The police arrived in riot gear and, unprovoked and unthreatened, shot wooden bullets and beanbags at the activists. Three members of the media, nine longshoremen, and fifty activists were injured. I saw bloody welts as big as half grapefruits on the backs of some young men and a swelling the size of an egg on the jaw of a delicate yoga instructor. But the violence inspired the union dockworkers to form closer alliances with antiwar activists and underscored the connections between local and global issues. We picketed again a month later, with no violence. This time, the longshoremen acted in solidarity with the picketers, and—for the first time in anyone's memory—the shipping companies canceled the work shift rather than face the protesters. After the picket was broken up, one immigrant truck driver pulled over to ask for a peace sign for his rig. I pierced holes in it so he could bungee-cord it to the chrome grille. He was turned back at the gates—the ships wouldn't accept deliveries from antiwar truckers. When I saw him next, he was sitting on a curb behind police lines, looking cheerful and fearless. Who knows what will ultimately come of the spontaneous courage of this man with a job on the line?

ᔋᕽᔋ

"There is no time left for anything but to make
peace work a dimension of our every waking activity."
—Elise Boulding

THE ART OF MISBEHAVIN'

DIANE WILSON

Diane Wilson is a mother of five and a fourth-generation shrimper from the Texas Gulf Coast. Through hunger strikes and other direct action, she has been putting pressure on chemical companies to stop poisoning the bay. A longtime environmentalist and peace activist, Wilson is one of the founding members of CODEPINK.

I went to Iraq with a group of CODEPINK women just before the U.S. invasion in March 2003. Before I left, I had heard a lot about how the Iraqis hated Americans and envied our lifestyle and freedom. With that in mind, I was totally surprised with what I experienced in Baghdad—instead of hatred and suspicion and grudges galore, I met people who were open and curious and generous. When I asked them if they were angry about the Americans on the verge of bombing their country, they all said, "We know it isn't the American people at fault, but the administration." Unlike so many people in the United States who think all Arabs are terrorists, Iraqis understood the difference between the American people and U.S. government policies.

Despite their unfailing graciousness, the Iraqis were quite afraid of the U.S. invasion. The waiters in our Baghdad hotel begged us not to leave. The children who met us every morning after our coffee—and who charmed us with their sales of pastries and scarves and shoe shines—hung on to our arms on our last day there and cried tears of desperation. They acted as if somehow, if we remained, the bombs wouldn't fall.

The Iraqi people had no idea what to do to protect themselves and, in a futile gesture, taped up their windows. It reminded me a lot of what happens in my own hometown when a hurricane threatens the Gulf Coast: it's almost surreal. A monumental thing is fixing to happen and there's not much you can do to prepare for it, but you know it's going to change your life.

Even before I'd arrived in Baghdad, I had been opposed to the war. I was raised in a small coastal fishing town in a state where concealed handguns are legal and hunting is equated with ritual. But I had developed a total aversion to killing. During my time as an army medic in the Vietnam War, I saw firsthand (in a boot camp in Georgia and in a medical ward in Fort Sam Houston) what happens to eighteen-year-old boys conscripted into wartime service: their descent from innocent enthusiasm into a hell of drugs and violence and numbing withdrawal. In the wards where I worked, patients

Twenty-third Street, New York City, March 20, 2004: Banner drop of the infamous CODEPINK "pink slip."
© Fred Askew

constantly swiped needles to shoot up. A pot haze hung in the air like smoke from a lingering fire. This was a lost generation of boys.

This wasn't something I wanted to see again. So before the war began, I went with Medea Benjamin to Washington, D.C., and we disrupted a House Armed Services Committee hearing where Donald Rumsfeld, the secretary of defense, was stating his case for war with Iraq. It was a spontaneous moment spurred by our wish to do something to stop the war, and it made national news because we did it while the TV cameras in the room were rolling.

One month later, a group of women from across the nation staged a hunger strike and vigil at Lafayette Park in front of the White House. We remained in the park, in the dead of winter, protesting the war and promoting peace for several months. During one protest, I scaled the fence in front of the White House with an antiwar banner and stayed up there for about five minutes until I was shoved to the ground by the Secret Service. For that action, I was arrested, jailed, and banned from Washington for an entire year. The Secret Service felt so threatened by our nonviolent antiwar protests that they even followed me to my hometown in Seadrift!

Still, I felt compelled to do more than just sit in Seadrift and grieve. So on the day before half a million Americans took to the streets of New York and people around the globe protested the invasion, a delegation of CODEPINK women assembled before the UN gate to protest. I climbed the fence and chained myself to it. I was then arrested and sent to trial. Later, back in Texas, two other protesters and I stood in the state capitol and shouted down a resolution supporting the war. For that I got four days in a women's correctional facility outside Austin.

But still, I didn't do enough. I don't think I've ever regretted any failure as much. A war rages, children die, families are blown apart—and we are all too well behaved.

I'm a fourth-generation commercial fisherwoman, born and raised in Texas and baptized in a river by a Pentecostal preacher. I've also been an environmental activist fighting the destruction on the Texas bays for years. My environmental activism flowed into the peace movement, and that flowed into CODEPINK. Just like the ecosystem where I shrimp, it's all connected. The corporations like Formosa and Dupont and Dow are destroying the Texas bays and killing small communities like my town, and the federal government is bombing a whole country to control its oil. It's the same destructive mentality at work.

When we say we don't want war, those can't just be words. Stopping a war takes a real commitment, and that means putting ourselves at risk. We have to pursue peace as aggressively as others want to make war. In our own American history, people have laid their lives on the line for their beliefs. To paraphrase one of them, Dr. Martin Luther King Jr.: If you don't have something in your life that you'd die for, then you don't have much to live for.

So we need to be bold and imaginative and brave. We've got to be heroes.

∾o∾

"No single person can liberate a country.
You can only liberate a country if you act as a collective."

—Nelson Mandela

NURTURE NEW ACTIVISTS

MARTI HIKEN

Marti Hiken is the cochair of the Military Law Task Force of the National Lawyers Guild.

When I first started college at the University of California Riverside during the Vietnam War, I merrily went to classes. I was young, I was away from home for the first time, and I was pro-war. Every day at noon, I walked across the courtyard to go to one of my classes, and one day there was a woman there from UC Berkeley—you know, a wild hippie—who was antiwar. She was arguing with a group of people about Vietnam. She went around in a circle and talked to everyone there. At one point she singled me out because I was so pro-war. We argued and argued. The next day I was walking through the courtyard and saw her again. I stopped and listened and argued. This went on for weeks. Every day she would take me on—going over the same points, trying to convince me.

Then one day I was walking through the courtyard and she wasn't there. I felt this loneliness, but then I suddenly realized that I didn't need her anymore, that she had fulfilled her purpose for being there: I was now against the war. I never learned her name, but I learned that a real exchange of ideas can change people's lives—it certainly changed mine.

NOT RONALD REAGAN'S
ANTIWAR MOVEMENT

BECKY BOND

Becky Bond is a creative producer for Working Assets.

The work of stopping the next war started with broad-based opposition to the preemptive invasion of Iraq. When a large swath of the American public is moved to take a stand, only to discover that their thoughtful protest is ignored by those who purport to represent them, they return to fight with renewed strength. If we want to win, we must continue to be an inclusive movement and push for success where we settled for narrow defeat in the past. And we must fight as though we are entitled to victory.

Even though we did not stop the preemptive attack on Iraq, the millions of Americans who opposed the war laid the groundwork for preventing the next war. Citizens did their job by lobbying the president and Congress with e-mails, calls, and letters protesting the rush to preemptive war. But in a cynical move, progressive leaders in both houses joined the pro-war forces in hopes of burnishing their credentials for a far-off presidential race.

We were defeated. But when the peace groups sat down to plan the protests in the streets, the unexpected occurred. It wasn't just the regular suspects who showed up. Everybody marched, a group as diverse as it was broad.

March after march, from coast to coast, protesters came on their own terms, with their own slogans. When asked his opinion of antiwar activists of another era, president Ronald Reagan famously quipped that they acted like Tarzan, looked like Jane, and smelled like Cheetah. But today's antiwar demonstration was not Ronald Reagan's protest. Something very different was going on. Suburbanites took advantage of an online protest RSVP form from Working Assets, which printed and assembled ready-made placards with a range of slogans that allowed even busy people to express themselves with a customized message. The messages ranged from the earnest "Go solar, not ballistic," "How many lives per gallon," and "Register to vote for peace" to the edgier "Draft SUV drivers first" and "Draft the Bush twins!"

In collaboration with the environmental community, Working Assets also organized an "Environmentalists against the War" rally featuring the first ever antiwar hybrid, electric, and biofuel car convoy. More than a hundred vehicles took part, from Priuses to battery-powered Volkswagen Beetles and a Berkeley biofueled garbage truck. Many people were moved to attend the protest (some from hundreds of miles away), in large part because this was the first time they were asked to demonstrate in their green cars. These peaceful environmentalists now had the opportunity to connect their conservationist beliefs to a principled opposition to an unjust war.

What we learned in the process was that the movement had the potential to be much broader—you just had to reach out and ask people to come. And you needed to let them march under their own banners, not just a few themes decided by a committee of conveners. In this way, the people who oppose all wars were joined by the folks who just oppose unilateral preemptive war, and the people who believe in the absolute sovereignty of even totalitarian regimes enjoyed the company of marchers who simply felt diplomacy needed more time. Clergy walked with their congregations in tow. Francophiles marched with baguettes held aloft. Student activists were, for once, outnumbered by parents pushing strollers.

After we marched, we gave money to fund relief efforts in Iraq, to cover the cost of the next protest, and to put up billboards that demanded, "Bring the troops home now." And then we went to work making sure that more people than ever before participated in the 2004 election.

Citizens whose protests against the war were largely ignored in 2003 came out in full force the following year to volunteer and vote. The growing antiwar movement had a profound effect on the presidential debates, with people from both parties beginning to question the rationale for the increasingly costly venture.

Although we failed to stop the war, with steadfast opposition we may well stop subsequent invasions. It would pay to keep a few things in mind along the way:

- Recognize that if you don't speak out, volunteer, or give money to worthy groups, you cannot effect change, no matter how admirable your views. Getting active not only helps the movement, but will also make you feel better.
- Elect and support leaders who will fight, and hold them accountable, both at the ballot box on election day and with e-mails, calls, and letters throughout their terms.
- Finding common cause means making room for people in the movement who don't agree with you on every issue. Welcome new allies and let them fight for peace on their own terms. You can still be picky about whom you let into your own affinity group.
- Remember that sometimes we win. Not even Bush could persuade the American people to accept more arsenic in our water. And the Senate has successfully filibustered the administration's most extreme federal judicial nominees. Don't forget that meaningful universal enfranchisement in this country was won just forty years ago. Big changes can happen in our lifetimes.
- Bring a friend. If we want to become the majority we think we are, more people will simply have to show up.
- Seek out people who share your values and who have a sense of humor. Politics is depressing enough. The work of stopping wars is hard, and it takes time. We won't make it if we can't have some fun along the way.

There is a joke going around that the difference between Vietnam and Iraq is that George W. Bush had a plan for getting out of Vietnam. For people who oppose preemptive invasions as a foreign-policy tool, the difference between stopping the Iraq invasion and stopping the next wars, may mean helping less on left politics as usual and more on creating and executing a plausible play for peace.

Chapter 4

STRENGTHENING
WOMEN'S
VOICES

A NEW COUNTERTERRORISM STRATEGY: FEMINISM

BARBARA EHRENREICH

Barbara Ehrenreich has written more than ten books, including *Blood Rites* and *Nickel and Dimed*. She is a frequent contributor to *Esquire, Harper's Magazine, Mirabella*, the *Nation*, the *New Republic*, the *New York Times*, and *Time*. Ehrenreich became involved in political activism during the Vietnam War and has been an activist and feminist ever since.

I've been reading Bin Ladin—Carmen, that is, not her brother-in-law Osama (she spells the last name with an "i")—and I'd like to present a brand-new approach to terrorism, one that turns out to be more consistent with traditional American values. First, let's stop calling the enemy "terrorism," which is like saying we're fighting "bombings." Terrorism is only a method; the enemy is an extremist Islamic insurgency whose appeal lies in its claim to represent the Muslim masses against a bullying superpower.

But as Carmen Bin Ladin urgently reminds us in her book *Inside the Kingdom*, one glaring moral flaw of this insurgency, quite apart from its methods, is that it aims to push one-half of those masses down to a status only slightly above that of domestic animals. While Osama was getting pumped up for jihad, Carmen was getting up her nerve to walk across the street in a residential neighborhood in Jeddah—fully veiled but unescorted by a male, something that is an illegal act for a woman in Saudi Arabia. Eventually she left the kingdom and got a divorce because she didn't want her daughters to grow up in a place where women are kept "locked in and breeding."

So here in one word is my new counterterrorism strategy: feminism. Or, if that's too incendiary, try the phrase "human rights for women." I don't mean just a few opportunistic references to women, like those that accompanied the war on the Taliban and were quietly dropped by the Bush administration when that war was abandoned and Afghan women were locked back into their burqas. I'm talking about a sustained and serious effort.

We should announce plans to pour U.S. tax dollars into girls' education in places like Pakistan, where the high-end estimate for female literacy is 26 percent, and into scholarships for women seeking higher education in nations that typically discourage it. (Secular education for the boys wouldn't hurt,

Los Angeles women speak out just days after the Iraq invasion.
Photo by Jodie Evans

either.) Expand the grounds for asylum to all women fleeing gender totali-
tarianism, wherever it springs up. Reverse the Bush policies on global family
planning, which condemn seventy-eight thousand women to death each year
in makeshift abortions. Lead the global battle against the trafficking of women.

I'm not expecting such measures alone to incite a feminist insurgency within
the Islamist one. Carmen Bin Ladin found her rich Saudi sisters-in-law sunk
in bovine passivity, and some of the more spirited young women in the Muslim world have been adopting the head scarf as a gesture of defiance toward
American imperialism. We're going to need a thorough foreign policy
makeover—from Afghanistan to Israel—before we have the credibility to
stand up for anyone's human rights. You can't play the gender card with dirty
hands.

If this country were to embrace a feminist strategy against the insurgency,
we'd have to start by addressing our own dismal record on women's rights.
We'd be pushing for the immediate ratification of the UN Convention on
the Elimination of All Forms of Discrimination against Women, which has
been ratified by 169 countries but remains stalled in the U.S. Senate. We'd be

threatening to break off relations with Saudi Arabia until it acknowledged the humanity of women. And we'd be thundering about the shortage of women in the U.S. Senate and House, an internationally embarrassing 14 percent. We should be aiming for a representation of at least 25 percent, the same target the Transitional Administrative Law of Iraq has set for the federal assembly there.

If we want to beat Osama, we've got to start by listening to Carmen.

∽∽∽

"Women may be the one group that grows more radical with age."

—Gloria Steinem

MOTHERS OF ALL THE WORLD'S CHILDREN

BETH OSNES

Beth Osnes is the author of *Twice Alive*, a spiritual guide to mothering. She is a theater teacher, a mother of three, and a founding member of Mothers Acting Up.

Once my kids could walk and tie their own shoes, I took a good look at the world and saw it with new eyes. The glaring discrepancy between the conditions under which I was able to raise my children and the conditions under which so many other mothers were forced to raise *their* children—without access to clean water, health care, education, or safety—awakened within me a feeling of solidarity with mothers across economic and national boundaries. I knew I wanted to connect with them in some meaningful way, but at the time I lacked the means. As my kids started to grow and I found a little freedom in my schedule, I began to be a little more active in my community, attending political events and helping a struggling single mother with child care. I kept looking for avenues to make a difference.

Within my community of other mother friends in Boulder, Colorado, many of us had these same restless feelings, accompanied by newfound reserves of energy (now that our kids were mostly sleeping through the night) and a yearning for some outlet that matched our concerns. After a few attempts to get others to join us (don't ask us about the time we organized an outdoor rally in December and only loyal friends showed up, shivering in support), we created Mothers Acting Up (MAU). MAU is a movement to mobilize the gigantic political strength of mothers to ensure the health, education, and safety of every child, not just a privileged few.

To launch our movement, we hosted a Mothers Acting Up Mother's Day parade in May 2002. Amid audacious costumes of every sort—many of us donned stilts in the parade to show motherhood as a large, impressive force to be reckoned with—we launched MAU as a tool for mothers moving from concern to action. We created a Web site, www.mothersactingup.org, with suggestions for easy actions that women could take to address specific issues facing children. The Web site provides contact information for congressional representatives, advice on how to write powerful appeals to the government, and sample letters to the editor that a revved-up mama can send to her newspaper.

One of our early inspirations for this movement came from a "first wave" feminist and suffragist, Julia Ward Howe, best known as the author of "The Battle Hymn of the Republic." In 1870 she called for women to rise up and oppose war in all its forms and declared a Mother's Day for Peace. She asked the women of her nation, "Why do not the mothers of mankind interfere in these matters, to prevent the waste of that human life of which they alone bear and know the cost?" She attempted to organize an international council of women to determine the means "whereby the great human family could live in peace." Sadly, she was never able to achieve those dreams. Mother's Day became a national holiday after her death but only as a watered-down version of her original vision, without any hint of activism.

Nearly a century later, Howe's words are gaining an ever-increasing audience, thanks to the advent of the Internet and the ripeness of the moment for mothers to assert their values. In 2003, just one year after MAU's inception, eleven cities throughout the country hosted Mothers Acting Up Mother's Day events, celebrating the desire of mothers to speak out for the rights of children. In 2004, there were twenty-five events across the country, and in 2005, MAU's goal is to hold MAU Mother's Day celebrations in every state of the country.

For me, this movement feels like a true fit for my passions and abilities. I trust and love the women I work with, and I feel a lifelong commitment to our goals. I also like the fact that this work feels constructive rather than reactionary, unlike much political activism I've encountered. I, like many other women, recoil from confrontational, negative approaches to politics, so this celebratory and positive alternative feels like a comfortable home for my budding activism. Anger can't sustain my commitment or interest, but the belief in every child's right to health, education, and safety can.

Reaching out into the world through MAU has become a spiritual calling to the mother in me. It is a cousin to the urge to cook chicken soup for friends suffering from a loss, or the desire to put my sweater around the shoulders of a cold child on the playground. With MAU, though, my response to the needs of the world is not only personal but also political—because American politics has far-reaching effects on the quality of children's lives. Whether babies in South Africa get the antiviral AIDS drug they need is based on a political decision to allocate aid to that country. Whether millions of U.S. children receive quality preschool through Head Start is a political decision. Politicians determine the priorities for each nation's resources and allocate funds accordingly. Since nobody stands to make a profit from lobbying for the health, education, and safety of every child, then I must speak up and advocate on behalf of these children. Indeed, who else will give voice to the voiceless?

Mothers are a natural lobbying group for children. The gargantuan momentum of mothers mobilizing has the potential to catapult us to a future in which children's needs are prioritized and their rights protected. Let us whisper this to each other, sing it on the streets, yell it from our rooftops, and declare it in our houses of government: We will protect our children—wherever they live on earth—with our personal and political strength!

❧ MOTHER'S DAY PROCLAMATION ❧

JULIA WARD HOWE, BOSTON, 1870

Mother's day was originally started after the Civil War as a protest to the carnage by the women who had lost their sons. The following piece is the orginal proclamamation.

Arise then . . . women of this day!
Arise, all women who have hearts!
Whether your baptism be of water or of tears!
Say firmly:
"We will not have questions answered by irrelevant agencies,
Our husbands will not come to us, reeking with carnage,
For caresses and applause.
Our sons shall not be taken from us to unlearn
All that we have been able to teach them of charity, mercy and patience.

We, the women of one country,
Will be too tender of those of another country
To allow our sons to be trained to injure theirs."

From the voice of a devastated Earth a voice goes up with
Our own. It says: "Disarm! Disarm!
The sword of murder is not the balance of justice."
Blood does not wipe our dishonor,
Nor violence indicate possession.
As men have often forsaken the plough and the anvil
At the summons of war,
Let women now leave all that may be left of home
For a great and earnest day of counsel.
Let them meet first, as women, to bewail and commemorate the dead.
Let them solemnly take counsel with each other as to the means
Whereby the great human family can live in peace . . .
Each bearing after his own time the sacred impress, not of Caesar,
But of God—

In the name of womanhood and humanity, I earnestly ask
That a general congress of women without limit of nationality,
May be appointed and held at someplace deemed most convenient
And the earliest period consistent with its objects,
To promote the alliance of the different nationalities,
The amicable settlement of international questions,
The great and general interests of peace.

W STANDS FOR WAR

LAURA FLANDERS

Laura Flanders is the host of *The Laura Flanders Show* on Air America Radio and the author of several books, including *Bushwomen*.

After 9/11, to justify its attack on Afghanistan, the Bush administration deployed its women to cast its campaign not as a vengeful assault by the world's most powerful nation against one of planet's most underdeveloped states but as a rescue mission. Out came Laura Bush to say, "This isn't about revenge; this is about protection and defense, not just of Afghan women and girls, but of women and girls the world over."

Some Afghan women returned to schools, but liberation remains an unfinished business. In fact, Afghan women have been denied the support they were promised by the Bush administration during the bombing. Laura Bush was used to put a soft face, a kind of feminist-friendly face, on a devastating bombing campaign, but the Bush administration never made supporting Afghan women a priority. Few people know how much money was allocated in the administration's 2004 budget for the Women's Department in Afghanistan: not one cent. Only after women's organizations protested did some money get put in the budget.

While Bush is using the rhetoric of women's rights to advance an unpopular corporate agenda around the world, at home, his administration has been giving public jobs to religious extremists who'd set women's choices back decades. For all the talk of security, most women's lives today are more perilous. Bush's policies around the world are fueling anger against all things American—including equality for women. In some places that backlash is taking the form of extremist religious movements in the name of national resistance. At home that backlash is taking place beneath a veil of secrecy.

George W. Bush campaigned for the presidency on the slogan "W Stands for Women." The reality is that W has come to mean war—including war on women.

FEMINIST **VOICES** FOR PEACE

STARHAWK

Starhawk is the author and coauthor of ten books, including *The Spiral Dance*, about the neopagan movement, and the ecotopian novel *The Fifth Sacred Thing*. Starhawk's newest book is *The Earth Path*.

When outcries against the war and the occupation of Iraq echoed across the United States and around the globe, women were not silent. Groups like CODEPINK: Women for Peace disrupted congressional hearings and organized monthlong peace vigils at the White House. Women in Black held vigils in hundreds of communities around the world. Women Rising for Peace and Justice, the women's caucus of United for Peace, issued calls for nationwide women's actions against the war.

Women are deeply affected by war, racism, and poverty—the three evils named by Martin Luther King Jr. When we stand for peace as women, we are not doing it to make a case that we're victims but to represent a different vision of strength. The unique power in women-initiated and women-led actions comes not from excluding men—most of these actions welcome men as participants—but through embracing the joy and visionary potential that arise when we come together as women to defend the life-sustaining values that we hold dear.

No set of qualities is innately or exclusively female or male. Men can be compassionate, loving, and kind, just as women can be tough, brave, or callous. Wise feminists do not claim that women are essentially kinder or gentler than men, per se. If we did, the Margaret Thatchers and Condoleezza Rices of the world would soon prove us wrong. Nonetheless, we have seen throughout history that patriarchy assigns the qualities associated with aggression and competition to men and relegates to women the devalued roles of nurturing and service. Patriarchy values the hard over the soft; the tough over the tender; punishment, vengeance, and vindictiveness over compassion, negotiation, and reconciliation. The "hard" qualities are linked to power, success, and masculinity—and exalted. The "soft" qualities are identified with weakness, powerlessness, and femininity—and denigrated.

Under patriarchy, men are shamed and considered weak if they act in ways associated with femininity. Politicians win elections by being tough—tough on terror, tough on crime, tough on drugs, tough on welfare mothers. Calls for cooperation, negotiation, compassion, or a recognition of our interdependence are equated with womanly weakness. In the name of "toughness," the power holders deprive the poor of the means of life, the troubled and the ill of treatment and care, the ordinary citizen of privacy and civil rights. Force, punishment, and violence are patriarchy's answer to conflicts and social problems.

Patriarchy finds its ultimate expression in war. Soldiers can be coerced into dying or killing when their fear of being called womanlike or cowardly overrides their reluctance to face death or to inflict injury on others. War removes every argument for tenderness and dissolves all strictures on violence.

To counter the rabid cries for war, we need not just women's voices but raucous, incautious, feminist voices—for feminism allows us to analyze and pull apart patriarchy, the constellation of values, ideas, and beliefs that reinforces male control over women.

As the powers that be cynically use the instances of oppression against women in the Muslim world to justify racism and to encourage American support for military takeovers, only feminist voices can speak to issues of women's freedom and autonomy with candor and genuine concern for the welfare of Muslim women.

The United States and its allies, who now pose as the liberators of women in the Muslim world, are the same powers that gave the Taliban, Saddam Hussein, and Al-Qaeda their start-up funds—supporting them and putting them in power, with no consideration of their impact on women. The "liberators" of Afghan women ignored the grassroots women's organizations, like the Revolutionary Association of the Women of Afghanistan (RAWA), and installed a new government almost as oppressive as the Taliban, thereby excluding the heroic women who had risked their lives to educate their daughters and maintain some sense of freedom under oppressive rule.

We protest the hypocrisy that trumpets the oppression of women in Muslim societies as a rallying cry for war while entirely overlooking the oppression of women in Western societies—and the Western governments' complicity in it. (Similarly, the racism, economic oppression, and endemic violence of Western culture are notably ignored even as the United States appoints itself the flag bearer of freedom.) Women cannot walk safely through the streets of this country, nor can they be assured of a living wage, health care in illnesses, or care and support in old age.

We need feminist voices for peace to declare that those who truly care about life and freedom will work to support, not conquer, those women in every culture who are struggling for liberation and social justice. Real security can come only when we weave a global web of mutual aid and support. As we make larger connections and take action together, we must assert what we as women know to be true: compassion is not weakness, and brutality is not strength.

∾o∾

You were born with potential.
You were born with goodness and trust.
You were born with ideals and dreams.
You were born with wings.
You are not meant for crawling, so don't.
You have wings.
Learn to use them and fly.

—Rumi, thirteenth century

FREEDOM THROUGH SOLIDARITY—**THE LIE OF "LIBERATION"**

SONALI KOLHATKAR

Sonali Kolhatkar is the codirector of the Afghan Women's Mission, a U.S.-based non-profit agency founded in 2000 that helps fund the humanitarian and political work of the Revolutionary Association of the Women of Afghanistan. Kolhatkar is also the host and coproducer of *Uprising*, a daily drive-time morning program at KPFK, Los Angeles, part of the Pacifica Radio network.

"Our coalition has liberated Afghanistan and restored fundamental human rights and freedoms to Afghan women, and all the people of Afghanistan."
—PRESIDENT BUSH, PROCLAMATION 7584,
WOMEN'S EQUALITY DAY, AUGUST 23, 2002

Many American women supported the October 2001 invasion of Afghanistan because of claims by the Bush administration that the war would liberate Afghan women from the Taliban. The administration and the corporate media worked in tandem to effectively sensationalize the Taliban's abuse of women by keeping the message simple and palatable: Afghan women's oppression was limited to the burqa (veil), and burqa-clad women needed saving by Western governments. While the war of "Operation Enduring Freedom" toppled the Taliban and resulted in the repeal of forced-veiling laws, it also resulted in the brutal bombing deaths of thousands of women and children and the installation of warlords as fanatical as the Taliban.

The rhetoric of "liberation" conjures up an image of millions of brown faces awaiting the Western savior as they starve and sustain torture and imprisonment by native tyrants (Mullah Omar, Osama bin Laden, and Saddam Hussein) and their cronies (the Taliban, Al-Qaeda, and the Ba'ath Party). The idea of a more "advanced," powerful country "liberating" a weaker, "backward" nation and its women reveals the powerful nation's sense of superiority—it is sexist and racist logic. (Immediately after the Taliban fell, Christopher Hitchens of the *Nation*, in a November 2004 article, celebrated this false superiority when he made the smug proclamation, "The United States of America has just succeeded in bombing a country back out of the Stone Age.")

Older empires claimed to "civilize" their colonies with the same arrogance as today's "liberators," and with the same consequences. As described in *The Rise and Fall of the British Empire*, by Lawrence James, the British imperialists' "possession of an empire . . . encouraged a sense of superiority. . . . It also fostered racial arrogance. And yet at the same time, deeply rooted liberal and evangelical ideals produced a powerful sense of imperial duty and mission. The empire existed to civilize and uplift its subjects, or so its champions claimed."

In the case of the U.S. empire, the language of "liberation" allowed Bush to justify war and imperialism in the name of women's freedom. By perpetuating the burqa as the main visual symbol of women's oppression, the Bush administration tried to fool us into thinking that if the Taliban were ousted, and their laws on forced veiling removed, then Afghan women would instantly be free. But a closer look reveals that Bush's definition of "liberation" has not translated into tangible freedom for women. In fact, women are suffering as much as they did under the Taliban, and in some cases more so.

International human-rights organizations like Human Rights Watch and Amnesty International have exposed the lie of Afghan women's freedom. According to their reports, post-Taliban Afghanistan still poses grave dangers for Afghan women: armed warlords from the U.S.-backed Northern Alliance reign supreme and echo the Taliban's anti-woman ideology; sexual violence against women has soared; more and more women are burning themselves alive to escape their traumas; married women and girls have been barred from schools; a constitution upholding the supremacy of Islamic law has been ratified; permission for political demonstrations by women are routinely denied; and an outspoken critic of the warlords (Malalai Joya) has received threats on her life.

The rhetoric of "liberation" victimizes and dehumanizes women: it denies them their ability to determine their fate and instead subjects them to the whims of the "liberators." Conversely, to accept the humanity of Afghan women would mean acknowledging their dignity and right to self-determination, as well as their right and ability to resist the supremacist actions of foreign invaders and homegrown despots (who are often colluding with one another) and to decide what form foreign intervention should take.

In their self-serving focus on the plight of oppressed women in Afghanistan, the Bush administration and the corporate-controlled U.S. media ignored existing movements organized by women struggling for freedom. The women of RAWA (Revolutionary Association of the Women of Afghanistan), for example, have been waging nonviolent war on fundamentalism and foreign occupation since 1977. Why don't we ever see RAWA on the nightly network news? Because Afghan women like these are not voiceless and faceless victims who can be portrayed as dependent on the benevolence of foreigners.

On October 11, 2001, as the United States commenced the bombing of Afghanistan, RAWA released a statement: "We believe that once there is no foreign interference, especially of a fundamentalist type, all ethnic groups of all religions . . . will prove their solidarity for achieving the most sacred national interests for the sake of a proud and free Afghanistan." We would do well to follow RAWA's example, replacing the language of "liberation" with that of solidarity.

Clearly the people of the world, and especially Afghan women, do not need liberating. They need us to rein in our government, and its support of misogynist forces like the Northern Alliance and the Taliban, so that they can continue the difficult task of achieving their own freedom. Our solidarity must enable indigenous struggles to attain freedom by preventing the interference of imperial governments.

In the case of Afghanistan, solidarity can take the form of supporting the work of indigenous women's rights organizations like RAWA. Other important examples of solidarity include the recent anti-Iraq-war movement in the United States and elsewhere, the International Solidarity Movement in Palestine, and the East Timor Action Network. Whether we lend our support to the struggles of women in Afghanistan, or to other peoples oppressed by U.S.-backed governments or military actions around the world, our solidarity with the survivors of "liberation" is the most effective rejection of war.

∽o∾

"Now woman is confronted with the necessity of emancipating herself from emancipation, if she desires to be free."

Emma Goldman

GLOBAL WOMEN
FOR PEACE

KAVITA N. RAMDAS

Kavita N. Ramdas is the president and CEO of the Global Fund for Women, a U.S.-based grant-making organization. This piece is excerpted from an interview conducted by Gael Murphy on November 29, 2004.

Women are leading the struggle for peace and conflict resolution and see these as clearly linked to their own struggle for the full realization of their human rights. In the post-9/11 world, women outside the United States have been at the forefront of the global peace movement and have been at the table demanding alternative ways in which to resolve conflicts.

War takes a high toll on anybody living within a conflict zone. But the toll it takes on women, children, and the elderly is different. Human Rights Watch and other international agencies estimate that up to 70 percent of the casualties of any war are noncombatants or civilian casualties, and certainly the experience in Iraq bears that out. Women and children who are not supposedly in the line of fire pay a huge price, dismissed as "collateral damage" in military speak. This so-called collateral damage includes the destruction of the infrastructure that enables families to continue living. Women who become the primary providers for their families when their men are at war are now hugely affected.

They're also vulnerable to sexual exploitation, and in war after war, we see rape used systematically as a weapon. And—as has been well documented in the case of Vietnam veterans—in the aftermath of conflict, even though the women may have been traumatized themselves, it is they who bear the primary responsibility for dealing with men who come back with psychological damage.

Given all the ways in which war affects women, women in most parts of the world see it as self-evident that commitment to a just peace is essential. Women pay a huge amount of attention to the issue of constitution building and to women's participation in it. Afghan women took great risks to be able to be present at the Loya Jirga, which is a sort of council of elders, and they begged the United States to support them in their demand for a 50 percent representation of women in the Loya Jirga discussions. Our government refused to back them, arguing that even in the United States there was only

Women in Maheshwar, India, protest the construction of the Narmada Dam, 1999.
© Ian Berry/MAGNUM

a 14 percent representation of women in the House and Senate—how could they require that Afghan women should have a 50 percent representation? The Afghan women responded, "Just because you're backward, why should we be?"

Women's lawyers associations in conflict zones and nonconflict zones are working on ways in which to ensure that women's human rights are protected within the fabric of those societies. The way in which women are treated in a society can tell you a lot about how that society will choose to deal with conflict.

One Global Fund for Women grantee, the Mano River Women's Peace Network, is a network of activists from Guinea, Sierra Leone, and Liberia. The Mano River Network is an effort to bring women together at the negotiating table. One of its especially successful efforts was getting regional leaders to sit down for peace talks. The organization is also doing extraordinary work documenting the high environmental costs of war, something that is rarely taken into account.

To women's organizations in the rest of the world, the women's movement here in the United States appears to be so disconnected from an understanding that peace and security ought to be central to a women's-rights struggle. They can't understand why women in the United States seem to have such a hard time understanding that the so-called war on terror and the unchecked expansion of American militarism around the world are a threat to women's security. You essentially root out the feminine aspects of any culture as that culture becomes discordantly masculine, and that has huge repercussions on how women are treated.

There is much work to be done to strengthen the notion of a global women's movement. I think that many women, particularly in the developing world, do not see women in the West as understanding or supporting their struggles. Whether we can stop the next war will really depend, to a great extent, on our ability to build strong connections with women in the rest of the world. Because they can't do it without us.

If you talk to Israeli and Palestinian women, they will tell you that without U.S. intervention, that situation is not going to be resolved. The United States will only intervene if there is sufficient domestic pressure to do so. The big question for women here is, can we get to a point where we see ourselves as so strongly allied with the international women's movement that we make it a priority to push for those outcomes?

We would be doing it in coordination with a number of other social movements. What is really exciting to me is the networking and building of alliances across movements. I believe that if the women's movement wants to do something, it can do so, even if it is unable to do it via existing forums like the United Nations. What if we had a huge convening of social movements to put pressure on our governments, just by pure force and presence? I know we have the capability. Recall February 15, 2003, when the world stood still in protest against the Iraq war.

Women also have to support their sisters in the United States. The Bush administration's second term is going to be a time when women here will need our global sisters more than ever before. We will need their solidarity, and we will need them to speak up for us in international venues. We will need them to remind the world that America is not monolithic, that it's not homogenous, and that there are many different perspectives and races and visions inside this country. The more they can talk to and learn from women like us, the more they can take that message and share it with the rest of the world.

EMPOWERING
THE SILENT MAJORITY

NEELA MARIKKAR

Neela Marikkar is a Sri Lankan businesswoman who built Sri Lanka First, a group of business leaders advocating a negotiated settlement between the government of Sri Lanka and the Liberation Tigers of Tamil Eelam.

For fifteen years, I experienced war while living in Sri Lanka. My husband's company was devastated when a car bomb exploded outside his office building in 1991. When the Central Bank was bombed in 1996, the building was damaged again. But for me the turning point was on July 24, 2001, when the international airport was attacked and SriLankan Airlines—one of my biggest clients—lost half its fleet.

All over the world there were severe warnings not to visit Sri Lanka because of the danger. Insurance premiums went up. Every aircraft that wanted to land was to be charged $150,000. Every ship that called on our port was going to be charged $100,000. It meant that tourism, one of our key industries, crashed overnight. It meant we couldn't get our exports out or imports in because ships had stopped calling.

That was a dire situation. We'd had terrible media fallout internationally, so I volunteered to do damage control with a group of people directly affected. While I was working with this group and looking at what went wrong with airport security, I came to the realization that patchwork solutions were not enough. No fence is high enough to guarantee security, so putting up a ten-foot electric fence wasn't the answer. Bringing in a foreign security company to take care of the airport wasn't the answer. Going back to the root cause was the answer. The only way to stop terrorism was to stop the war, and the only way to stop the war was to get back to the negotiating table.

The more I thought, the clearer it was that I had to get a group together to start looking at the conflict in our country. July 24 was a wake-up call for the Sri Lankan business community: it was time to get involved and put pressure on our political leaders to put the interests of the country ahead of their party agendas. We called ourselves Sri Lanka First. The idea was that we had to put the country first—not our businesses, not our party agendas. Nothing.

We knew we had to have grassroots support, so we went all out to educate people about the cost of the war and the need for a settlement. The high point of our campaign was a peaceful demonstration. We had advertised widely, asking everyone to step outside at noon on September 19, 2001, and hold hands to let the government know that they wanted peace. It was an experiment. We didn't know whether anyone would really come out and stand.

I woke up that day thinking, What if nobody comes out? That was a tremendous concern, especially because the 9/11 attacks in the United States had happened just a week before. The whole world was saying, "We've got to wipe out terrorism," and here we were saying, "No, we want to talk. Let's try to resolve this through negotiation. Let's not continue this war."

We took a deep breath and went ahead with the campaign. Out of a population of almost eighteen million, more than a million came out into the streets. It was an amazing sight. They poured out of their homes and offices and stood holding hands for fifteen minutes in the midday sun. The turnout proved to Sri Lanka's political leaders that our people were committed to peace. We were able to marginalize the extreme voices and empower the silent majority—the moderate voices—by organizing this very simple demonstration. You just had to come out of your building. You didn't have to hold cards or protest. It was a very gentle display of solidarity.

Not long after the demonstration, the government faced a no-confidence vote, Parliament was dissolved, and we had new elections. A new government won on the peace mandate, and on December 24, 2001, we had a cessation of hostilities. A final cease-fire agreement was signed in February 2002, and it is still holding.

Being an active member of Sri Lanka First has been an enormous personal challenge. My day job is running Sri Lanka's largest marketing communications company; my night job is working for peace and development. Making time for my family hasn't been easy. But this experience has been extremely fulfilling—my life is richer, and my heart is more forgiving. I'm grateful for the chance to have contributed in some small way to a peaceful resolution of my country's devastating war.

Chapter 5

THE HUMANITY
WE SHARE

WE REFUSE
TO BE ENEMIES

SUMAYA FARHAT-NASER AND GILA SVIRSKY

Dr. Sumaya Farhat-Naser, a Palestinian woman, is the cofounder and former director of the Jerusalem Center for Women, a Palestinian organization committed to Middle East peace based on justice, human rights, and women's rights. Gila Svirsky is a Jewish Israeli peace activist. She was the head of the peace groups Bat Shalom and B'Tselem and a cofounder of the Coalition of Women for Peace.

Although the news has not yet reached the international media, we would like the world to know that women in Israel and Palestine are ready to make peace.

For the past thirteen years, women have been the most vibrant, daring, and progressive part of the peace movement on both sides of our divide. Palestinian and Israeli women have been meeting and negotiating with each other for years, even when the very act of speaking to each other was illegal in Israel and prohibited in Palestine.

These negotiations began in secret years ago in local homes and churches. Then we felt safer meeting in Basel, Berlin, Brussels, Bologna, and other European cities. Today, we meet openly when we can, often in symbolic venues, such as the Notre Dame Center on the border between Palestinian and Israeli Jerusalem.

While there have been dissension and debate, and while we have often held these discussions in painful circumstances, we have always held aloft the common vision of peace. Were it left to us, we would long ago have reached a peace agreement that settles the difficult issues between us.

We women advocate an end to the situation of occupier and occupied. We want to see Israel and Palestine as two separate states, side by side, with Jerusalem the shared capital of both. We desire a just solution to end the suffering of the refugees. We believe that each nation has an equal right to statehood, independence, freedom, security, development, and a life of dignity. And, in a crucial point of agreement, we condemn all forms of brutality, violence, and terrorism—whether by individuals, political groups, governments, or the military. We have had enough of the killing, on both sides. Too many Palestinian and Israeli children are now dead or orphaned or maimed for life. And too many of our own sons, fathers, and brothers have done that killing—

for war not only victimizes the innocent but also brutalizes the perpetrators.

As Israeli and Palestinian women, we have tried to educate our own peoples about the validity of both claims to this territory; we've worked against our societies' efforts to demonize the other side. We have promoted dialogue between women, paid mutual condolence calls to the families of victims on both sides, been arrested for protesting actions that violate our national consensus, and spoken out in a clear voice to demand a just solution.

And, apart from our public organizational activity, we women also operate as secret agents. We are not just the mothers, teachers, nurses, and social workers of our societies. We also serve up politics with dinner and teach the lessons of nonviolence to every child in our classrooms, every patient in our care, every client we advise, every son and daughter we love. We plant subversive ideas of peace in the minds of the young before the agents of war have even noticed. This is a long process whose results are not visible overnight, but we believe in its ultimate success.

The women's peace movement in Palestine and in Israel believes that the time has come to end the bloodshed, to lay down our weapons and our fears. We refuse to accept more warfare in our lives, our communities, our nations. We refuse to go along with the fear. We refuse to give in to the violence. We refuse to be enemies.

∞∞

"If we have no peace, it is because we have forgotten
that we belong to each other."

—Mother Teresa of Calcutta

THE PILLARS OF PEACE

SHIRIN EBADI

In 2003, Shirin Ebadi became the first Iranian and the first Muslim woman to win the Nobel Peace Prize. One of the first female judges in Iran, Ebadi served as president of the city court of Tehran before she was forced to resign after the revolution in 1979. In her decades of work as a human-rights activist, she has been imprisoned many times.

Violence, terror, humiliation, and torture are an affront to all cultures. Those Islamists who use the excuse of cultural relativism to reject democracy and human rights are ossified oppressors. They have put a straitjacket on culture in the name of "nationalism," with the intent of denying their own people their rights. They take small things that have nothing to do with the Islamic religion, and are actually in conflict with Islam, and turn these issues into an excuse to go to war.

Democracy and human rights are common needs of all human cultures. Muslims should not be deceived by the claim that Islam is incompatible with democracy and that we must choose between accepting democracy or the tradition of our ancestors. We can have both.

On the other hand, the Western world should not vilify Islam. In the U.S. media, we hear the term "Islamic terrorism" over and over again. Like those in power in America, the media rarely make an effort to separate the crimes of individuals from their religious affiliations. If an Islamic person kills someone else, this misdeed should not be recorded in the Islamic report card. It should not be counted against Islam, just as the misdeeds of some people in Bosnia should not be attributed to Christianity. Similarly, Israel's disregard for the numerous resolutions of the United Nations about Israel and Palestine should not be blamed on the Jewish religion. Moses was a harbinger of justice, and Jesus was a prophet who advocated peace.

We must not foment a war between the civilizations, which would take the entire world to war. Instead, we must talk about cooperation among civilizations, and we must understand that peace is lasting only when it is based on two pillars: democracy and justice. Without those, it is not truly peace: those who make people quiet through jails and bullets may achieve a silence that feels like peace, but that silence is the quiet of cemeteries. Let's not forget that for seventy years in the former Soviet Union there was silence but not peace.

But what is democracy? It is not something that occurs overnight. It is not a gift delivered on a golden tray. Democracy is a long process of fighting, challenging accepted ideas, and perpetually striving for freedom. Like a seed that has to be watered every day to become a flower, democracy needs constant attention and care.

Many people who are truly fighting for democracy and human rights face prison, intimidation, and even death. I and many other political prisoners were locked up in Iran, and unfortunately, many of the writers, journalists, political and social activists, and university students who have been fighting for our rights remain in prison. I plead for their freedom and mourn the many others who have lost their lives in this struggle.

Large and powerful countries should not attack other countries on the pretext of bringing democracy and human rights. The United Nations was established to address violations of democratic principles around the world. When Iraq attacked Kuwait, the United Nations coordinated an international effort to free Kuwait. But when the United States invaded Iraq in this most recent war, it did so despite the objections of the United Nations Security Council, thereby circumventing the global community and ignoring its reservations.

But you cannot export democracy with weapons. You cannot pour human rights on people's heads with cluster bombs. Military attacks, even with good intentions, do not create democracy. They will only harm democracy as society degenerates into violence.

If one country sincerely wants to support democracy in another country that is under dictatorial rule, the only thing to do is to support the freedom fighters who stand for the democratic institutions of that country. Done this way, the sapling of democracy will bear the flower of freedom.

∽⚬∾

"When I despair, I remember that all through history the
way of truth and love has always won. There have been
tyrants and murderers and for a time they seem invincible but
in the end, they always fall—think of it, always."

—Mahatma Gandhi

PEACE PRAYERS

HINDU PEACE PRAYER

I desire neither earthly kingdom, nor even freedom from birth and death. I desire only the deliverance from grief of all those afflicted by misery. O Lord, lead us from the unreal to the real; from darkness to light; from death to immortality. May there be peace in celestial regions. May there be peace on earth. May the waters be appeasing. May herbs be wholesome and may trees and plants bring peace to all. May all beneficent beings bring peace to us. May thy wisdom spread peace all through the world. May all things be a source of peace to all and to me. Om Shanti, Shanti, Shanti (Peace, Peace, Peace).

ISLAMIC PEACE PRAYER

We think of Thee, worship Thee, bow to Thee as the Creator of this Universe; we seek refuge in Thee, the Truth, our only support. Thou art the Ruler, the barge in this ocean of endless births and deaths. In the name of Allah, the beneficent, the merciful. Praise be to the Lord of the Universe who has created us and made us into tribes and nations. Give us wisdom that we may know each other and not despise all things. We shall abide by thy Peace. And, we shall remember the servants of God are those who walk on this earth in humility and, when we address them, we shall say Peace Unto Us All.

CHRISTIAN PEACE PRAYER

Blessed are the peacemakers, for they shall be known as the Children of God. But I say to you: love your enemy, do good to those who hate you, bless those who curse you, pray for those who abuse you. To those who strike you on the cheek, offer the other also; and from those who take away your cloak, do not withhold your coat as well. Give to everyone who begs from you; and, to those who take away your goods, do not ask them again. And as you wish that others would do unto you, do so unto them as well.

JEWISH PEACE PRAYER

Come let us go up to the mountain of the Lord, that we may walk the paths of the Most High. And we shall beat our swords into plowshares and our spears into pruning hooks. Nation shall not lift up sword against nation— neither shall they learn war anymore. And none shall be afraid, for the mouth of the Lord of Hosts has spoken.

SHINTO PEACE PRAYER

Although the people living across the ocean surrounding us are all our brothers and sisters why, O Lord, is there trouble in this world? Why do winds and waves rise in the ocean surrounding us? I earnestly wish the wind will soon blow away all the clouds hanging over the tops of the mountains.

A MOTHER'S **PLEA**

NURIT PELED-ELHANAN

Nurit Peled-Elhanan is an Israeli peace activist and a professor of language and education at Hebrew University. Her only daughter, Smadar Elhanan, was thirteen years old when she was killed by a suicide bomber in Jerusalem in 1997. Peled-Elhanan received the 2001 European Parliament Sakharov Prize for Freedom of Thought and Human Rights.

Most of the following is extracted from a speech delivered at the Israel-Palestine

I would like to dedicate this piece to a thirteen-year-old Palestinian girl, Iman El-Hamas, who, on October 4, 2004, joined my own thirteen-year-old girl in the underground kingdom of dead children, which is growing and growing and growing under our feet as I speak. I would like to tell her not to worry: "You will be well received there, Iman, and no one will hurt you just because you wandered off on your way to school or because you wore a scarf on your head. Rest in peace, little girl; everyone is equally worthy in your new world."

Thank you for inviting me to share with you the struggle for peace in my country. I say "my" country, but I don't even know if this term is correct anymore. What is mine in this country depends very much on what I identify with, and today it is very hard to identify with anything in a place that has let Death have dominion over it.

And Death has created a new identity for me and has given me a new voice, a new voice that is as ancient as the world itself, the voice of our biblical mother Rachel, weeping for her children, refusing to be comforted, for they are not. This new identity and voice transcend nationalities, religions, and even time; the identity overshadows all other identities and the voice deafens all the other voices I have been given by life.

My little girl was killed just because she was born Israeli, by a young man who felt hopeless to the point of murder and suicide just because he was born a Palestinian. A reporter asked me how I can accept condolences from the other side. I said to her very spontaneously that I do not accept condolences from the other side, and that when the mayor of Jerusalem came to offer his condolences, I went to my room because I didn't want to speak to him or shake his hand. But for me, the other side is not the Palestinians.

For me the whole population of the area, and of the world, has always been divided into two distinct groups: peace lovers and war lovers. Today, on the face of the earth, there rules the kingdom of evil, where for the last thirty-seven years, people who call themselves leaders have earned, through democratic means, the right to kill and destroy and be as vile and corrupt as they please, to have young boys become expert killers, whether in the name of "God," the "good of the nation," or "honor" and "courage."

But these evil people have created yet another kingdom, a glorious kingdom that flourishes and grows larger and larger every day, a kingdom that lives and breathes under our feet, beneath the earth we walk on. That is where my little daughter dwells, side by side with Palestinian children, and where I dwell side by side with Palestinian parents who, for the most part, have never held a gun and have never obeyed orders to kill anyone. There she lies, alongside her murderer, whose blood is mingled with hers on Jerusalem's stones, which have long grown indifferent to blood.

There they both lie, deceived. He, because his act of murder and suicide did not change anything, did not end Israel's cruel occupation, did not bring him to heaven, while the people who promised him his act would be meaningful carry on as if he had never existed. She, because she believed her life was safe, that her parents and her country were protecting her from evil, and that no harm could come to little girls who are good and gentle and go through the streets of their own cities to a dance class.

And they were both deceived because the world goes on living as if their blood had never been shed. Both are victims of so-called leaders who keep on playing their murderous games, using our children as their puppets and our grief as fuel to continue with their vindictive campaigns. Children are abstract entities for them, numbers, and grief is a political tool. They know that all they have to do to draw more young, enthusiastic little soldiers into their units is to find a God to ordain this killing. And each finds him in his Bible, in his mythologies. In the name of the Jewish God and the Muslim God, they commit their crimes, while in Ireland and Eastern Europe they kill each other for different versions of their Christian God. And now the enlightened leaders of the West kill in the name of the God of freedom and democracy. But, in fact, all of these warmongers recruit man-made gods to their sides—the God of racism and the God of greed and megalomania.

This is not new in the history of man. People have always used God as an excuse for their crimes. Our children, from a very tender age, learn about Joshua, the glorified leader who murdered the whole population of Jericho in the name of God. Then they learn about the prophet Eliyahu, who killed the 450 priests of the Baal because they practiced a different religion, and then they learn about Elisha, who brought death, with the help of God, upon 42 children who mocked him by calling him bald. Not to mention the adored King David and his terrible deeds.

In a culture that allows killing as a means of solving social and religious problems, and in which people see themselves as the descendants of biblical heroes, these stories overshadow the story about the God who said, "Lay not thy hand upon the child." But children can also learn about the God who

Iraqi street kids, July 2003.
Photo by Gael Murphy

said, "I will have mercy upon them who have not obtained mercy, and I will say to them who were not my people, 'Thou art my people.'" I believe very strongly that only by educating our children that killing, starving, or humiliating the innocent are unforgivable crimes can we save them from joining the evil forces—the evil forces of Israel and of the Palestinians.

Israel, through long and cruel occupation, is making it very easy for young Palestinians to turn to the path of terrorism. But terrorism dominates both forces. An organized army that terrorizes a whole population is even more criminal than any guerrilla group. An "enlightened" first-world government that ordains the killing of the innocent is just as evil as any third-world guerrilla leader who is hardly known and never seen. For me, Saddam Hussein, Ariel Sharon, and George Bush, father and son, are the same, for all have inflicted pain and death upon innocent populations. If we don't tell our children that these people are unscrupulous murderers, we shall never have leaders who rule out killing as a solution to social and political problems.

Today, when there is no meaningful opposition in Israel, the political distinctions between "left" and "right" don't matter, for everyone consents to the atrocities. That's why I believe that world condemnation of those deeds and their doers is critically important. It's time to make it clear that the death of one child, any child, be it Serbian, Albanian, Iraqi, or Jewish, is the death of the whole world, its past and its future.

This is the cry that has never, never been heard by politicians and generals, especially not in Jerusalem, which everybody thinks is made of gold but which is really made of stones and iron and lead. It is time for this cry to be heard above all others, for after the violence this is the only voice that really understands the meaning of the end of all things, including war. This is the voice that understands what's well known in the underground kingdom of our murdered children, namely, that all blood is equal, and that it takes so little to kill a child and so much to keep her alive. It understands that ending a war means supporting negotiations that are true dialogues, conversations in which both sides come to terms, not bring each other to their knees. Ending a war means that I don't care what flag is put on which mountain, that I don't care who looks where when they pray, that nothing is more important than securing a little girl's way to her dance class.

I call on all parents who have not yet lost their children and all who are about to: if we don't stand up to the politicians by teaching our children not to follow their murderous ways, if we don't listen to the voice of peace coming from underneath, very soon there will be nothing left to say, nothing left to write or read or listen to except the perpetual cry of mourning and the muted voices of dead children.

Therefore I have come here to ask you: please help us save the children that are left to us. Help us make the world stop for a moment to look at the small body of Iman, pierced by twenty bullets, and at the twenty-first hole at her smooth temple and ask with us, Why does that streak of blood rip the petal of her cheek?

∽o∾

I am no longer intimidated by experts, critics, and the name callers.
After all, my daughter stood in front of a bulldozer to protect a
Palestinian home. I have a responsibility as a mother to demand that the
experts, the policymakers, Congress and the White House reflect
our beliefs in the sanctity of each life, in the equality of
each human being, and in justice and the rule of law.

—Cindy Corrie, mother of Rachel Corrie

PILGRIMAGE FOR PEACE

RABIA ROBERTS

Rabia Elizabeth Roberts is the codirector, with her husband, Elias Amidon, of the Boulder Institute for Nature and the Human Spirit. Several years ago, they quit their jobs and sold their home to become full-time "pilgrims of peace," traveling around the world to conflict areas such as Iraq and Palestine.

I n America, the idea of us Syrians is that we eat foreigners," joked Mahat El-Khoury, a seventy-one-year-old human-rights worker and recent Damascus "Woman of the Year." "We Syrians feel misunderstood by the West. You don't understand our religions, our family ways, our history, or our politics. You think we're terrorists. We like American people, but we feel poorly treated by your government and its policies." Mahat's feelings were echoed by many people my husband and I spoke with during our pilgrimage to Syria.

On this pilgrimage, fifteen people from six Western countries joined us to bear witness to Muslim-Christian relations in this ancient land, to Arab-Western relations in general, and to the realities facing the Syrian people at this time of tension and distrust between the United States and Syria. Above all else, we came to make friends and to listen. While these "pilgrimages of peace" are modest gestures, we hope that others who hear of this kind of spiritual "citizen diplomacy" might be inspired to do something similar. Magnified a hundredfold, these encounters could heal a city; by a hundred thousand, a nation; by a few million, a world.

Building peace in this way offers us a powerful gift: a breakthrough in our fears of the "other." On this trip, tension was high for the pilgrims and their families back home. Many reported the long talks they had had with their children or parents about the wisdom of going to Syria. One man told his mother he was only going to London (a far riskier place!), and another woman told us later that during the first day she was convinced we were going to be kidnapped or stoned. Nothing could have been further from the welcome each one of us received throughout our time in Damascus. In the scores of encounters we had with a variety of people—men and women, young and old, Muslim and Christian—we were met with kindness, generosity, hospitality, dignity, humor, and a genuine appreciation of our intentions.

On the second morning, we asked our fellow pilgrims to wander in Damascus alone or in small groups of two and three to initiate conversations with ordinary Syrians, and to ask them ever-deeper questions about their feelings and beliefs. The idea of this experience always causes much consternation at the outset, but afterward people speak of it as a watershed event, one that has shifted their experiences of the world from those of a tourist to those of a pilgrim. It's a crash course in human trust.

In subsequent days we met with all kinds of people: students from Damascus University, young architects, teachers, businesspeople, Christian priests, Muslim sheikhs, social workers, and others. We visited churches, mosques, shrines, schools, offices, homes, and monasteries. As word of our presence spread, more and more invitations to meet and talk came to us. People were eager to have their stories heard. Though we did not always agree with what we were told, our task was not to persuade anyone of our opinions, but to try to understand. What have these people been taught? What are their fears? What are their dreams for their children?

Like a small stone dropped in a vast lake, our effort produced ever-widening ripples. My husband, Elias, and Shabda Kahn, a guest teacher on the pilgrimage, were interviewed on Syria's leading TV news commentary program. A pilgrimage participant who is a state representative for the international Sister Cities project met with Syrian officials in the Ministry of Urban Affairs and received assurances of cooperation in setting up American-Syrian sister-city partnerships. The Abu Nour Islamic Foundation, the largest Muslim nongovernmental organization in Syria, agreed to join the Nonviolent Peaceforce as a member organization.

Our presence provided an opportunity for Sheikh Nabil Hilbawi, one of Syria's most respected Shi'ite clerics, to meet with Christian leaders and discuss projects of mutual concern. Because we were there, a special interfaith concert was performed in our honor at the new opera house; a Mevlevi Sufi choir with whirling dervishes and a seventy-five-member Christian choir shared the same stage, singing anthems of peace together in the finale.

In a particularly stirring moment, we were welcomed as guests at Friday prayers in the largest mosque in Damascus, the seat of the grand mufti, Syria's leading Islamic cleric. The men of our group were seated in the front of the mosque beside the raised dais of the mufti, with the women looking down from the balcony above. When the mufti's sermon was finished, my husband was asked to speak to the several thousand people present. Elias spoke of the humiliation that so many Muslims feel in our times, both as a result of Western policies and as a result of self-betrayal.

The mirror he held up for them reflected their long and sophisticated culture, their religious integrity and commitment to family life, their spontaneous kindness and expressions of generosity. He thanked them for welcoming us so warmly and apologized for the lack of fairness and understanding in

America's recent policies toward Syria. He concluded with these words: "The policies and politicians of the world are failing us. To protect our children, we all must do everything we can to break through the masks that are being painted on our faces. When we truly meet each other, we will have peace. Let nothing stop our getting to know each other."

The mosque was quiet, and when we all stood to leave we were swarmed by men below and women above. With tears in their eyes, they wanted to thank us, to wish us well, to invite us to their homes. The talk at the mosque, along with the entire service, was broadcast on TV and radio throughout the country. An Orthodox priest congratulated us that evening: "You give us hope, you feel with us, you show there are Americans who care." Another seed of understanding was planted in this rocky soil.

But all was not love and light. If you listen and question long enough, the Syrians' anger and suspicion emerge. For millennia, empires have come to rule this land and these people. With an American occupation of Iraq on their eastern border and Israel's occupation of the West Bank and Gaza to their southwest, most Syrians fear that foreign interests might set out to expand their territories and take over Syrian land. Many Syrians quoted to us an inscription written over Israel's Knesset, to the effect that the true land of Zion extends from the Euphrates to the Nile. This proves, they said, that Israel wants to conquer Syria. Part of our witness was to hear this anger, this distrust, and (in some cases) a desire for justice that bordered on vengeance.

Sheikh Salah Kuftaro, head of the largest Muslim social service organization in Syria and a liberal proponent of a just peace in the Middle East, summed up our thinking when he stated, "There will not be peace in our world until there is peace among the religions. And there will not be peace among the religions until the adherents come to understand one another. Muslims, Christians, and Jews all want peace and harmony. But we have been taught different things. It is important to listen to one another. There is a great future for this part of the world if the religious traditions learn to cooperate to achieve these expressed goals. But this process is not an easy one. It may be easy to dream about or talk about, but what we need today is people who are prepared to commit themselves in very practical ways to achieving this goal."

Citizens reaching across borders in acts of spiritual diplomacy are some of these "practical ways." Our own pilgrimage is not just about the journey of the two of us, or the five or ten of us, or however many people join each trip. We are the visible aspect of a much larger community of people, many of whom have never met but who share a commitment to changing how the story of our time is being told and who contribute to making these things happen.

We have a dream of communities of people coming together to send pilgrims or emissaries like us to places of conflict to extend friendship, humility, and openhearted listening. Once we declare our intentions, doors open, opportunities appear, and networks of friends emerge. We have been on the road for over four years now in different parts of the world and have not been disappointed yet in the willingness of people everywhere to make friends.

P.S. by Rabia's husband, Elias Amidon: There's one more lesson, or gift, of this journey I'd like to mention: it has expanded my notion of family. I remember telling stories to wide-eyed tribal kids—and adults—in bamboo huts in remote villages in northern Thailand. I remember a long session of singing *dhikr* with a group of young Muslim men in Morocco. I remember taking *jukaiv*, Zen Buddhist initiation, with a group of ten women in New Mexico, sewing together in silence for hours and hours as we made the intricate apron that signifies the robe of the Buddha. In each case, and in hundreds of others, I have come away with a new idea of who my family is and who my people are. The "other" is my family. We are all brothers and sisters, fathers and mothers, sons and daughters, to each other.

❧

"That's all nonviolence is—organized love."

—Joan Baez

A LETTER TO MY IMAGINARY AMERICAN FRIEND

JASMINA TESANOVIC

Jasmina Tesanovic is a renowned Serbian writer, editor, publisher, and filmmaker and an active member of Women in Black. She is the author of *The Diary of a Political Idiot* and the coeditor of *The Suitcase*, a collection of memoirs from refugees fleeing Bosnia and Croatia. She is also a founding editor of 94, the first feminist publisher in Serbia.

Belgrade, November 22, 2004
Four years ago, I wrote in my first letter to my virtual friend from Baghdad, Nuha al Radi: "We should be enemies. You are a Muslim, I am a Christian. You are dark, I am white. But we both are

women, we both write diaries, we both are pacifists. . . ." Unfortunately, Nuha died and we never managed to meet. Our love and understanding was virtual, transnational, and global, yet far more valuable than our relationships with most of our "natural" allies in our own communities. We shared two hundred pages of questions, emotions, and insights, unveiling the universality of militarism and patriarchy.

Our common enemy should have been the United States. Nuha wrote, "I could never live in the USA," and I said, "I could never, ever fall in love with an American." We both had to eat our words: Nuha received medical treatment in the United States, and I now love Americans. Ever since Bush won for the second time, ever since the American economy went to pieces and threatened global disorder, ever since the U.S. government's raving antiterrorism measures have turned the whole world into an internment camp, I have had a feeling that the "decent people" from the United States who have raised their voices against the enemy within their own country need the world's support in order to set us all free.

As I said to Nuha, and now I say to you, my imaginary American friend: We should be enemies. Your country bombed us and killed innocent people with sanctions, but I know it was not you who did it. I know because it happened to me, too. My country also bombed and killed innocent people, and it was not me doing it. It is easy to be against the "other," to oppose the obvious enemy. Yet it is not only wrong but also dangerous to fail to see the real enemies, which are in our homes and sometimes inside ourselves: militarism and nationalism. They are lethal, killers without faces or names or races.

At the 2003 international conference in Italy of Women in Black, I declared: "World beware, Women in Black are everywhere. They don't have to be women; they don't even have to wear black. We are all Women in Black."

We who say, "Not in our names, not with our money," we who are labeled traitors, we who are antipatriots, we who are spreading the politics of women's solidarity, we who accept the mark of social shame, we who transform the sense of guilt into acts of responsibility, we who support the conscientious objectors, we who transgress ethnic barriers, we who condemn every war, we who support the victims of war, we who demand accountability for war and war crimes: we are all Women in Black. And we are building an alternative world that is not only possible but already here.

When I think of the United States, I don't think of Bush, of frenetic militarism, of global warming, of racism. I think of my editor and coauthor, Steph. I think of my young friend Violeta, half Serbian and half Albanian, who married an American and has an American child. I think of Andy Warhol, Laurie Anderson, Patti Smith, bell hooks. I think of rock music, of the Internet, of dreams of freedom and multiculturalism, dreams for which so many Americans have died. I think of a new continent available to all of us eager to leave behind the trenches of national history. I think of all those American friends (and there were many) who sent me packages, letters, and books during our dark times of Milošević.

And I want to tell them now, because I found it out myself, written in scars all over my body: Nobody can save you, lead you, or destroy you but yourselves. We are never alone but only lonely.

MAKING AMERICA
A HATE-FREE ZONE

PRAMILA JAYAPAL

Over her life, Pramila Jayapal has gone from investment banker to meditative writer and pilgrim to community activist. Since 9/11, with the escalation of abuses against Arab and South Asian communities, Jayapal has been at the forefront of community organizing against racism; she founded Hate-Free Zone Washington to build solidarity at the local level. The following piece was adapted from an interview with Anne Lappe.

September 11, 2001, was on a Tuesday. By Saturday, I had already received a number of calls from people living in immigrant communities I was close to: South Asians, East Asians, East Africans. Many were being attacked,

CODEPINK cofounder Gael Murphy with Palestinian women protesting the Israeli wall.
Photo by Medea Benjamin

physically and verbally. They were afraid to leave their homes. Teacher friends called to say kids were missing. Parents were afraid to send their children to school. It was one of those times when you cry, and then you wipe your tears and ask, What can I do?

By Monday I had met with U.S. representative Jim McDermott of Seattle and presented a plan for a statewide campaign that included political advocacy, direct community support, education and training, and public awareness and media relations. By Tuesday, Representative Jim McDermott, myself, and others held a press conference with the governor, the mayor of Seattle, the county council, the chief of police, and the chief of schools, and we launched the Hate-Free Zone Campaign of Washington.

We started out thinking we'd focus on hate crimes by individuals against individuals, but we soon discovered an enormous need to oppose government actions targeting immigrant communities of color. Immigrant communities are—in some deep, dark way—becoming an endangered species.

Since 9/11, we have seen the federal government arrest or detain massive numbers of immigrants from the Middle East, often holding detainees without declaring any charges whatsoever. Once in custody, immigrants find themselves vulnerable to deportation on the grounds of minor visa infractions (such as not reporting a change of address within ten days of moving), not to mention being subject to the humiliation that comes from their captors' misunderstanding of their religion or culture. One day, as I was leaving a detention center, I saw a Sikh man with a towel wrapped around his head as a turban. He was trying to communicate with a guard who was demanding he remove it. I explained to the officer that taking off this towel went against the man's religion. In Sikhism, I explained, you must always keep your hair covered. I then talked to the director of the detention center and explained the situation. He eventually agreed to let the man keep his turban. For a Sikh man, having your turban taken off is not unlike having your pants removed and being forced to expose your penis. That's what the officials had tried to do to him.

It is very difficult to know the scope of the post-9/11 detentions, raids, and arrests because the U.S. government has consistently maintained that revealing such information is a threat to national security. Now all federal agencies can claim blanket exemption from the Freedom of Information Act and refuse to provide information.

The lack of information about exactly what these agencies are doing makes it difficult to police the authorities—and to know the difference between legitimate law-enforcement activities and unscrupulous abuses of power. At one community meeting, a Somali man said he'd been getting calls from a man who claimed to be from the FBI and who asked prying questions about his family members. In another case, a man also claiming to be from the FBI arrived at someone's home and asked to listen to the answering machine. I myself received a call from someone who said he was with the Department of Defense, but when I called the Department of Defense, no one had heard of him.

And it's not only the federal government we have to worry about—the increased authority of local cops is also a cause for concern. Immigration offenses are classified as civil violations (conveniently so for our government, because people charged with immigration violations do not need to be provided with public defenders!). Local cops enforce criminal violations. This distinction has been critical for the safety of immigrant communities; because of it, immigrants have felt safe reporting crimes without worrying that their immigration status will be challenged. Now that's on the verge of changing. The state of Florida, working with the U.S. attorney general's office, signed an order deputizing all local law-enforcement officers as INS officials.

We can't always control what the federal government does, but we can mobilize locally. Hate-Free Zone worked with the Seattle mayor and the Seattle Police Department to establish a policy that police officers will not ask people about their immigration status. (The police were all too happy to comply, since they often don't have the resources to handle immigration issues and they don't want to be involved with such disputes.)

Meanwhile, though, the government is still effectively deputizing ordinary citizens, encouraging every American to report "suspicious activity." But what is that? If you are an Arab-looking man taking pictures of public buildings, are you suspicious? If you are a Muslim woman in *hajib* walking in a neighborhood you don't know, are you suspicious? With no clear criteria to define suspicious activity, many people make judgments based on what a person looks like.

And what is all this doing to control terrorism? Does it make you feel safer to know that more than two thousand people have been detained, yielding no concrete information about potential terrorist attacks (according to the Justice Department's own report)? Does it make you feel safer that Operation Tarmac's raid on airport workers led to 375 workers (primarily Latino and Filipino) being deported? Does it make you feel safer to know that the government is prohibiting people from working because of their countries of origin? Does it make you feel safer to know that the USDA pulled all foreign graduate research students out of their labs, citing fears of bioterrorism?

For most of us, any improvements in our day-to-day security are vague or intangible at best, while some of us have become remarkably less safe—these are the newest Americans, those with no money, no status, no voice. What they do possess, which would do much to boost our nation right now, is an impressive resilience, a faith in their own inner strength and the strength of their communities, rather than an overwhelming fear of others.

∽∘∾

"It's time for greatness, not greed. Idealism, not ideology. It's a time not just for compassionate words, but compassionate action."

—Marian Wright Edelman

WHAT WE EXPECT
FROM AMERICA

MARY ROBINSON

Mary Robinson is the former president of Ireland and the former UN high Commissioner for human rights. This essay appeared in a slightly different form in *The American Prospect*.

U.S. leadership was critical in building the global human-rights agenda from the ground up, beginning with the 1948 Universal Declaration of Human Rights. More than half a century later, that agenda and the movement it inspired urgently need renewed U.S. leadership at every level, from grass-roots activism to government policy and actions, nationally and globally.

The reluctance of the United States to embrace fully the international human-rights system it did so much to establish has weakened efforts to promote democracy and social justice in the United States and abroad. Witness what has happened following the terrorist attacks of 9/11: since then, the U.S. government has decided to hold detainees at Guantánamo Bay, Cuba, without Geneva Convention hearings; to monitor, detain, and deport immigrants against whom no charges have been made; and to restrict visitors and immigrants alike from many parts of the world.

In lowering its own standards, the United States has, often inadvertently, given other governments an opening to ignore international rights commitments. I saw this firsthand as the United Nations' high commissioner for human rights. A number of countries have introduced repressive laws and detention practices, all broadly justified by U.S. actions and the international war on terrorism. I will never forget how one ambassador put it to me bluntly: "Don't you see, High Commissioner? The standards have changed."

We must challenge this view and do everything possible to maintain the integrity of international human rights and humanitarian-law norms in light of heightened security tensions. Yet we must do more. We must also win the war of ideas and make the case that true security is possible only when the full range of human rights—civil and political as well as economic, social, and cultural—is guaranteed for all people.

This thinking isn't new. In fact, it draws on the best traditions of U.S. leadership, epitomized by president Franklin Delano Roosevelt's celebrated 1944 State of the Union address. But succeeding U.S. administrations have rejected the idea that education, health care, adequate housing, and food are rights citizens are entitled to, sometimes contending that these are aspirations, not justifiable rights. Some of our leaders have voiced fears that U.S. sovereignty and states' rights would be put at risk by ratifying international human-rights agreements. These philosophical and legal issues have long been debated. But we've spent far less time considering the advantages of committing ourselves to human rights around the world: namely, that the vision, legal framework, methods, and strategies of the human-rights movement could support and strengthen U.S. efforts to promote democracy and social justice today.

I am encouraged by the emergence of a U.S. movement that advocates the rights of people across the globe. For example, a growing number of academics at U.S. medical schools and groups such as Physicians for Human Rights are defending everyone's right to the highest attainable standard of health—and demonstrating the impact this shift would have on the way decisions are made about health spending and access to health services, especially for the most vulnerable. At human-rights conventions, U.S. development and humanitarian organizations increasingly empower grassroots civil-society groups to press their governments to take appropriate actions. The U.S. labor movement (through new initiatives such as American Rights at Work) and networks of women's- and children's-advocacy organizations are recognizing the potential power of the international human-rights agenda.

Reclaiming American traditions that contributed so much to the creation of the international human-rights movement will be an uphill journey. We must begin close to home, while being mindful that each step will have a profound impact on the realization of human rights around the world.

∽∽

"Warfare is only an invention—not a biological necessity."

—Margaret Mead

PART II:

A CHALLENGE TO THE SUPPORT STRUCTURE OF WAR AND VIOLENCE

Chapter 6

UNSPIN
THE MEDIA

THE GUARDS ARE SLEEPING: AN INTERVIEW WITH HELEN THOMAS

GAEL MURPHY

Helen Thomas, known as "the first lady" of the press, was a White House correspondent for four decades, sitting in the front row during presidential press conferences, asking the tough questions. She was the first woman to hold posts in the White House Correspondents' Association and the National Press Club. She now writes a syndicated column twice a week for the Hearst newspapers. She was one of the only "mainstream" journalists who vehemently opposed the invasion of Iraq and challenged the Bush administration on the fabrications and distortions that led the United States to war. The following is a conversation between Helen Thomas and CODEPINK cofounder Gael Murphy.

Q: *Our so-called independent media, the cornerstone of our democracy, have truly failed us in the most recent events around Iraq. They didn't do the investigations or critical analyses of the administration's policy toward Iraq. They didn't take into account opposing voices, alternative sources, and the millions of protesters. Why do you think the corporate media paid so little attention to exposing the flaws in the Bush administration's justification to go to war?*

A: I think that the media really went into a coma and rolled over and played dead, just as Congress did. It was a politics of fear after 9/11. Everybody, even reporters, started wearing flags after 9/11. At these White House briefings there was an atmosphere among the reporters that you would be considered unpatriotic or un-American if you were asking any tough questions. Then it segued into a war where you'd be seen as jeopardizing the troops if you asked certain questions.

And the administration did an amazing job of linking Saddam Hussein and terrorism. In every briefing I attended in the lead-up to the war, the spokespeople would say, "Saddam Hussein, 9/11"—"Saddam Hussein, 9/11" in the same breath. Obviously they had put the two together and wanted the media to as well. Then a week or so before the war they said there was no connection. Well, by this time, the job was done. It was a beautiful propaganda message, and it worked.

Another problem is that there are no investigative reporters anymore.

Washington Square Park, New York City, March 27, 2003.
© Fred Askew

During the unraveling of the Watergate scandal, the *Washington Post* had eighteen reporters on the story and the *New York Times* had an equal number, digging in everywhere. In this case, no one was around, really, to challenge the administration.

Q: *But there were a lot of alternative sources of news and investigative journalism, and there was also the world press doing its job. Don't mainstream journalists look at these other sources?*

A: We have a herd mentality here. It was groupthink. Nobody wanted to get out of line. Reporters felt that they shouldn't push too hard. I didn't feel that way. I was against this war from day one, and I kept challenging the White House spokesperson, Ari Fleischer. One day, about six months before the U.S. invasion, I said, "Ari, why does the president want to kill thousands of people?" I mean that's about as simplistic as I could put it. And he said, "Why are you saying that, Helen? They have a dictator! They have no say in their country!" I said, "Neither do we."

I went up to Condoleezza Rice after the U.S. invasion and said, "Where are the weapons? Where's the smoking gun? Where's the mushroom cloud?" She said, "Saddam used these weapons twelve years ago, he had them. . . ." And then she went up in smoke herself. She flew out of there with her eyes blazing, so angry that she should be challenged.

Q: *Regarding the White House press corps, is it sort of the cream of the crop of journalists who get to be part of those briefings?*

A: Every new administration comes in with a new crop of reporters who have been on the campaign with them and have gotten to know them, and their bosses say, "You're going to the White House because you know intimately so-and-so and can call them up and get an interview." So not only do they tend to be young, but they tend not to question what is said.

Q: *It almost sounds like reporters are embedded with a presidential candidate and then inherit the White House as their reward.*

A: That's certainly true. They get to the White House because they've done a good job on the campaign, they've gotten to know the players, and they're supposed to have this kind of entrée and closeness. And then they engage in self-censorship instead of challenging everything that's being said.

I remember Bush's press conference a few days before the war. It was a fiasco, because everybody knew we were going to war and asked things like Do you pray? instead of asking the hard-news questions like: Why are we going to war? Why haven't you done more to avoid it? Why haven't you used diplomacy? Under what justification can you go into someone else's country?

I'm also one of the few reporters who push the Pentagon on Iraqi casualties. When I'm writing a column about war casualties, I call the Pentagon and say, "Well, now, how many fatalities?" They'll readily say how many, in battle and in accidents. Then I ask about the wounded soldiers, and they reluctantly tell me about the wounded. Then I say, "How many Iraqis?" And the answer I'd get is, "We don't track that. They don't count." So once I called back and I said, "Look, aren't we supposed to be liberating these people? What do you mean they don't count? I want a rationale for why you don't count them." And they said, "Look, our purpose is not to kill, but if there is resistance, we do our job and don't count the numbers."

Iraqis don't want foreigners in their country, and some will resort to terrible things to get rid of them. But what right do we have to be there? That's the bottom line. I can assure you no reporter has asked that question. What right do we have to be there?

Q: *Did you ever challenge your colleagues about their reporting?*

A: No. They knew how I felt, they could hear me, but there is an unwritten rule that you do not challenge your colleagues. Except I must say that the *Wall Street Journal* called me the crazy aunt in the attic, and so did Fox, for questioning the war. Well, I want to know, who is the crazy aunt in the attic now? I think the *Wall Street Journal* owes me an apology.

Q: *Have you always questioned U.S. military involvement?*

A: I was in favor of U.S. involvement in World War II. It was absolutely necessary. We were attacked. And our country was unified—we believed in it.

I'm critical of unnecessary wars. I hated the Vietnam War, not from the moment Kennedy and Johnson put their foot in the door, but from the time of French colonialism from 1948 and the battle of Dien Bien Phu in 1953. I certainly thought it was wrong for us to go into Indochina after the French had been defeated.

I did support the invasion of Afghanistan. I thought we had to go to the core and find out more about Al-Qaeda. But I thought Iraq was absolutely wrong. It was just out of the blue, when Bush came into power and decided that he was going to have a regime change in Iraq.

And then Congress signed on the dotted line, giving a blank check without asking any questions!

I couldn't believe the people in Congress who actually did that. I couldn't believe Senator Kerry—he went to Vietnam and came back saying, "War is horrible. This is a horrible war and we shouldn't be in it." I suppose that eighteen years in the Senate can make you an Establishment person, and you forget. The authorization to go into Iraq is practically word for word from the Gulf of Tonkin resolution. Why didn't bells ring? How on earth could Kerry have just signed on? Because he was running for president and thought it would get him more votes?

Q: *So how do we get journalists and the media to do their job, to be critical of administrations and the policies that are not in the best interests of the public? How do we wake up America?*

A: I think journalists are coming out of their coma now. I think they're getting a little more feisty. I think the public kind of bore down on the press and the press started to respond, although there is certainly a lot more we need to do.

I think the public should reach out to the editorial writers and the publishers and take them to task for their pro-war positions. People should get meetings with the editorial departments of the major papers and the local papers and say, "Look, your paper came out for this war. Can you explain why? And what do you have to say now? Have you changed your mind? Have you printed your new position?" Ask them if they'll do a mea culpa. I'm sure most of them won't, but they should be encouraged to do it.

People should also go to the TV stations, including the talk shows. They should complain about the one-sided nature of the guests on the show. They should ask why, every Sunday, did we hear from Colin Powell and Condoleezza Rice and Donald Rumsfeld and Dick Cheney, but not equally from the antiwar side? Remember, a free and independent press is the basis of democracy. Journalism is the last resort against a government with such imperial motives, and we have to hold their feet to the fire.

I think that we should shame Congress for signing on the bottom line but not asking the tough questions they should have asked. They defaulted on the most important privilege they have in the Constitution—the right to declare war. They let the Constitution down. They let the country down. I think everyone who voted to authorize the president to go to war should be pinned down. [John D. Rockefeller IV, of West Virginia] was the vice chairman of the Senate Intelligence Committee. He said that if he knew then what he knows now, he would not have voted to go to war. I would go to every congressman, every senator, who voted for the war, and say, "Knowing what you know now, would you still have voted the same way? And if you would, why?" Reporters should put them on the line, and so should their constituents.

Reporters should put presidents on the line as well, and the public should demand that presidents have regular press conferences. During the campaign we should make them say that they will hold regular news conferences every two weeks. Bush hated talking to the press and only did when forced to. He had a seating chart and would pick the journalists he wanted. He was told to not call on me because I would ask a very tough question. He didn't allow any follow-up questions and would get mad if a reporter asked a two-part question. I mean, c'mon. The president of the United States should be able to answer any question, or at least dance around it. Presidents should be obligated—early and often—to submit to questioning and be held accountable. The presidential news conference is the only forum in our society, the only institution, where a president can be questioned. If a leader is not questioned, he can rule by edict or executive order. He can be a king or a dictator. Who's to challenge him?

Q: *So in terms of the media, looking toward the future, what hope do you see?*

A: My hope is that we'll all wake up and realize our tremendous collective failure. Maybe we could have saved lives. Maybe we could have stopped Bush from the folly of invading Iraq. We certainly must learn from our mistakes—not being aggressive enough, not being curious enough, not demanding enough—so that we can help to stop the next folly of war.

And my hope is that people will begin to hold their government leaders accountable, and that we'll have true leaders who understand the horror of war and who do everything in their power to work for peace.

∾〇∾

> "The paper was not front-paging stuff," said Pentagon correspondent Thomas Ricks. "Administration assertions were on the front page. Things that challenged the administration were on A18 on Sunday or A24 on Monday. There was an attitude among editors: Look, we're going to war, why do we even worry about all this contrary stuff?"
>
> —Howard Kurtz, *Washington Post*, August 12, 2004

HEADING INTO THE CAVE
WITH A TORCH

KATRINA VANDEN HEUVEL

Katrina vanden Heuvel is the editor of the *Nation* magazine and the coeditor of the book *Taking Back America*. She is a frequent TV commentator on American and international politics and a member of the Council on Foreign Relations. This essay was adapted from a talk given in New York City with the Dalai Lama September 23, 2003.

How do those of us in the media, living at a time when our government lies and deceives its own people, search out the truth? How can we create media that do not make citizens passive, fearful spectators but rather informed and compassionate ones?

Sadly, most of our media—especially in the last few years—have lacked the courage to question authority, to raise tough questions, to perform the basic duties required of a free press in a democracy. They have been too easily intimidated by an administration that has used fear to make its case for war, to label its critics traitors, to silence dissent, to pervert the meaning of patriotism and compassion, and to push for legislation that would invade our privacy and destroy our dignity.

But in life and in history, there are always alternatives, so I'd like to propose an alternative way of looking at the media.

Media can also mean the "surrounding environments in which something functions and thrives." Scientists use the term to refer to substances they use to nurture a particular organism. Media in a petri dish might be used to grow penicillin, or anthrax. I choose those two germs on purpose because our media are in some ways just as neutral a transmission belt: they can carry news that enlightens as easily as they carry news that poisons minds. If we understand that mass communication in this country helps to create the environment in which society functions, then the question for those of us who would like to bring about a more ethical society is, What kind of information is to be disseminated, by whom, and for what purpose?

Columnist Pete Hamill has described the reporter as the member of the tribe who is sent to the back of the cave to find out what's there. The report must be accurate. If there's a rabbit hiding in the darkness, it cannot be transformed into a dragon. Bad reporting, after all, could deprive people of shelter and warmth and survival on an arctic night. But if there is, in fact, a dragon lurking in the dark, it can't be described as a rabbit. The survival of the tribe could depend on that person with the torch.

We Americans are very lucky to have a rich tradition of torchbearers poking around the dark corners of the caves of the powerful. I'm thinking of muckrakers like Jacob Riis, Lincoln Steffens, Ida Tarbell, and Upton Sinclair, who rooted out political corruption, corporate greed, and dangerous working conditions, sparking vital movements for reform. I'm thinking of Rachel Carson, who examined the effects of pesticides on the environment; of I. F. Stone, who revealed how the Gulf of Tonkin incident was used by Lyndon Johnson to justify the Vietnam War; of Seymour Hersh and Ron Ridenhour, for unearthing the massacre at My Lai; of Allan Nairn, who showed the connections between the CIA and Latin American death squads. And the list goes on.

A democratic and ethical society can function and thrive only when the media alert the public to the difference between what the powers that be promise and what they deliver, defend the weak against the strong, and ensure that no person is above the law, no matter how powerful.

To perform these functions, our media must be independent from government interference, from the more subtle pressures imposed by would-be moralists who think they know what the public should read and see, and from base considerations of private profit that are causing many news outlets to turn away from hard news and toward what we now call "infotainment."

In the Soviet Union, people knew when they opened *Pravda* that they were not getting the truth, and so they became experts at reading between the lines of the official lies and discerning the truth for themselves. Those of us who live in democratic or nonauthoritarian societies have a similar task, but perhaps a harder one because, while our mainstream media are not officially controlled by those in power, journalists are nevertheless under pressure to shy away from reporting hard truths.

Too much of the press has become subservient to the manipulations of the White House and the gatekeepers of other powerful private institutions. Many journalists fear losing access to the powerful, and tailor their reporting accordingly. Thus we have seen a tremendous increase in sycophantic press coverage of the president and his administration. Add to that this administration's obsession with secrecy and control and you have a very dangerous situation.

But I am a realistic idealist, and I think there are extraordinary opportunities to change our media. First of all, the tradition of independent investigative reporting is not dead, and you can find vibrant examples of it in both the alternative media—at the *Nation* or on Amy Goodman's *Democracy Now!*— as well as in some corporate outlets. For example, the careful investigative reporting of two journalists at the *Chicago Tribune* in 1999 revealed deeply ingrained problems in Illinois' system of capital punishment and ultimately led to the commutation of the sentences of all the inmates on death row by the state's Republican governor.

At the same time, the technologies of the Internet and digital video have fostered a new generation of independent journalism, created directly by the participants in political movements and campaigns. Instead of being mere subjects of the mass media, millions of people are making their own media and talking back to the official journalists in ways that are slowly changing and broadening the definition of "news."

Can the Internet, with its culture of freewheeling grassroots debate, and the media democracy movement, with its goal of breaking up the giant media monopolies, somehow supplant the top-down, profit-oriented, power-following media conglomerates? I don't know, but I believe it's our best hope. Media made by people who are responsive to the real interests of their audiences, as opposed to the interests of their owners or their advertisers, are far more likely to be media that nurture civic society, see the world in its complex interdependence, look for solutions to problems, and help bring about a more peaceful world.

If there is to be an ethical revival in the media, it won't be because we've somehow changed the human nature of the people who work in the media;

it will be because we've changed the structures they have to work in, so they can be their own better selves. In the end, I believe that the full story will come out—it always does—because someone is heading into the cave with a torch.

∽o∾

"The inappropriate fit between the country's major media and the country's political system has starved voters of relevant information. It has eroded the central requirement of a democracy that those who are governed give not only their consent but their informed consent."

—Ben H. Bagdikian

THE POWER OF DISSENT

AMY GOODMAN

Amy Goodman hosts *Democracy Now!* a daily news hour that appears on NPR, Pacifica Radio, public access television, and PBS stations across the country. *Exception to the Rulers*, by Amy and David Goodman, was published in 2004.

The U.S. media are among the most powerful institutions on earth. They are not only among the wealthiest, but they are also the way the whole world views us and we view each other.

There was a piece in the *Wall Street Journal* the other day about the difference between CNN and CNN International, two networks owned by the same company. The day the statue was pulled down [in Baghdad], on CNN we watched that statue get pulled down and go back up and get pulled down again all day.

On CNN International they also showed the statue pulled down, but it was on a split screen—and on half the screen they showed the casualties of war. Now, I'm not talking about the difference between CNN and Al-Jazeera. I'm talking about the difference between CNN and CNN International. It means that that company knows exactly what it's doing—what it provides for domestic consumption and what it provides to the rest of the world.

I really do think that if for one week in the United States we saw the true face of war, if we saw people's limbs sheared off, saw kids blown apart, war would be eradicated. Instead what we see in the U.S. media is the video war game. Those gray, grainy photographs with a target down on the ground. It would be more accurate to show the target on the forehead of a little Iraqi girl, because that's who dies in war. The overwhelming majority of people who die are innocent civilians.

Dissent does matter. It's what makes this country healthy. And the media have a responsibility to go to where the silence is, to present the views of people all over this country and not simply beat the drums for war. And that's precisely what it did in this lead-up to the invasion.

We get the "news" from reporters embedded with the military and a parade of retired generals who are on the networks' payrolls.

Why is it that they have these retired generals on the payroll, and they don't have peace activists and peace leaders on the payroll? Let's see the same number of reporters embedded with Iraqi families and embedded in the peace movement all over the world. Maybe then we'll get some picture of what's going on.

Think about Dan Rather the night that the bombs started falling on Iraq: "Good morning, Baghdad," he said. Tom Brokaw said, "We don't want to destroy the infrastructure of Iraq, because we're going to own it in a few days."

Peter Jennings was interviewing Chris Cuomo, a reporter for ABC, who was out on the street in Times Square, where thousands of people had come out to protest the war in the freezing rain. They had all sorts of signs that were sopping wet, and people were trying to keep the umbrellas up, and the police charged a part of the crowd.

Jennings said to Cuomo, "What are they doing out there? What are they saying?" And he answered, "Well, they have these signs that say, 'No blood for oil,' but when you ask them what that means, they seem very confused. I don't think they know why they're out here." I guess they got caught in a traffic jam. Why not have Peter Jennings invite one of the protesters into the studio and then have a real discussion as he does with the generals?

That is not an independent media. That is a media that is hell-bent on war, and it is violating our sacred responsibility to be fair.

As the Federal Communications Commission and its chairman, Michael Powell, continue the process of deregulating the media, we have seen a concentration of ownership. Clear Channel went from owning forty-seven radio stations to fourteen hundred in no time at all. Clear Channel's management is sponsoring pro-war rallies and refusing to play music that is critical of war.

It is essential that the media provide a forum for all views. Pacifica Radio and NPR and PBS are not the only ones using the public airwaves. The commercial, corporate-controlled media do, too. They are leasing those airwaves. And responsibilities come with that.

There is a whole chapter in *Exception to the Rulers* about the direction broadcasting has gone at the FCC under Michael Powell, although it goes back to the Clinton administration as well. Powell, the son of Colin Powell, leads the war on the diversity of voices at home. He has thought he could get away with it, and he tried to hold only one public hearing on the largest overhaul of media consolidation regulations in this country's history.

Pacifica Radio broadcasted the informal hearings that the dissident commissioners, Michael Copps and Jonathan Adelstein, held in early 2003 all over the country to get the public's views.

It was remarkable. When people heard about the proposed consolidation rules, they revolted—and the anger crossed the political spectrum. Congress and the FCC got more than two million responses. People said: no, it is not healthy for a media mogul to own the newspaper, a television network affiliate, and a radio station in one town.

That level of response was not due to the corporate media. They hardly covered the story all year. Instead, behind the scenes, media owners were filing joint briefs in support of deregulation, because they will benefit. The public demands better than that.

This country has parallel worlds. For some it's the greatest democracy on earth. There is no question about that. But others, such as immigrants now in detention facilities, have no rights, not even to a lawyer. Independent reporters have to be there to watch and to listen, to tell their stories until they can tell their own.

That's why I think *Democracy Now!* is a good model for the rest of the media, as are the Independent Media Centers all over the country and the world. They are built on almost nothing except the goodwill and the passion of people who are tired of seeing their friends and neighbors through a corporate lens.

Dissent is what makes this country healthy. And the media have to fight for that, as the rest of us have to fight for an independent media.

∞

"People should fear art, film, and theatre. This is where ideas happen.
This is where somebody goes into a dark room and starts to
watch something and their perspective can be completely questioned …
the very seeds of activism are empathy and imagination."

—Susan Sarandon

BUILDING
A BETTER MEDIA

JANINE JACKSON

Janine Jackson is the program director at FAIR (Fairness & Accuracy in Reporting), the national media watch group, and the producer-host of CounterSpin, FAIR's nationally syndicated radio show.

> "I take a grave view of the press. It has become the weak slat under the bed of democracy. It is an anomaly that information, the one thing most necessary to our survival as choosers of our own way, should be a commodity subject to the same merchandising rules as chewing gum, while armament, a secondary instrument of liberty, is a government concern. A man is not free if he cannot see where he is going, even if he has a gun to help him get there."
>
> — A. J. LIEBLING

When the Bush administration made clear its intention to turn the nation's grief and anger over the 9/11 attacks into an open-ended, ill-defined war on terror, the U.S. media had a choice: whether to serve as an independent, critical check on the government or to act primarily as mouthpieces for the administration, echoing and amplifying the official line. No clear-eyed survey of major U.S. media's coverage of the subsequent violent interventions in Afghanistan and Iraq will leave any question as to which course they took.

But if we are to fight for better media, it helps to be hopeful—to imagine the media we would like to see. In their failures, the mainstream media's reporting on the Bush administration's wars helps us define what sort of news reporting would truly serve democracy. That sort of journalism would:

REPORT ALL THE FACTS.

War involves violence, death, and destruction, and a presentation of war that pretends otherwise is inaccurate and misleading. Yet much of the press corps seemed to accept the White House's spin that coverage of the "bad news" that naturally comes with a violent military action constitutes "bad press," or unfairly biased media treatment. This cautiousness led the media to undercover or ignore numerous stories critical to an understanding of the effects of war.

Union Square, New York City, September 8, 2002.
© Fred Askew

Civilian deaths resulting from U.S.-led attacks were routinely downplayed. When dozens of civilians, including children, were killed in U.S. air strikes on the Afghan village Niazi Kala in December 2002, overseas newspapers carried headlines like "U.S. Accused of Killing Over 100 Villagers in Airstrike" (*Guardian*) and "100 Villagers Killed in U.S. Airstrike" (*London Times*). In contrast, the *New York Times* first reported the deaths at Niazi Kala under the headline "Afghan Leader Warily Backs U.S. Bombing." Earlier, saying that it would be "perverse" for the media to "focus too much on the casualties or hardship in Afghanistan," CNN chair Walter Isaacson had ordered his staff to "balance" imagery of the devastation of Afghan cities with explicit reminders to viewers that the Taliban harbored murderous terrorists (*Washington Post*, October 31, 2001).

More recently, the *New York Times* persisted in describing civilian casualty figures from the April 2004 U.S.-led attack on the Iraqi city of Fallujah as "unconfirmed," without offering any explanation as to why the numerous accounts of widespread death are to be disbelieved. An independent press corps would fearlessly investigate all of the impacts of war, so that the public could know what is being done in its name.

QUESTION THE POWERFUL.

Reporters can't be afraid to ask tough questions of political leaders. But the U.S. press failed to demand a credible and coherent accounting from the Bush administration with regard to the case for the attacks on Afghanistan and Iraq, as subsequent editorial mea culpas from outlets like the *Washington Post* and the *New York Times* partially acknowledged.

Journalists' failure to challenge the politically powerful is a reflection of the unhealthy closeness that exists between the government and the corporate-owned media. But it also results from the attitude of many reporters who see no problem with shedding their journalistic independence in a "crisis." As a guest on David Letterman's show in 2002, TV and radio pundit Cokie Roberts announced that she was "a total sucker for the guys who stand up with all the [military] ribbons on and stuff," explaining that "when they say stuff, I tend to believe it." And who can forget veteran CBS anchor Dan Rather's declaration: "George Bush is the president, he makes the decisions. . . . Wherever he wants me to line up, just tell me where." The notion that patriotism is best served by the media's uncritical treatment of powerful figures is the opposite of a democratic value.

PRESENT A WIDE DEBATE.

In October 2002, *Time* magazine ran a pair of opinion columns to illustrate the debate on the imminent invasion of Iraq. Their headlines read, "Let's Wait to Attack" and "No, Let's Not Waste Any Time." Indeed, media debate over the Afghanistan and Iraq wars was generally limited to questions of strategy and tactics; the deeper questions of the soundness of the rationales offered for war, as well as the wars' legality and myriad potential impacts, were off the major media's radar, despite being very much on the public's mind.

A FAIR (Fairness & Accuracy in Reporting) study of network newscasts on ABC, CBS, NBC, and PBS in the weeks before the Iraq invasion found that, of 393 on-air sources in news stories about Iraq, just 3 were opposed to the war. At the time, CNN and Gallup polls were showing some 27 percent of the public critical of the war. The truncated debate was the predictable result of commercial media's overreliance on official sources: 76 percent of all sources on the four networks were current or former government officials. That didn't leave much room for independent or grassroots voices.

Resist demonization: Everyone knows there's a tendency for governments to "dehumanize" official enemies, especially in a time of war. Journalists, however, have a responsibility to resist such oversimplified characterizations of people and history. In contrast to the thoughtful, culturally sensitive conversations we might have had in the wake of the 9/11 attacks, many in the U.S. press were nearly hysterical in banging the drums for war. "Let them eat sand," declared Fox News Channel's Bill O'Reilly, calling—on September 17, 2001—for the United States to bomb not just Afghanistan but Iraq and Libya as well. "The U.S. should bomb the Afghan infrastructure to rubble—the airport, the power plants, their water facilities and the roads," he said. On September 13, 2001, the popular TV pundit and *National Review* editor Rich Lowry used the op-ed page of the *Washington Post* to declare, "If we flatten part of Damascus or Tehran or whatever it takes, that is part of the solution." It seems a minimum expectation for a democratic society that the debate in the dominant media not give pride of place to calls for widespread war crimes.

Activists pushed for improvements in the U.S. media's post-9/11 coverage, and sometimes won. For example, the *New York Times* and NPR ran stories seriously undercounting the size of the crowd at a Washington, D.C., protest against the Iraq war in October 2002. After complaints from hundreds of activists, as well as critical attention in the alternative press, NPR corrected its story, and while the *New York Times* did not acknowledge its error, the paper took the highly unusual step of running a second, more accurate and inclusive article about the demonstration. Another FAIR campaign led to

HBO's adding a disclaimer to its movie about the first Gulf War, *Live from Baghdad*, clarifying scenes that seemed to endorse the fraudulent stories about Iraqi soldiers removing Kuwaiti babies from incubators.

Such efforts may seem quixotic, but they matter: they encourage people to consume media reports critically and actively, and they put the media on notice that the public expects, and increasingly demands, better, more complete, more honest, more inclusive reporting—not just in times of war but always.

Like anything else important, a more democratic media system will not simply evolve but will result from organized effort. We, as citizens, can bring it closer by speaking up to the press when they let us down, by calling for broader structural reforms to diversify the ownership of media outlets and make them more accountable, and by supporting those truly independent and alternative outlets that try to do things a different way.

That's a long fight, and a worthy one. But until we have a media that more fully reflects our society, we have to do something else, too: there's just no substitute for informing yourself independently, for looking beyond the newspapers and the television for an understanding of the world. If the question is, What can we do about the media? then actions like reading this book and talking about it with friends and family are a big part of the answer.

BE THE MEDIA

ANDREA BUFFA

Andrea Buffa is the peace campaign coordinator at Global Exchange; she was previously the executive director of Media Alliance.

U.S. news reports of the assault on Fallujah, Iraq, in November 2004 epitomized the problems with the corporate media coverage of war and showed how much those of us working for peace need to change the media if we are ever to stop the next war before it starts. U.S. warplanes dropped bombs on Fallujah's neighborhoods, decimating homes, government buildings, and mosques; and thousands of U.S. troops stormed the city, shooting at anything in sight. Thirty to sixty thousand Fallujans were barricaded into their houses, without access to running water, electricity, or food.

Rather than show the reality of what must have happened in Fallujah—destruction that ended the lives of some seventy-one soldiers and two thousand Iraqis—reports from embedded journalists revealed hardly a drop of blood. There was never a mention of the tens of thousands of civilians still in Fallujah during the assault, much less an attempt to determine how many were killed.

But the distortion of the Fallujah attack is only the tip of the iceberg. From the beginning, the U.S. media consistently underplayed the human costs of the Iraq war, ignored or ridiculed antiwar activists who argued that war would leave Americans less safe than before, and even left media consumers confused about the basic facts: to this day, many still believe that Saddam Hussein was involved in the 9/11 attacks and that weapons of mass destruction were found in Iraq.

If Americans are ever to be convinced of the need to change the government's militaristic policies, they must be informed about the devastating consequences of war and educated about peaceful alternatives. We cannot reach people without access to mass communications. We need to stop our media from acting as a mouthpiece of the Pentagon and make it start telling the truth, unpleasant as the truth may be.

Convincing Americans of the importance of peace and justice requires peace activists to be media activists as well. When Michael Powell, the head of the FCC, was about to relax the rules and give even more power to the news outlets that were cheerleading for the war, peace activists sprang into action to try to stop it.

MoveOn.org, United for Peace and Justice, and CODEPINK encouraged supporters to bombard the FCC with phone calls and e-mails opposing Powell's media-deregulation plan. Four days before the FCC vote, organizers mounted protests in a dozen U.S. cities outside radio stations owned by Clear Channel Communications, the poster child for what's wrong with media deregulation. Clear Channel owns some fourteen hundred radio stations nationwide, and its monopolistic practices have accelerated the homogenization of the airwaves. The company used its stations to promote a conservative political agenda when it sponsored pro-war rallies in cities around the country before and during the Iraq war.

Although the FCC ended up voting in favor of the radical media deregulation, a lawsuit by media activist groups has stopped the deregulation from being implemented, and widespread opposition has grown. But stopping the ruling didn't undo the fact that a handful of corporations controls 80 percent of what the American public sees and hears.

The most fundamental problem with the U.S. mass media is the way it is structured. Broadcast outlets are supposed to be regulated to operate in the public interest, but the FCC has instead worked for the interests of corporate profits. The Telecommunications Act of 1996 eliminated many of the previous restrictions on media-company ownership, and the deregulation proposal of 2003 would have done away with the few remaining restrictions if there hadn't been such a huge outcry.

Meanwhile, public radio and television are just as bad. Their funding depends on the benevolence of Congress, which means that public radio and TV managers are reluctant to be too critical of government policy. Congress could propose to eliminate funding to the Corporation for Public Broadcasting at any time, which is what Newt Gingrich's Congress attempted in 1995.

A radical restructuring of media ownership would certainly be nice, but there are more realistic reforms that would also improve the quality and quantity of programming. Taking the following actions could significantly improve the coverage of community and social-justice issues, including war:

Bring back the Fairness Doctrine. From 1949 to 1987, the "Fairness Doctrine" required broadcast media outlets to offer opposing viewpoints on issues and to do so in a "fair" manner. If the Fairness Doctrine were in effect today, right-wing radio hosts would be required to provide some balance and to interview people whose views differed from theirs on issues like the Iraq war.

Push for the licensing of additional low-power FM radio stations. It's not likely that any peace groups are regular guests on commercial radio stations, but peace activists are often interviewed on community radio. Low-power FM stations are small radio stations run by nonprofits and community groups. They fit in between commercial stations on the radio dial. In 2000, the FCC approved licenses for a limited number of low-power FM radio stations, bringing a slew of political and music programming to the airwaves. With more licenses, there could be community radio stations everywhere in America.

Make broadcasters pay for their use of the spectrum. It's crazy, but corporations that make millions of dollars get to use the public airwaves for free. These corporations should have to pay for their broadcast licenses, and the money that's collected for the licenses could go toward public media or the development of independent programming.

Bring back requirements for local programming and more public affairs programming. Americans need and want programming that educates them about the issues that affect their lives. If the broadcasters aren't going to pay for their licenses, they should at least be required to meet basic requirements like providing several hours a day of local and public affairs programming.

Set aside part of the dial for community and nonprofit stations. The airwaves are owned by the public and should be regulated in the public interest. Because for-profit media outlets are always going to prioritize the bottom line over the public interest, a good part of the broadcast spectrum, including the digital spectrum, should be set aside for nonprofit, community-based media.

Defeat the new Telecommunications Act! Unfortunately, rather than a strengthening of ownership regulations, in the next few years we're looking at a probable attempt to roll them back. The big media companies and major telephone companies have persuaded Congress to rewrite the Telecommunications Act of 1996, starting this year. Any telecommunications act created under the Bush administration and the Republican-dominated House and Senate is bound to be a boon for corporate interests and a disaster for the rest of us.

During the next four years, peace activists must not only fight to end the occupation of Iraq but must also rally to take back the country's media. To make a real difference, the people need to be the media.

It is unrealistic to depend on Fox News and the *Washington Post* to adequately cover the war and the antiwar movement. New media must be created to expose violence and injustice and to express a variety of perspectives on how things can be done differently. More and more activists are doing just that, through Web sites, low-power FM radio stations, and public access TV shows. Since there is so little local news coverage on TV and radio these days, local groups can fill the gap by reporting on local issues and activism.

Not enough people know about alternative news sources such as local independent newsweeklies; Web sites like AlterNet (www.alternet.org), Common Dreams (www.commondreams.org), the Independent Media Centers (www.indymedia.org), TomDispatch (www.tomdispatch.com), TomPaine.com (www.tompaine.com), and ZNet (www.zmag.org); pioneering television programs such as those on Free Speech TV (www.freespeech.org) and Link TV (www.worldlinktv.org); and progressive radio networks like Pacifica Radio and Air America. And the award-winning daily news program *Democracy Now!*

Peace activists also need to be media activists, to hold our media accountable and to push media outlets to uphold basic standards of fairness and accuracy. Media activism can work. It stopped the conservative company Sinclair Broadcasting from airing an anti–John Kerry propaganda film on its sixty-two television stations in the weeks before the presidential election. It blocked the FCC's plan to allow greater media monopolization and homogenization.

Through vigorous watchdogging of the mainstream media and the robust creation of alternative news sources, media activists can be a major force in preventing the next war before it starts.

MEDIA ACTIVIST RESOURCES

Center for Digital Democracy, www.democraticmedia.org

Common Cause, www.commoncause.org

FAIR, www.fair.org

The Free Press, www.freepress.org

Media Access Project, www.mediaaccess.org

Media Alliance, www.media-alliance.org

MediaChannel, www.mediachannel.org

Media Tank, www.mediatank.org

Prometheus Radio Project, www.prometheusradio.org

Reclaim the Media, www.reclaimthemedia.org

ഇ൦ഇ

"The cororate grip on opinion in the United States is one of the wonders of the western world. No first world country has ever managed to eliminate so entirely from its media all objectivity—much less dissent."

—Gore Vidal

HOPE VERSUS CYNICISM

NINA ROTHSCHILD UTNE

Nina Utne, the chair and CEO of *Utne* magazine, is a writer, political activist, mother, and community builder. Utne is a founding member of both UnReasonable Women for the Earth and CODEPINK. She is married to *Utne* founder Eric Utne and is the mother of three sons and the stepmother of one.

A t a conference recently, a woman came up and grabbed me. Several years ago, she said, she had become so demoralized by what was going on in our country that she became an expatriate. But some months ago in Fiji, she came across the issue of *Utne* magazine with the Statue of Liberty on the cover, the one that proclaimed "CODEPINK: The Birth of a Movement." She lay in a hammock reading for five hours, and when she got up, she knew she had to come home and become an activist. Now she and her two daughters are involved with CODEPINK and she wanted to thank me.

It awes me to be part of that kind of power—the power to transform lives by the quality of a story. And that, for good and for evil, is the power of the media. The media amplify stories that instill terror or inspire hope. The stories that dominate our individual and collective awareness, and the feelings they stir up, form the raw material of our imagination. What we as a society take in and how we interpret it determine our vision of the future, our sense of possibility.

Yes, we need to know the atrocities that are being perpetuated in our name. We need media that ask hard questions persistently enough to get answers. But once we know the facts, we need to find the will, the courage, and the stamina to confront them. Those are to be found in the inspiring examples of maverick creativity, joyful service, and courageous resistance that exist all around us. At *Utne* magazine, the editors look for those kinds of stories, populated by people who provide examples of how to best live their own lives. Those who know gratitude and perceive grace in the midst of chaos and crisis have much to teach the rest of us—and they can do just that with the help of journalists who think with their hearts as well as their heads, whose hope is stronger than their cynicism. For all of us, learning to cultivate creativity and courage, gratitude and grace, is what will sustain us in what Chinese lore called the "curse of living in interesting times."

Whether we have fled to Fiji or into the morass of our own hopelessness, we must heed the call to come home to our own strength and convictions, to devote ourselves to what we care about. It is the job of the media to issue that call. And it is our job as citizens to settle for nothing less.

⌘

> "Of course it matters if our government lies to us. Why do you think
> people were so angry at Lyndon Johnson over the Gulf of Tonkin?
> At Richard Nixon over the "secret war" in Cambodia? Even Bill Clinton
> over the less cosmic matter of sex with 'that woman'?
> If it makes no difference whether the government lies,
> why does journalism exist at all?"
>
> —Molly Ivins

KILLING THE MESSENGER
WITH KINDNESS

TAD BARTIMUS

When Tad Bartimus isn't writing her nationally syndicated weekly column, creating a book, or teaching a workshop, she's interviewing visitors at her Hana, Maui, fruit stand. In an earlier life, she spent twenty-five years reporting for the Associated Press on four continents.

W hen I was a young Associated Press war correspondent in Vietnam I hitchhiked to the war. Throughout Vietnam, Laos, and Cambodia in 1973–74, I reported as many stories as my journalistic instincts, fear, and dumb luck permitted. I thumbed or bought access via CIA and American military aircraft, generous or corrupt Vietnamese chopper pilots, and all manner of hired private conveyances, from one-passenger cyclos pedaled by barefoot peasants to Mercedes limousines driven by white-gloved chauffeurs. To get to enemy territory I once even chartered a Mekong riverboat that made the *African Queen* look seaworthy.

My professional colleagues also relied on their wits and experience to ferret out their firsthand versions of the truth. The occasional organized "fact-finding" junket was a great way to hear the official story, but the best reporting came from independent roaming among troops and civilians, on the battlefield and behind the scenes.

It was this journalistic autonomy that led most of the press corps to the same conclusion: America could not win the war in Indochina no matter how much smoke or how many mirrors the military and White House threw at the biggest war story of my generation.

When Richard Nixon's administration finally negotiated a cease-fire and pullout in 1973, after ten years and fifty-eight thousand U.S. casualties, the hawks blamed the press and vowed never again to allow journalists unrestricted, uncensored access during armed conflicts.

Some of the Vietnam-era captains and majors who believed the media was the reason America lost the war now run the U.S. military and the White House. Out of their antipress mind-set has emerged a new kind of battlefield journalist: "the embed."

To be embedded is to eat, sleep, hit the dirt, and travel with a single military unit, to be an unarmed appendage who reports only on "their" soldiers' narrow view of the big picture.

When I hear *embed*, I think "in bed." Three decades of reporting around the globe has taught me what the cub reporter covering city hall may not yet have learned: to live with sources is to be co-opted by them. It may not be intentional or overt, but an attachment inevitably forms between people thrown together in extreme danger under constant stress.

Becoming an integral part of any story is dangerous for a journalist. No matter how innocent the bonding between witness and source, there is a natural instinct for the witness to become a gatekeeper, particularly if the source is helping to keep the reporter alive.

When journalists hold back, however slightly, for fear their reporting could negatively reflect on the soldiers risking their lives beside them, the first draft of history is incomplete because they aren't fully doing their job.

That's what happened in Iraq. The Pentagon's "embed" strategy fostered the journalists' emotional and physical codependence on the troops, and the result, in too many dispatches, was information skewed by a docile, manipulated, and woefully inexperienced media.

Months before the March 2003 invasion, the administration correctly guessed that up-close-and-personal journalism focused on brave young soldiers, delivered by scared embeds high on adrenaline, would sway hearts and minds in favor of president George W. Bush's preemptive strike.

Breathless television reports, minute-by-minute feature stories, and dramatic photographs and video provided by embeds captured the urgency and danger facing U.S. and allied forces advancing against Saddam Hussein's regime.

We saw gun battles in real time, heard orders as they were given, read of heroic deeds almost as they occurred. Media coverage was almost all about the fighting, delivered by embeds who experienced it firsthand.

Some of the reporting and writing was in the finest journalistic tradition of Ernie Pyle in World War II, Marguerite Higgins in Korea, and Neil Sheehan in Vietnam. The *New York Times*' Dexter Filkins, embedded with Bravo Company of the First Battalion, Eighth Marines, took the reader into hand-to-hand combat during the November 2004 battle for Fallujah:

"The sounds, sights and feel of the battle were as old as war itself, and as new as the Pentagon's latest weapons system," Filkins wrote in a November 21 story in the *Times*.

> The glow of the insurgents' flares, throwing daylight over a landscape to help them spot their targets: us.
>
> The nervous shove of a marine scrambling for space along a brick wall as tracer rounds ricocheted above.

The silence between the ping of the shell leaving its mortar tube and the explosion when it strikes.

The screams of the marines when one of their comrades . . . lost part of his jaw to a hand grenade.

"No, no, no!" the marines shouted as they dragged [him] from the darkened house where the bomb went off . . . "No, no, no!"

Nothing in the combat I saw even remotely resembled the scenes regularly flashed across movie screens; even so, they seemed no more real.

What news consumers didn't see or read much about was the collateral damage; the administration's postinvasion plans to turn Iraq over to its people; solidly researched estimates of the cost of the war, reconstruction, and peacekeeping efforts; and informed analysis of what Iraqis thought of it all.

The best of these more complex stories were often written by a small band of unembedded reporters known as "unilaterals." Their coverage was uncensored and filed without obligation to allied forces.

Unilaterals didn't travel in armored vehicles, aboard helicopters assaulting rebel strongholds, or in the middle of camouflaged ground forces fighting house to house. Because they were not embedded they operated on the increasingly dangerous fringes of a war where insurgent forces don't hesitate to behead and kidnap perceived enemies.

Of the fifty-four journalists killed in the line of work in 2004, the Committee to Protect Journalists said, twenty-three of them died reporting the Iraq war. CNN executive vice president and chief news executive Eason Jordan told a group of news executives in Portugal in November 2004 that unilaterals in Iraq faced arrest and even torture by the U.S. military.

"Actions speak louder than words," Jordan was quoted by the *Guardian* newspaper as saying. "The reality is that at least 10 journalists have been killed by the U.S. military . . . and the fact that no one has been reprimanded would indicate that no one is taking responsibility."

His allegation was denied by Bryan Whitman, a spokesman for defense Secretary Donald Rumsfeld, who insisted American military commanders were "very enlightened with respect to the freedom of the press."

But being un-embedded continued to prove more dangerous than being "in bedded." Paul Workman, who filed stories for the Canadian Broadcasting Corporation as a unilateral, claimed news consumers were more likely to see what he called a "glorified view of American power and morality, in a war much of the world considers unnecessary, unjustified, or plain wrong" because the embedded press corps was "sleeping with the winner."

As the Iraq war drags on, it gets harder for all journalists to report on its multiple fronts. When I covered Vietnam, and afterward the sectarian violence in Northern Ireland and the guerrilla movements in Latin America in the last half of the 1970s, I believed all journalists had a modicum of protection because most of us tried hard to be objective and fair and our efforts to stay neutral were frequently recognized by news sources.

The veil was ripped off personal partisanship when American TV anchors began wearing American flag lapel pins following the September 11, 2001, terrorist attacks. Now it's commonplace for cable TV anchors as well as pundits to ignore the once-sacrosanct line separating fact from opinion.

It's hard for me, in these most dangerous and politically polarized times, to encourage young journalists to go to war anywhere. In 2004, journalists all over the world were attacked for doing their job. In Moscow, the editor of the Russian edition of *Forbes* magazine was shot dead as he left his office. A crusading broadcaster, Roger Mariano, was en route home in the Philippines when he was shot more than a dozen times and left for dead along a country road. Reporters in China, Turkmenistan, and Iran were arrested, interrogated, and held incommunicado for days before being released.

In Providence, Rhode Island, television reporter Jim Taricani was found guilty of contempt by a U.S. district judge and sentenced to six months' house arrest for refusing to reveal a news source. Other U.S. journalists face possible prosecution in 2005 for the same reason.

If we journalists are no longer free to gather news and information for the public good in our own country, why bother to go abroad to defend the people's right to know? Why not stay and fight for our constitutionally guaranteed rights here?

If I were in their combat boots, I'd have to answer three questions in the affirmative before I booked my plane ticket to be a war correspondent:

- Will my being there make a difference in discovering the truth?
- Will disseminating the truth as I find it alleviate suffering, save lives, and positively influence humanitarian policies?
- Is this war worth dying for?

If the answer to any of those questions is "hell no!" then stay home and protect the beleaguered First Amendment.

Chapter 7

HOLD OUR LEADERS **ACCOUNTABLE**

ON **NOT PASSING** THE BUCK

PATRICIA SCOTT SCHROEDER

Patricia Schroeder is a former congresswoman who represented Denver, Colorado, in the House of Representatives for twenty-four years. She was the first woman to serve on the House Armed Services Committee and was an outspoken critic of wasteful Defense Department spending.

I was honored to be asked to write about how to influence today's policy makers. I started this essay and began to realize that the things I was going to say don't fit today's political climate. Think about it. How do you influence officials when we hear such things as: "He tripled the national debt, but has such charisma," or "Star Wars is an expensive fantasy, but I love his infectious optimism," or "The war in Iraq *is* wrong, but I feel I could have a beer with this guy." I hope you get my point that our first task is to work on the electorate! Many of us have friends who said similar things. If we hold elected leaders accountable for their actions only when they have no personality, appear stiff, or are not "regular" guys, then I don't know how you influence policy makers. What happened? Don't we teach civics in the schools anymore?

When I was in Congress, the buzz in the cloakroom was: "There go the people, and I must get in front of them because I'm their leader." That worked for getting the United States out of Vietnam, pushing the nuclear-freeze movement, and resolving other war and peace issues. When the people mobilized, wrote, marched, picketed, visited offices, and engaged in civic life, their representatives changed positions. Now it appears that if a representative has an engaging personality, political positions and votes don't matter. The charm offensive seems to be working against the voters. The charm offensive guts the foundations of democracy, which are responsibility and accountability.

So in this new environment, people have to understand that someone calls the shots and if we don't hold that someone accountable, we may as well have a king. President Harry S. Truman prided himself in saying, "The buck stops here." That sure hasn't been said in recent years! It's time we go back to teaching Democracy 101.

Let's look at the military issues. Clearly, those who manufacture military hardware drive the agenda because they have the money to give to campaigns. It is sad that Congress is more and more like a coin-operated legislative machine. When you look at the hardware your representatives are buying, it doesn't fit the threat! Military personnel and their families never get the same legislative attention because they don't give money. In the Iraq war, we see U.S. military families buying body armor and sending it to their family members. We hear the troops complaining that they don't have armored vehicles. But Congress funds Star Wars, the B-2 bombers, and so on. Whether people are for or against the war in Iraq, they ought to be upset that legislators are spending huge sums of taxpayers' money to reward campaign contributors! We would never tolerate such waste in any other part of the budget.

The good news is that the younger generation doesn't buy into this notion that the best leader in these times is the guy who seems the most "macho." They believe that trying to negotiate with people who don't agree with you on all issues doesn't make you a "girlie man" or a "Frenchman." They understand this is a fragile universe. The younger generation just needs to learn how to organize, and the Internet makes it easier than ever.

In a democracy, an educated electorate is essential. Yes, it takes time, but how else can a democracy flourish? Absolute power does corrupt absolutely in any system. If the people are asleep, uninterested, uncaring, or uneducated, we are in trouble. So the best way to make a difference, the best way to prevent future wars, is to roll up your sleeves and get to work influencing those around you. The tools we have today make it easier than ever, and it can even be fun. We had a wonderful time when we discovered the Pentagon had paid a ridiculous amount of money for a toilet seat. Everyone understood how outrageous it was, and they were furious. Let's bring that accountability back!

∽○∽

"When the power of love replaces the love of power,
then we begin our journey of awakening."

—Anonymous

DEMOCRACY IS A
LIFESTYLE

DORIS "GRANNY D" HADDOCK

Granny D is a lifelong activist, spearheading campaigns on nuclear proliferation and electoral reform. On January 1, 1999, at the age of eightynine, she began a walk across the country to demonstrate her concern for campaign reform, walking ten miles each day for fourteen months and making speeches along the way. She also ran for the Senate in 2004.

Our present emergency is upon us because our civic society has been dumbed down by dumbed-down newspapers and radio and television news, by dumbed-down schools, and by a corporate-run economic rat race that keeps people so busy trying to make ends meet that they have no time or energy left for the civic affairs of their towns or nation. Democracy cannot long survive when the people are not well informed, interested, and supplied with sufficient time and resources to participate.

But there is another thing that has been dumbed down over the past two or three generations, and that is the art of politics.

If the politics of a century ago can be likened to a banquet, the politics of today is like a fast-food burger. Let me tell you what it used to be like. Everybody used to be involved. You went to your Elks club or your women's club, but you went to your party meetings too. You worked your neighborhoods. You talked up your issues and candidates. It was a fairly constant thing, not just during the election season. Why? Because democracy is a lifestyle, not a fringe benefit of paying your taxes. Self-governance is a lot of work, but it's where you make your best friends and find your deepest satisfactions, after your family.

In 2004, I embarked on a twenty-thousand-mile road trip to register voters. I visited many housing projects and low-income neighborhoods where nobody had dropped by to talk politics since the last election—and even then, those who came to stump for candidates weren't there to listen to the people's problems or to help them craft political solutions. When you come around begging for votes, but you don't give a crouton in return, those are downright exploitative politics. And it's no surprise that the low-income people came to the conclusion that no matter who won the election, their own lives wouldn't change much.

Politics is about creatively serving the needs of your people, and the election is just the report card that reflects how you are doing, how many people you have helped, and how many people are following your leadership because you were there for them. Politicians and political campaigns must organize not just to win elections but also to deserve to win elections.

My friends at Iowa Citizens for Community Improvement know this well. They offer people help fighting predatory mortgage lenders, and those who are helped then become involved in campaign-finance reform and other large-scale issues. Solve people's personal problems—or even just try to—and they will march with you. That's the key to an enriched progressive movement.

Let us imagine a plan to create responsible communities with members who go to town councils to set goals in a wide variety of areas. We can pass a resolution that our town, for example, shall use 50 percent renewable energy within ten years, or that our state budget shall spend $5 in prevention and education for every $1 spent on police and prisons. The Bill of Rights Defense Committee (www.bordc.org/whatyoucando.html), which defends the Bill of Rights against the intrusive USA Patriot Act, provides a good model and specific tactics for how we can move national issues through town and city councils, and then through state legislatures, to affect national policy.

We must repair our old ship of Liberty with some new sails and masts, starting with the public funding of our elections and thereby the removal of special-interest campaign donations. We must stop our laws from being sold to the highest bidder, and our Congress from turning into a bawdy house where anything and everything is done for a price. Maine and Arizona already have good "clean elections" systems with full public financing, and similar plans are in the works in Florida, Iowa, Kentucky, North Carolina, Oregon, West Virginia, and many other states. These efforts, which are under attack by right-wing business groups, deserve our support (go to www.publicam paign.org/states/index.htm to find contacts in your state).

We must work for other improvements, too, such as instant runoff voting, where you can rank your favorite candidates and not risk splitting the vote. Instant runoff voting allows each voter to rank his or her choices; if the first choice does not gain a majority, the next-ranked choice then applies. That way, everyone can vote their hearts without "spoiling" their votes, and third parties can rise in influence. And we must return to paper ballots or paper receipts, to address the lack of public trust in computerized voting. We must have a way to verify ballots at the precinct level, with citizens watching.

It is not enough to elect representatives, give them a slim list of ideas, and send them off to speak for us. If we do not keep these boys and girls busy, they will always get into trouble. We must energize our communities and use this energy to instruct our elected representatives. This is the responsibility of every adult American, from native to newcomer, and from young worker to the long retired. If we are hypnotized by television and overwhelmed by life on a corporate-consumer treadmill, let us regain our lives as a fearlessly outspoken people who have time for each other and our communities.

This is an amazing moment in all of our lives, and in the life of our great nation. Never has our democracy been so challenged, and never have so many patriots of every age risen up to take their part in its defense. Never have I been less proud of my government or more proud of its people. This is a great time. We need to renew the spirit of our great American Revolution, town by town, neighbor by neighbor.

Let us do deep politics that starts and ends with the needs of our people. Let us remember that we are the people of an imperfect union, the ordinary people of a great republic still in the making. And in that we are no ordinary people at all.

∽о∾

"All I know is that those who are going to be killed
aren't those who preside on Capitol Hill."
—Ani DiFranco

MAKING OUR
VOICES HEARD

CHELLIE PINGREE

Chellie Pingree has been the president and CEO of Common Cause since March 2003. Previously, she served for eight years in the Maine senate, including four years as majority leader. During her terms, she sponsored legislation championing the interests of women and low-income families.

When it comes to fixing the system, the most important thing that we as Americans can do is make the right choice when we elect our leaders. Because the next time you travel to France, they're going to say, "Why did your country do that?" and none of us are going to be able to say, "Well, that

Protesters wearing pig snouts, costumes, chant and toss "Hallibacon Bucks" at a Halliburton protest in New York during the 2004 Republican National Convention.
© Dean Cox/AP

wasn't me. Those are some other people. That's the government. I don't have anything to do with them." This is a democracy. We elect our government, and we reap what we sow.

But it's also not quite so simple as that: the system has a large hand in the problem, and within our electoral system it has become harder and harder for an individual to have a voice—largely because of manipulations by our elected officials. There is a fairly long list of problems that we all need to care about, even though they seem somewhat obscure (for example, how the district lines are drawn so that they do not protect incumbents). In our political system, those with money continue to hold a lot more sway than those without. Huge special interests like defense companies are allowed to invest a tremendous amount of money in politicians who then feel compelled to act on the special interests' behalf, in order to attract financial support for their next campaign.

Consolidated media ownership has also contributed to a very uneven playing field—the political orientations of the select few corporations that now own this country's major media outlets have begun to distort our news, with blatant interference by CEOs and an all-too-common crossing of the line between opinion pieces and serious journalism. But local citizens can fight these changes by challenging licenses, boycotting advertisers, e-mailing their concerns to the Federal Communications Commission, and letting their congressional representatives know how they're feeling.

We also can't discount the serious role that Congress has played in limiting our voices. The fact is that many members of Congress voted to go ahead with this war, and while I understand that they were frustrated by the same lack of information that many of the citizens in this country experienced, we expect them to take a stronger role in overseeing matters of national importance and to make hard decisions regardless of politics (and regardless of those who would call them unpatriotic for raising questions about the war). There's a reason we have sent our representatives to Washington, and that is to counter an administration that chooses not to listen to the voices and concerns of citizens.

Democracy requires eternal vigilance—engaging in civic life need not be as unpleasant as taking a daily dose of cod liver oil, but it should be something you think about doing every day, every week, every so often. It could mean attending your local city council, or standing outside your local TV station with a sign that says, "I want this to be really fair and balanced."

In the last few years, we in the progressive movement have developed phenomenally good methods of communicating with people. A lot of ordinary

Americans now receive an Internet alert from one of five organizations that tells them what to do about Sinclair Broadcasting, or how to ask Tom DeLay to step down because of his ethics violations and the way he misuses money in Congress. And I think this has to keep going—the conversations that go on between members of a community, the dialogue that happens during a political campaign—these have to remain a part of people's everyday lives.

Today America has arrived at a huge fork in the road. One path, the one we're leaning toward, leads to a place where major corporations speak with a stronger voice than individual citizens, where politicians are more and more reluctant to exercise the power that we give them, and where we disgrace ourselves around the world by the way we act.

And on the other track, I see enormous opportunities ahead—I see a land with more energized citizens, more voters, more people who speak their minds and who take risks to change what's diseased about our system, to bring us closer to perfecting this experiment called democracy.

✂◦❧

"Dissent, rebellion, and all-around hell-raising
remain the true duty of patriots."

—Barbara Ehrenreich

GET **SMART**: A BETTER RESPONSE TO TERRORISM

LYNN WOOLSEY

Representing the Sixth Congressional District of California, Lynn Woolsey first took office in the U.S. House of Representatives in 1992 and is the chair of the Democratic Caucus Task Force on Children and Families and the ranking member of the House Education Committee's Subcommittee on Education Reform.

The Bush administration "has failed in the primary responsibilities of preserving national security and providing world leadership." Those are not my words. They come from a nonpartisan group of twenty-seven former senior diplomats and military officials, men and women with broad national-security expertise. Their June 16, 2004, statement continues: "Instead of building upon America's great economic and moral strength to address the causes of terrorism and stifle its resources, the Administration, motivated more by ideology than by reasoned analysis . . . led the United States into an ill-planned and costly war from which exit is uncertain."

Since the war in Iraq began, the Bush administration has done everything in its power to cajole and deceive soldiers into serving longer than they want to or agreed to, resulting in a shameful, behind-the-scenes "backdoor" draft. Depending on members of the army reserve and the National Guard—who almost always serve the country only here at home—to serve in Iraq was just the tip of the iceberg. Poor young men and women from rural areas, who enlisted because the military helped them pay for a college education they wouldn't have been able to get otherwise, have been targeted. Many soldiers have been manipulated into extending their contracts with the army, warned that if they do not reenlist on time, their brigades could be shipped to Iraq or Afghanistan.

I agree with President Bush that keeping Americans safe should be our most urgent priority. But there are more effective ways to protect America than throwing our weight around, alienating our friends and riling our enemies in the process—not to mention manipulating our young people into risking their lives.

We need to focus on preventing war, not engaging in preemptive war. It is time for change. That is why I have introduced HR 392, a SMART Security Platform for the twenty-first century. "SMART" stands for "Sensible, Multilateral, American Response to Terrorism." This plan would dramatically overhaul our approach to national security. Specifically, it has five components:

Prevent future acts of terrorism. Instead of military force, SMART emphasizes multilateral partnerships and stronger intelligence to track and detain terrorists while still respecting human rights and civil liberties. For example, we would work with other nations to freeze various bank accounts of terrorist organizations and provide more adequate funding for local intelligence.

Stop the spread of weapons of mass destruction. The SMART approach calls for strengthening nonproliferation treaties, not abandoning them. SMART also calls on the United States to set an example for the world by renouncing the development of new nuclear weapons. We need to work with the Russian Federation to dismantle nuclear warheads and secure nuclear materials in Russia, and we must stop selling weapons to countries like Rwanda and Uganda, who in turn sell them to the Republic of the Congo for use in armed conflict.

Address terrorism's root causes. This has to be the first front in the war on terrorism—confronting the despair and deprivation that foster it. SMART security includes an ambitious international development agenda: democracy building, human-rights education, sustainable development, and education for women and girls. Before sending troops, let's send scientists, teachers, urban planners, agricultural experts, and small-business loans to troubled parts of the world. We must engage actively with the international community to resolve the Israeli-Palestinian conflict; ensure the equal sharing of coveted sources of water, especially in Africa and the Middle East; and increase aid to the poorest countries like Haiti and Liberia.

Reprioritize our spending. SMART security would make stronger investments in peacekeeping and reconstruction. Energy independence—especially economic support for the development of renewable energy sources—is another centerpiece of SMART security, because nothing threatens us more than reliance on Middle Eastern oil.

Find alternatives to war. SMART security would make war a very last resort, to be considered only after every diplomatic solution has been exhausted. The legislation includes more effective conflict-assessment and early-warning systems, multilateral rapid-response mechanisms, human-rights monitoring, and investments in civil society and fair judicial systems. Civilian policing and effective justice systems (like the International Criminal Court, which the Bush administration opposes) are key.

It is time we stopped equating security with military might. SMART security would protect Americans without resorting to belligerence and warfare. SMART security is tough but diplomatic, aggressive but peaceful, pragmatic but idealistic. What better way to show love for our country than by embracing a national-security policy that defends America by relying on the very best of America—our capacity for global leadership, our compassion for the people of the world, and our commitment to peace and freedom.

∽○∽

"The very least you can do in your life is to figure out what you hope for and the most you can do is live inside that hope."

—Barbara Kingsolver

CREATING A DEPARTMENT OF PEACE

MEDEA BENJAMIN

Our bloated, overactive Department of War (called the Department of Defense) sucks up more than $400 billion of our tax dollars, but where is the Department of Peace? Where is the government body dedicated to preventing war and violence?

Thanks to U.S. representative Dennis Kucinich, there is a piece of legislation in Congress that would create a Department of Peace. The bill establishes nonviolence as an organizing principle of American society, providing the U.S. president with an array of peace-building policy options for domestic and international use. Domestically, the department would be responsible for developing policies that address domestic violence, child abuse, mistreatment of the elderly, and the like. Internationally, the department would analyze foreign policy and make recommendations to the president on how to address the root causes of war and intervene before violence begins.

For those concerned with the costs of a new federal department, spending just 2 percent of the current defense budget (which is what the legislation calls for) would surely save billions by preventing violence before it starts. Getting this legislation passed will require sustained pressure from a grassroots movement intent on ending armed conflict. Remember, the passage of the Thirteenth Amendment abolishing slavery took many years. The Nineteenth Amendment providing women's suffrage was a long time coming. The Civil Rights Act of the 1960s entailed much persistence and struggle. Legislation creating a Department of Peace will be a similarly historic act reflecting the deep yearnings of our generation to eradicate violence.

What you can do:

Go to the Department of Peace Web site, www.dopcampaign.org, to learn more, see the status of current legislation, and find out if your congressional representative has signed up as a cosponsor of the bill. If she has, thank him/her and focus on encouraging this member to become more active in urging her colleagues to join her, especially key committee chairs.

If your congressperson has not sponsored the bill, flood him/her with calls and letters from the community and set up a face-to-face meeting with supportive local leaders. Also, attend forums where your congressperson will be speaking, or set up your own community forum on the subject and invite him/her to speak—a community forum is also a good way to create more public support for the bill.

FINDING OUR
CONSCIENCE AGAIN

BARBARA LEE

Congresswoman Barbara Lee was the lone dissenting voice when Congress authorized President Bush to use "all necessary and appropriate force" in response to the 9/11 attack. She was one of only five U.S. Representatives to vote against a resolution supporting the December 1998 bombing of Iraq and the only member of congress to vote against a March 24, 1999, resolution regarding use of military force in Kosovo. Her continued stance for a nonviolent foreign policy has been deemed "courageous" by her constituents and by peace activists nationwide.

Not a day goes by when I do not think of the horrific attacks of September 11, 2001. I remember my sorrow and prayers for the victims and their families, whose lives were senselessly destroyed in one terrible instant.

I believed then, as I still do, that giving the Bush administration a blank check to wage war would not prevent further acts of terrorism, and that as progressives we have a responsibility not only to counsel restraint when it is needed, but also to offer alternatives to the rash policies that are only making us, and the world, less safe.

Since 9/11, the peace movement has helped this country to find its conscience. When you think back to the period immediately after the terrorist attacks, there was just so much fear. People were scared, and the Bush administration was skilled at using that fear to its advantage. The administration created the image of a president who couldn't be criticized, and the majority of the press and politicians blindly accepted that caricature.

The peace movement has played a critical role in breaking down the right-wing campaign to shut down democracy. Many members of Congress, other elected officials, individuals, and organizations have been empowered to openly dissent and criticize the administration's misguided policies. They also have been strengthened by people in the streets and by the public debate generated by the peace movement.

We have a lot of work ahead of us. It's not just opposing the ideologically driven policies of the Bush administration. We need to develop both a clear vision of the future and a proactive agenda to see that vision realized, and we must reach out to build a broad-based coalition that will take action to make that vision a reality.

Protestors outside Senator Hillary Clinton's office, New York City, March 8, 2003.
© Fred Askew

We must redefine the debate about security priorities. Currently, the debate about security and terrorism is defined by a small group of right-wing extremists who have used it to move their ideological agenda forward. The threat posed by terrorism is real. If we are going to be successful about overcoming it, we have to acknowledge the fact that the war in Iraq has made our country and the world *less* safe. After $200 billion and thousands of U.S. and Iraqi casualties, we have created a terrorist recruitment camp and fanned the flames of anti-Americanism around the world.

We need to keep building a peace movement, and that means continuing to protest. We must also continue to engage in effective political action. We must keep the pressure on our elected officials. And we must urge them not only to speak out but also to actively support legislation promoting global security and peace. Two people should be singled out for their leadership on these issues: my colleague Lynn Woolsey, who introduced a bill on SMART security, and my colleague Dennis Kucinich, who introduced a bill to create a cabinet-level Department of Peace.

We have to continue to broaden our coalition. That means understanding the concerns of all Americans. We must redefine national security to encompass economic security. Economic security—through cleaner air, healthy kids, safer communities—is a cornerstone to our national security. We must reject the tired math that tells us that paying for our national defense equals bankrupting our schools.

The task is not simply stopping a war, but changing the prevailing wisdom that makes wars possible. We have to continue to broaden our movement and we can't ever shy away from fighting in the electoral and legislative arenas. We are going to keep developing alternative policies and making sure that the debate on security priorities is redefined.

Dr. King once said that peace is not the absence of tension, but the presence of justice. Our job is to continue the fight for peace and justice.

∽o∾

"No pessimist ever discovered the secret of the stars, or sailed to an uncharted land, or opened a new doorway for the human spirit."

—Helen Keller

Chapter 8

DISARM
THE WORLD

A WORLD
WORKING TOGETHER

JODY WILLIAMS

Jody Williams, together with the International Campaign to Ban Landmines (ICBL), received the Nobel Peace Prize in 1997. She now serves as a campaign ambassador for the ICBL, which she helped create. Prior to her work on landmines, Jody spent eleven years building public awareness about U.S. policy toward Central America.

The heinous crime of September 11, 2001, sowed fear and uncertainty not only in the United States but also around the globe. Terrorism is a threat that must be countered—but when it comes to solving the problem of terrorism, the U.S. government has offered only one answer: war. This has made the world even more unstable, exacerbating a fundamental tension between those who feel that one nation, or a small handful of nations, should determine how to meet the multitude of threats facing us all, and those who want to see those decisions made by a community of nations, international bodies, and civil society all joining together to take a truly multilateral path.

Understanding the terrorist threat does not mean simply being able to identify the countries the terrorists come from. We must recognize the underlying political forces that make people willing to die and to kill others in their efforts to bring attention to their causes. In a world increasingly dominated by the few, who seem not to care about the many, it's no surprise that some of the disenfranchised see drastic action as their only option. Until we work together as a global community to address the common threats to human security posed by these gross inequalities, we will not live in a secure world.

Examples of the world coming together to solve common threats do exist—I have seen it myself. In 1992, when a group of nongovernmental organizations (NGOs) launched the International Campaign to Ban Landmines (ICBL), we had no idea what we could ultimately accomplish. We started the campaign because we wanted to help victims of war. But for me, the landmine issue was also a launching point; from there, we could begin to talk about larger issues, such as the laws of war and the means and methods of warfare. The decades-long impact of landmines could be a powerful symbol of other long-term impacts of war.

In the beginning, every government we met with thought that banning landmines was a "nice idea" but a utopian dream that would never come true. After all, virtually every fighting force in the world had been using land-mines since World War I. Millions of mines contaminated eighty countries around the world and claimed thousands of new mine victims every year. Some fifty-five countries produced landmines, and tens of millions of mines were stockpiled. Few believed that eliminating the weapon was possible, since no conventional weapon in common use had ever been widely banned.

But we believed that what we were doing was right and that no matter what the outcome was, we would build public awareness so that citizens around the world would pressure their governments to get rid of the weapon. And to our amazement, it worked! The ICBL was able to capture the public conscience and propel governments to join with us in common cause to address the humanitarian crisis in the shortest time possible.

In less than a year, the Mine Ban Treaty was negotiated. It was signed in Ottawa, Canada, on December 3 and 4, 1997, by 122 nations. It is an elegant, simple, yet comprehensive international convention that provides the framework for ridding the world of the scourge of antipersonnel mines. Key provisions of the treaty require participating nations to stop producing, acquiring, or using antipersonnel mines; to destroy mines in their stockpiles; to clear mines in their territories within ten years; and to provide for the needs of landmine survivors.

By the end of 2004, some 143 nations were party to the treaty, and another 8 were signatories. Those who have signed on include most former mine producers and users. Unfortunately, though, the United States has refused to sign the treaty. While the U.S. government has offered various excuses, many of us at the ICBL believe that the issue for the United States has little to do with antipersonnel landmines. Surely, if all of our major military allies, including NATO members and Japan, are willing to give up landmines, then the country with the most sophisticated military in the world can give them up, too. In my opinion, the U.S. military is afraid that responding to pressure from civilians on this particular weapon will set an uncomfortable precedent, perhaps pushing the military down a long and slippery slope on which they will have to surrender other weapons for humanitarian reasons. We still, however, continue to pressure the U.S. government to join the majority of the world community and adopt the treaty.

The process that led to the signing of the Mine Ban Treaty has been described as unorthodox, historic, and unique. Why?

- The ICBL worked at the regional, national, and international levels to build the political will necessary to ban the weapon.
- The ICBL successfully pressed governments to take individual steps toward

banning landmines. The October 1996 Canadian challenge to other "pro-ban" governments to negotiate the treaty within a year resulted in the "Ottawa Process," which yielded the Mine Ban Treaty.

- For the first time, small- and medium-size powers (from Mozambique to South Africa to Mexico to Norway and Austria) took the lead and were not held back by some of the superpowers that had not yet agreed to ban landmines (such as the United States, China, and Russia).
- The process took place outside the official UN system, and governments were required to "opt in"—meaning that governments attending the treaty negotiation conference had to agree on the basic text beforehand. This, together with strong leadership at the negotiating conferences, prevented a few governments from watering down the treaty or slowing down the negotiations.
- Not only was the negotiation process extremely quick—the treaty was negotiated within a year, unprecedented for an international agreement of this nature—but it also took only nine months for forty countries to ratify the treaty.
- The treaty is a unique hybrid—successfully combining arms-control provisions with issues of international humanitarian law.
- The ICBL encouraged continued citizen participation. While governments were signing the Mine Ban Treaty in Ottawa, ordinary citizens were invited to make their pledges to the People's Treaty against Landmines. Similarly, youth across the world promoted their own peace treaties, declaring: "We want no more war. We want no more landmines. We want no more mine victims. We promise to work for peace in our world." The Youth against War Treaty was launched in Ottawa on the first anniversary of the signing of the Mine Ban Treaty. It was later translated into many languages and taken up by campaigns from Italy to Brazil to Pakistan.
- The treaty was the product of an unusually cohesive partnership among NGOs, UN organizations, and governments. Whereas in other treaty negotiations NGOs are often excluded or limited to observer status, in this case the ICBL participated in conferences about the treaty. That partnership has continued to this day, to ensure that the Mine Ban Treaty is fully implemented.

For those who want to work in coalitions to bring about social change, it's important to understand the importance of NGOs forming strategic partnerships with governments and UN organizations. It's not easy to form such partnerships (and such partnerships are not necessarily appropriate for all issues activists are working on), and it requires a lot of work on the part of NGOs. In our case, we had to first prove that we had the ability to provide expertise on the issues, and credible documentation to back up the expertise; to articulate our goals and messages clearly and simply; to maintain a flexible coalition structure, inclusive and diverse, while still managing to speak with one voice on our issues; to communicate key developments to members of the coalition itself, as well as to governments and other agencies involved in the issue; to organize; to formulate action plans with deadlines—and to always follow up so that the goals of the action plans were achieved, building momentum and excitement.

Thanks to this broad-based campaign, today only about a dozen countries continue to produce landmines, and there have been no significant exports in the world in years. Stockpiled landmines are being destroyed. Mine action programs are operating in countries all over the world. And, most important, the number of new mine victims is beginning to decrease.

Our work is far from over. Until all countries are party to the treaty and everyone obeys it—until, in other words, all the mines are destroyed and victims are fully taken care of—our work is not finished.

But in this terribly unstable and insecure world, the ICBL and the Mine Ban Treaty offer us hope: the possibility that we will one day live in a world free of the daily terror of landmines, and the proof that there are alternative models for addressing our common problems. The process that the ICBL spurred shows people everywhere that governments, international bodies, and civil society can work together to find solutions to critical humanitarian and security issues.

CALL TO ACTION: TEN THINGS **YOU** CAN DO FOR A MINE-FREE WORLD!

1. Visit the ICBL Web site to learn more about the problem and the solution at www.icbl.org, then join or start a local campaign.
2. Call, fax, e-mail, or visit the president, secretary of state, secretary of defense, your senator, and your congressional representative and tell them to support the United States' signing the 1997 Mine Ban Treaty *now*!
3. Call, fax, e-mail, or visit your state, district, and county representatives; the mayo; and other prominent local decision makers (school board members, Rotary club officers, church leaders). Ask them to support the

United States' signing the 1997 Mine Ban Treaty *now!* Ask for a written proclamation or resolution of support for the ban declaring your town, city, or state a landmine-free zone.

4. Get the word out: Write an opinion piece for your local newspaper, call up a radio station, and send information to your friends. For publicity tips go to www.icbl.org/resources/campaignkit/publicise/index.html.

5. Call, fax, e-mail, or visit your local newspapers, radio stations, and television stations, asking them to support the United States' signing the 1997 Mine Ban Treaty *now!* Contact the ICBL or the U.S. Campaign organizations for audio and video footage that local TV stations can use.

6. Call, fax, e-mail, or visit U.S. manufacturers of antipersonnel landmines. These are identified in the 1997 Human Rights Watch report *Exposing the Source*, available from the HRW office (1-202-612-4321) and its Web site: www.hrw.org/hrw/campaigns/mines/index.html.

7. Promote the Mine Ban Treaty: Write to the countries that have not signed the treaty. Urge them to get on board right away! You can find a list of these countries at www.icbl.org/treaty/members/non_sp. Use the ICBL database to find contact information for governments and embassies. Look at our country pages and action alerts for message ideas and sample letters.

8. Act for a mine-free world: Do something! Organize a photo or art exhibition, arrange a film screening, start a landmine-awareness day or week, set up a letter-writing event, hold a public demonstration, host a benefit conference! More action ideas are at www.icbl.org/resources/campaign kit/pubevent.html.

9. Sponsor a mine-detection dog: Raise money for a mine-detection dog to help clear mines and safeguard lives and livelihoods! Check them out at www.sponsor-a-minedog.org.

10. Make a donation or work for us: Every bit counts! Support the ICBL by telephone, mail, or online (www.icbl.org/campaign/donate), or find out about volunteering, interning, or working for the ICBL (www.icbl.org/campaign/opportunities).

∽o∾

"The best preparedness is the one that disarms the hostility
of other nations and makes friends of them."

—Helen Keller

SEATING WOMEN
AT THE PEACE TABLE

NOELEEN HEYZER

Noeleen Heyzer is the executive director of the United Nations Development Fund for Women (UNIFEM), where she serves as the UN's chief advocate for advancing women's issues. She is also a founding member of Development Alternatives with Women for a New Era (DAWN), a network of women leaders.

We are living in a time of great fear and insecurity. This is particularly true for women. Thousands of women are raped at gunpoint in countries experiencing war; countless women and their children lose their limbs to landmines; hundreds of thousands sit in refugee camps, displaced by the bombing of their towns and villages.

Those women know that wars are no longer fought on battlefields separate from homes and communities. Today's battlefields are our schools, our villages, our communities—even women's bodies.

During the genocide in Rwanda in 1994, some five hundred thousand women were raped; tens of thousands of women suffered a similar fate in Bosnia, Sierra Leone, and East Timor. Already in the twenty-first century, some forty million people have fled their homes as a consequence of armed conflicts from Afghanistan to Liberia and Colombia. Eighty percent of these refugees are women and children. Unprotected and unable to provide for their children, these women are particularly vulnerable to sexual exploitation, which includes the slow murder from infection by HIV.

Weapons-based security has certainly not delivered peace for women. So what does security look like through women's eyes?

Women who have been invited to the peace table have been able to tell us. In the 2002 meetings that set up the interim government of Afghanistan, only three women were officially involved, but the United Nations Development Fund for Women brought more than sixty women from the Afghan diaspora, the refugee camps, Kabul, and across all the provinces and ethnic groups of Afghanistan to participate at a roundtable with UN agencies. These women forged an agenda that was incorporated into a transitional program at the UN, putting at the forefront education, health, economic security, human rights, and women's rights.

Women who have sat at the peacekeeping table tend to agree on a number of points: for example, that we can start building peace only by ending the violence in our homes, our schools, and our streets; and that sustainable peace hinges on the presence of economic and social systems that put the majority of people and their needs at the center of development. As Gandhi said, "There is enough in the world for all our needs, but never enough for one man's greed."

If women allocated the world's resources, they would surely choose to invest in the much broader notion of human security—through the economic development of poorer nations, environmental protections, and social services—instead of buying more weapons or helping corporate America become ever wealthier. Women would see HIV/AIDS as a real security threat faced by millions and would provide money for drugs instead of fighter jets.

But women do not yet enjoy democratic representation in the world's powerful institutions. Very few women participate in meetings that determine the conditions of security and the distribution of resources, and fewer still are hammering out peace agreements around negotiating tables.

However, in October 2000, for the first time in its history, the UN Security Council passed a resolution, Resolution 1325, that called not only for the protection of women in conflict zones but also for their participation in the decision-making process at the peace table. In passing this resolution, the Security Council acknowledged that women are essential for waging peace.

Even in those countries where atrocities against women were particularly widespread and horrific and where efforts at peace and reconciliation have mostly consisted of men forgiving men for crimes against women, women have started to find a seat at the table. In southeastern Europe, women from Kosovo's new assembly have banded together across party lines to form a women's caucus, a nonpartisan effort in a community traumatized by conflict and ethnic strife.

Creating a world without war is too important to be the responsibility of any single government or institution, no matter how powerful. The United Nations, the peace movement, the women's movement, the human-rights movement, and the economic-rights movement must all come together.

Let us, as we move further into the twenty-first century, assure women their proper role in putting an end to the unspeakable horrors of war and in rediscovering our shared humanity. Let us give women the opportunity to unlock the frozen rivers of our hearts so the healing waters can flow.

༈

> "History tells us that every oppressed class gained true
> liberation from its masters through its own efforts. It is necessary
> that woman learn that lesson, that she realize that her freedom
> will reach as far as her power to achieve her freedoms."
>
> —Emma Goldman

ENDING THE NUCLEAR CRISIS: A PRESCRIPTION FOR SURVIVAL

HELEN CALDICOTT

Helen Caldicott is an Australian-born pediatrician and the author of five books, including *The New Nuclear Danger*. President emerita of Physicians for Social Responsibility, she also founded Women's Action for Nuclear Disarmament in 1980. Currently she is president of the Nuclear Policy Research Institute. This essay was excerpted from an interview with Julia Scott that took place on Chicago Public Radio's *Worldview* on October 12, 2004.

When the Cold War ended in 1989, I was thrilled. I was in Australia at the time, and I went into my garden and thought, That's it. They'll get rid of the bombs. The first President Bush unilaterally eliminated ten thousand bombs. Never before had a U.S. president done that. It wasn't until 1997 that I found out that nothing had changed—the weapons were all on hair-trigger alert, with America still determined to win a nuclear war against Russia, which could cause partial nuclear winter and end most life on earth. When I found that out, I thought, How did that happen? Why didn't they get rid of the bombs?

President Clinton set up a nuclear-posture review in 1994, which the Joint Chiefs of Staff, who liked their missiles, destroyed. One general was overheard saying, "If you threaten our missiles and our early-warning system, baby, that's threatening the family jewels." America then developed a policy called "lead and hedge"—lead in the development of nuclear weapons, and hedge our bets. The United States has more than five thousand hydrogen bombs targeted on Russia. Since the Cold War, we have increased the number of our targets, to include China. And Russia keeps its own bombs at the ready.

What's really dangerous is not just proliferation, but the sheer number of hydrogen bombs that still exist: thirty thousand, of which Russia and America own 97 percent. They're the true "rogue" states, facing off just as they did in the Cold War and maintaining a huge storehouse of bombs that could be captured by terrorists. The Chechen rebels, for example, could seize control of the command system in Russia just as they took over that theater in Moscow or the school in Beslan. A nuclear war could happen tonight, by accident. It could happen in the United States, even, if computer hackers broke into the early-warning system.

America is in the process of building and testing five hundred new nuclear weapons every year. Clinton started that, but it continued under Bush, and it will create lateral proliferation as other countries look at America and say, "Well, if you're doing it, we will too."

As a physician, I see the earth as a patient in the intensive care unit. We have an acute clinical crisis on our hands and must take urgent action. My prescription for survival is that the American people rise up as they did in the 1980s, when 80 percent of Americans supported the nuclear weapons freeze. We must force the administration to negotiate with Vladimir Putin to set up a process to eliminate nuclear weapons between Russia and America in the next five years.

We must also close down the 103 nuclear-power plants in America and generate our electricity with plentiful supplies of wind and sunlight instead. As it is, terrorists don't need to build nuclear weapons—weapons of this magnitude are available all over the country, in the form of nuclear reactors. The cooling pools inside the reactors contain up to thirty times as much radiation as the reactor core—enough to equal a thousand Hiroshima bombs.

If we close the plants down, we at least won't make any more nuclear waste. What we can do with the nuclear waste inside the core and the cooling pools I really don't know, and neither does anybody else. I've been debating with the nuclear industry for thirty-five years, and its representatives have always said, "Don't worry, we'll work out what to do with the waste." I used to reply, "That's like my saying to you, 'You've got pancreatic cancer and you'll die in six months, but don't worry, I'll find the cure in twenty years.'"

The industry's solution is to package the waste and deliver fifteen hundred shipments every year for the next thirty years to Yucca Mountain in Nevada, a site transected by thirty earthquake faults. Vice president Dick Cheney is in favor of the Yucca Mountain project, and he wants to build fifty new nuclear power plants in the next twenty years. Here is a man who doesn't understand what he's doing, yet he is making the most profound decisions for the rest of the human race, for the rest of time.

It's been estimated that fewer than 3 percent of the people in Congress are scientifically literate, yet they're taking actions with extraordinary medical consequences. In this age of profound scientific discovery, it's terribly important for people to understand the health implications of government initiatives, especially nuclear ones. And it's equally important for physicians to teach the American public about the dangers of nuclear power and nuclear war—for example, the increased risk of cancer, especially for children, who are much more sensitive to the carcinogenic effects of radiation than adults are.

We've got to return to sanity and decide we're going to save the earth for our children, if we indeed want them to have a future.

∽o∾

"The pens which write against disarmament are made
with the same steel from which guns are made."

—Aristide Briand, French statesman, Nobel Peace Prize laureate, 1926

NONPROLIFERATION:
THE U.S. IMPERIAL DOUBLE STANDARD

RANDALL FORSBERG

Dr. Randall Caroline Forsberg is the executive director of the Institute for Defense and Disarmament Studies and the publisher of the monthly *Arms Control Reporter*. She helped found the Freeze movement and authored the 1980 Nuclear Weapon Freeze proposal. Forsberg was appointed by President Clinton to the Advisory Committee of the U.S. Arms Control and Disarmament Agency.

One of the most shocking developments of recent years has been President Bush's rejection of treaties meant to help stop the spread of weapons of mass destruction. The Bush administration arrogated to the United States the "right" to invade a country, overthrow its government, and launch a multiyear occupation in flagrant violation of U.S. and international laws on the grounds that Iraq might have had some chemical-weapon remnants left from the 1980s, and could theoretically have become involved in a military or terrorist threat against us. At the same time, the United States systematically blocked and undermined the very international treaties designed to prevent the global spread of weapons of mass destruction (WMD) and to verifiably reduce the nuclear, chemical, and biological weapons that exist today—on the grounds that these treaties might limit America's freedom to acquire, test, deploy, and even use such weapons!

The hypocrisy and imperial arrogance of this double standard (proclaiming to other nations, particularly Arab and other non-Western countries, that they should do as we say and not as we do) have played a major role in provoking worldwide anger and disrespect for the United States and in strengthening support for the terrorist acts that continue to be carried out by Muslim fundamentalists.

The United States has blocked or weakened nearly every international agreement intended to help reduce proliferation dangers:

A reduction of our own nuclear arsenal. In 2001, Russia proposed that each side cut its arsenal from around ten thousand nuclear weapons to just fifteen hundred, and that the withdrawn weapons be verifiably dismantled. President Bush refused this excellent offer. Instead, the Bush administration limited the latest Strategic Offensive Reduction Treaty (SORT), signed in 2002, to "de-alerting" several thousand warheads (that is, putting them in reserve). But there is no dismantlement requirement or verification mechanism, and the treaty limits do not take effect for ten years—and then expire the next day!

A global ban on all nuclear-test explosions. The United States has actively pursued negotiation of this treaty starting in 1963 and signed it when it was agreed upon at the United Nations in 1996. Then the Republican-controlled Senate refused to ratify it. As a result, India and Pakistan were free to conduct their first nuclear-weapons tests in 1998, making them the latest additions to the "nuclear club." Repeatedly, from 2002 to 2004, the United States was virtually the only country in the world to vote against a resolution expressing support for this treaty. Without American support, the Comprehensive Test Ban Treaty cannot enter into force, even though work to complete a global verification network is proceeding on schedule.

Verification of the biological-weapons ban. Between 1996 and 2001, the Conference on Disarmament in Geneva, with representatives from more than fifty nations, worked hard to negotiate a "protocol" to enforce the 1972 ban on the possession and use of biological weapons. This new protocol would permit on-site inspection to ensure the compliance of treaty parties. (Such a protocol would have been helpful in Iraq and Libya, among many other places.) When the Bush administration took over, it announced abruptly that the United States opposed the verification protocol because it might lead to the exposure of industrial secrets of biotech firms. Although many countries had spent years developing a process that would avoid this consequence, the Conference on Disarmament proceeds by consensus, so once the United States refused to continue the talks, the hard-fought accomplishments of many nations were simply discarded.

A ban on weapons in outer space. The United States alone has opposed the start of talks in the Conference on Disarmament to draft a treaty that would prevent the use or placement of weapons in outer space, for example, for the purpose of destroying satellites placed there by other countries. Again, since the conference proceeds by consensus, this has prevented any discussion of such a treaty. The United States is currently the only country with programs to develop weapons that could be used in space.

Missile nonproliferation and the ABM Treaty. Claiming that the United States needed to defend itself and other countries against a "rogue state" armed with a small number of long-range nuclear-tipped missiles, in 2002 the United States unilaterally withdrew from the Anti-Ballistic Missile (ABM) Treaty, which had been in effect since 1968. Widely protested around the world, this nullification of the treaty with Russia allowed the United States to begin testing antiballistic missiles. Then, in another unprecedented step, in 2004 the Bush administration approved the deployment of a costly new antimissile system that has failed in tests and been publicly described by the secretary of defense as not effective—but that would, officials claim, be improved over the years. At the same time, the Bush team reversed the previous administration's policy of negotiating an agreement with North Korea to permanently end its testing and export of all missiles with a range of more than two hundred miles. Since North Korea has been the source of all longer-range missiles acquired by so-called rogue states, this decision virtually guaranteed that new missile threats would continue to emerge—thereby justifying the U.S. government's $100-billion to $200-billion investment in the nonoperational antimissile system.

A permanent halt in the production of fissile material. The production of nuclear weapons requires the use of fissile material, either uranium or plutonium. All countries that have nuclear weapons have offered to negotiate a global ban on any further production of fissile material, by any country. Along with a comprehensive nuclear-test ban, this would make the spread of nuclear weapons far more difficult than it is today. The United States, with many times more fissile material than any other country, has supported this ban. China, however, concerned that U.S. antimissile and space weapon programs would compromise its defenses, has made talks on a fissile material cutoff contingent on simultaneous talks about banning weapons in space. Instead of agreeing to discuss both issues, the United States has chosen to discuss neither.

The nonproliferation treaty. Last but not least, the Bush administration has violated and weakened the main international treaty intended to stop the spread of weapons of mass destruction, the Nuclear Non-Proliferation Treaty (NPT). Since 1970, under the NPT, non-nuclear nations have agreed not to acquire nuclear weapons, while nuclear nations agreed to negotiate in good faith to reduce and eventually eliminate the weapons they have. The Bush administration's actions have demonstrated beyond any doubt that the United States is not negotiating in good faith to move toward nuclear disarmament. Moreover, as a condition for agreeing to the NPT, many non-nuclear states demanded that the nuclear-weapon states never threaten them with the use of nuclear weapons. When the treaty was signed, the United States, the USSR, Britain, France, and China all made unilateral declarations that non-nuclear states would not be threatened as long as they were not engaged in a war in alliance with a nuclear state. However, the Bush administration's nuclear-posture review, leaked in 2002, threatened the use of nuclear weapons against a number of countries, including non-nuclear nations such as Cuba, Syria, and Iran. Under George W. Bush, the United States also violated a separate agreement it had made with North Korea in 1994 not to threaten the use of nuclear weapons against that country.

In addition to blocking, undermining, and violating treaties to stop the spread of nuclear weapons, the Bush administration has requested funds to beef up the U.S. nuclear-weapons program, including funding to shorten the time needed to resume underground nuclear weapons tests (eighteen months instead of twenty-four to thirty-six months), and money for a modern pit facility so that we can produce twice as many plutonium cores for nuclear weapons.

It is hard to imagine a set of policy initiatives that could do more than the Bush administration has done to foster the spread of weapons of mass destruction. Clearly, putting all of our eggs in the military basket—renouncing international law, multilateral diplomacy, and arms-control protocols—has not helped to stop or reverse the proliferation of WMD. The very methods of arms control and disarmament that George W. has trashed constitute our best agenda for working to abolish weapons of mass destruction and to end international terrorism.

∽○∾

"Terrorism has no location or boundaries, it does not reside in a geography of its own; its homeland is disillusionment and despair. The best weapon to eradicate terrorism from the soul lies in the solidarity of the international world, in respecting the rights of all peoples of this globe to live in harmony and by reducing the ever-increasing gap between north and south. And the most effective way to defend freedom is through fully realizing the meaning of justice."

—Mahmoud Darwish

COLONIZING THE GLOBE,
ONE BASE AT A TIME

JOSEPH GERSON

Joseph Gerson is the director of programs of the American Friends Service Committee in New England. His books include *The Sun Never Sets*, about U.S. military bases abroad, *With Hiroshima Eyes*, and *The Deadly Connection*, which analyzes nuclear war and U.S. intervention. This essay is based on a talk delivered at the 2004 Japan Peace Conference in Sasebo, Japan.

When I first traveled to Japan for an antinuclear conference, I was amazed to learn that the United States still had more than a hundred military bases and installations across Japan. I was shocked as I listened to Okinawans describe what it meant to live in communities routinely terrorized by the shattering sounds of low-altitude flights and night-landing exercises, by unpunished crimes committed by GIs, and by the pervasiveness of prostitution and sexual harassment of local women near those bases. The Japanese shared their painful memories of deadly military accidents: planes and helicopters falling into people's homes and schools, drunken military drivers careening into civilian cars.

Their anguished words brought back memories from elementary school. My fourth-grade teacher had taught us that the U.S. Declaration of Independence proclaimed the necessity of fighting the War of Independence against Britain because King George III had "kept among us in times of peace . . . standing armies," which committed intolerable "abuses and usurpations." In subsequent years, it has been my privilege to learn from people who have been victims of similar "abuses and usurpations" by U.S. military bases in Korea, Okinawa, the Philippines, Britain, Germany, Belgium, Italy, Iceland, Spain, Turkey, Puerto Rico, Honduras, and other countries. Each base brings terrible consequences, including the loss of self-determination, human rights, and sovereignty. Military bases degrade the culture, values, health, and environment of host nations.

Why does the United States maintain more than seven hundred foreign military bases and installations in at least forty nations? Because the entire system makes imperial domination possible. These bases ensure access to key resources such as oil; they encircle enemies; they serve as training grounds for U.S. forces; they are jumping-off points for U.S. military interventions in foreign countries; they maintain American influence over the governments of host nations. Not even Genghis Khan, Alexander the Great, Julius Caesar, or Benjamin Disraeli could lay claim to such an array of mighty fortresses.

The Bush administration came to power with the commitment to make this infrastructure even stronger. Vice president Dick Cheney, secretary of defense Donald Rumsfeld, and their neocon allies let it be known that they modeled themselves after Teddy Roosevelt, Henry Cabot Lodge, and Admiral Alfred T. Mahan—the men who, in the 1880s and 1890s, envisioned the United States replacing Britain as the world's dominant power and then built the military needed to do it.

Some bases will be closed in the administration's latest reconfiguration, and some will be merged, but only to augment U.S. military power. In Asia, the plan is for "diversification": moving the concentration of U.S. bases from northeast Asia farther south. Why? To better encircle China, to fight the so-called war on terrorism across Southeast Asia, and to more completely control the sea-lanes over which Persian Gulf oil—the jugular vein of East Asia's economies—must travel. Troops will also be relocated to reinforce the power of Washington's "unsinkable aircraft carrier," Japan.

The invasions of Afghanistan and Iraq began the long-planned rearrangement of U.S. military bases abroad. Dictatorships in Kyrgyzstan, Pakistan, Tajikistan, and Uzbekistan were forced to surrender sovereignty and to invite the Pentagon to establish what will likely become permanent U.S. military bases. With Germany balking at joining the invasion of Iraq, Washington began "diversifying" its European military infrastructure, first threatening to punish Germany by withdrawing all U.S. bases from the country. Indeed, many troops—seventy thousand—are to be redeployed to the United States and other nations, including new bases in Romania and Bulgaria.

In the Middle East, under cover of preparations for war, Bush and company removed the vast majority of U.S. troops and bases in Saudi Arabia. One of the precipitating causes of the 9/11 attacks, these bases had been a constant affront to many Muslims, who felt that they sullied Islam's holiest land. While the troops in Saudi Arabia were transferred to Qatar and Kuwait, bases in Djibouti and Bahrain were expanded. And now U.S. military planners look forward to making Iraq a bastion of U.S. military power in the Middle East for decades to come.

In Africa, too, the Bush administration has been negotiating the creation of a "family" of military bases across the continent. The hosts for this new family include Algeria, Mali, and Guinea (which has also been targeted as a source of oil), with Senegal and Uganda providing refueling installations for the air force.

And Washington hasn't forgotten its own backyard: Latin America and South America. Although the Puerto Rican people's fifty-year struggle to close the base at Vieques finally prevailed, new military bases are sprouting across the Andean nations, and the United States is increasingly militarizing the Caribbean.

Two tactical military goals are driving Rumsfeld's reconfiguration of this infrastructure of global military power: flexibility and speed. If Germany, for example, is reluctant to permit U.S. military bases to launch missions against Iraq or Iran from its airspace, the Pentagon wants to be sure that it can launch those attacks from bases in other countries as quickly as possible. And new "lily pad" installations in countries like Lithuania and Tajikistan—jumping-off points for military interventions—are designed to allow U.S. troops to strike before their target can prepare its defenses.

As the people of Japan, Okinawa, South Korea, and other nations that already "host" U.S. military bases know all too well, these new bases will come with intolerable "abuses and usurpations" that must be resisted and overcome. I won't pretend that there are easy solutions to liberating people around the world from the daily intrusions and the dangers of war that accompany military bases. But there are several promising new initiatives, including a worldwide explosion of education and organizing against U.S. military bases. In Europe, a new network of activists is protesting at various U.S. bases across the continent, including the nuclear-weapons base in Belgium. In Asia, the Listserv initiated by Focus on Global South provides an important forum for people across the globe to exchange information and explore common actions. The annual meetings of the World Social Forum have also offered opportunities for anti-bases activists to collaborate.

The U.S. peace movement, if it is indeed going to try to stop future wars, must learn more about these issues and then join these international efforts to close overseas bases and repatriate U.S. troops.

∞○∞

"War is elective. It is not an inevitable state of affairs.
War is not the weather."

—Susan Sontag

ARMIES **FOR PEACE**

GAR SMITH

Gar Smith, is editor emeritus of *Earth Island Journal*, cofounder of Environmentalists Against War, and associate editor of *Common Ground* magazine, where this story originally appeared.

As the father of eight adopted children, Mel Duncan clearly has a stake in the future. This veteran community organizer from St. Paul, Minnesota, doesn't come across as a firebrand. Instead, the cherubic, puckish Duncan is blessed with a jokester's genial mien and the easy smile of a born salesman.

Duncan first conceived his vision of a global peace force during a stay at the Buddhist monastery where Thich Nhat Hanh teaches. It was one of Duncan's Sufi teachers who gave him his nonviolent marching orders: "Your job is to enlighten the heart of the enemy."

In 1999, Duncan attended the Hague Peace Conference in hopes of promoting his vision. But before Duncan could commandeer a microphone, a stranger stepped up to the podium to propose the same thing. The speaker was San Francisco's David Hartsough. Duncan raced to his side, introduced himself, and forged a life-altering friendship.

David Hartsough's Quaker parents set him on his spiritual path when they introduced him to the writings of Mahatma Gandhi at an early age. When

Ten thousand women march for peace on International Women's Day, March 8, 2003, in Washington, D.C.
Photo by Gael Murphy

Hartsough was in his twenties, he participated in a sit-in to desegregate a Southern restaurant. When an enraged racist threatened to kill him with a switchblade, Hartsough told the man, "Do what you think is right and I'll try to love you no matter what." The man's knife and jaw both dropped, and he walked away dumbfounded.

A decade later, Hartsough was with Vietnam veteran and antiwar activist Brian S. Willson when a Bay Area peace protest went horribly wrong. Willson was sitting cross-legged on the tracks just outside the navy weapons station at Port Chicago, hoping to block a train carrying explosives to El Salvador. Unbeknownst to the protesters, the military had ordered the train operator not to stop. The locomotive barreled over Willson, severing both his legs.

Willson went on to become an iconic figure of the antiwar movement, and Hartsough went on to found San Francisco's Peaceworkers organization, which has sent nonviolent volunteers to intervene in Chiapas, Mexico, and

Kosovo. During the NATO bombing campaign in the Balkans, Hartsough and five other Peaceworkers were thrown into a Serbian jail for several days, causing an international incident. Hartsough emerged from that Serbian cell determined to build a global peace army.

Within three years of its founding, the Nonviolent Peaceforce (NPF) had won the support of the Dalai Lama and seven Nobel Peace laureates. The NPF now has home offices in St. Paul and San Francisco and, as Duncan proudly notes, "ninety-two groups on every continent but Antarctica."

Their goal is to recruit two thousand paid professionals, four thousand reservists, and five thousand volunteers—all backed by an administrative organization and a research and training staff. Professional peace soldiers would enlist for a two-year tour of duty. Hartsough estimates that it will cost $1.6 million a year to finance the NPF. This seems like a lot until he points out that this is less money than the Pentagon will spend in the next two minutes. "With one-tenth of 1 percent of the U.S. military budget," Hartsough argues, "we could have a full-scale Nonviolent Peaceforce able to intervene in conflict areas in many parts of the world." And, he adds, this force would be able to respond more quickly than UN peacekeeping forces.

In December 2002, NPF representatives from more than forty peace and nonviolence organizations convened near New Delhi and selected Sri Lanka as the site for the NPF's first pilot project. During its twenty years of civil war, Duncan claims, "Sri Lanka has seen more suicide bombers than Israel and Palestine." The country is beset by landmines, child soldiers, and abductions, but a cease-fire in 2002—the fourth in twenty years—seemed to offer a window of opportunity.

Fourteen people from eleven countries formed the first group of volunteers, whose members ranged from young adults to a Vietnam veteran. The NPF dispatched two teams to Jaffna in the north of Sri Lanka (with members from Kenya and the Philippines), a team to Matara in the south (with members from Ghana, Japan, and the United States), and a team to Muthur and Trincomalee in the east (with members from Brazil, Germany, Palestine, and the United States).

In Sri Lanka, conflicts rage not only along religious lines (Christians versus Muslims) but also along linguistic lines, with Tamil and Sinhalese speakers frequently identifying the other as enemies solely because of the language they speak. Consequently, Peaceforce members had to learn both basic Tamil and Sinhalese in a grueling four-week crash course.

Linda Sartor, a former middle-school teacher from Sonoma County, California, was one of the peacemakers. Tormented by Washington's violent bombardment of Afghanistan in the wake of September 11, Sartor wanted to do more than attend protest rallies. She went to Palestine with the International Solidarity Movement, flew to Iraq before the invasion to act as a "witness," and then joined an NPF team in Sri Lanka. She soon found herself stationed in the village of Valachchenai, where Muslims and Tamils ran separate civic offices, schools, and buses, and where some neighbors remain so distrustful that they haven't spoken for a generation.

The NPF set up its office on a street lined with Muslim shops on one side and Tamil shops on the other, in hopes that the presence of foreigners could help ease the fear and tension. On April 9, a bloody confrontation erupted between political factions, causing thousands to flee. As the only group of internationals in the area, NPF worked with clergy, government officials, and the army to ensure shelter, food, and water for civilian refugees, some of whom had walked twenty kilometers to reach safety.

During the tense electoral period, NPF engaged in preelection monitoring and made repeated visits with police and military officials, as well as the Muslim residents of several internally displaced persons camps. On election day, NPF teams rose before dawn to visit more than thirty polling stations during the eight-hour voting period. NPF workers labored into the night, accompanying ballot boxes to counting stations and monitoring the counting of ballots. The outcome was reported in an official dispatch dated April 12, 2004: "Despite the gloomiest of forecasts, the election was the most violence-free that Sri Lanka had had for some time."

Oceans away in Iraq, a similar effort was pulled together in the wake of the U.S. attack on the holy cities of Najaf and Karbalā in April 2004. Appalled by the civilian deaths, Peter Lumsdaine, a San Francisco peace organizer, sent out a call for volunteers willing to nonviolently challenge the U.S. military offensive. Two weeks later, Lumsdaine's five-member Iraq Emergency Peace Team was making its way through Najaf's rubble-strewn streets and preparing to place their bodies between the city's mosques and the Pentagon's tanks.

"We understand the dangers of our journey, but we are determined to try and contribute in our own small way to peace and justice for the people of Najaf," the Peace Team's collective statement read. "Only when peacemakers are willing to shoulder some of the same risks that soldiers take in war can we begin to move away from the cycle of violence that grips human society at the dawn of the 21st century."

The efforts by this Peace Team or the Nonviolent Peaceforce may be dismissed as foolhardy or embraced as heroic. Granted, the likelihood of a small number of courageous and determined individuals derailing a billion-dollar military juggernaut is slim, but what might happen if the world had a standing nonviolent army of thousands?

While George W. Bush contends that there is no alternative to a future of endless war, the Nonviolent Peaceforce "is quietly attempting to institutionalize a proven alternative." If it succeeds, "the world will have two kinds of standing armies to choose from."

PEACEFORCE RESOURCES

Christian Peacemaker Teams, www.cpt.org

International Solidarity Movement, www.palsolidarity.org

Nonviolent Peaceforce, www.nonviolentpeaceforce.org

Peace Brigades International, www.peacebrigades.org

Voices in the Wilderness, www.vitw.org

Witness for Peace, www.witnessforpeace.org

Chapter 9

INDEPENDENCE FROM OIL

PROTECT AND **RESPECT RESOURCES**

VICTORY CARS

ARIANNA HUFFINGTON

Arianna Huffington is a nationally syndicated columnist and the author of ten books, including *How to Overthrow the Government, Pigs at the Trough,* and *Fanatics and Fools.*

On the way to my daughter's school this morning, I encountered the usual L.A. rush-hour road rally of elephantine sport-utility vehicles, many of them flying American flags. Taking the cake was a massive SUV proudly sporting half a dozen flags—one on each window and two on the bumper. My first thought was, "How patriotic!" My second was, "How much more patriotic it would be to trade in the gas-guzzling leviathan for something that sips, rather than gulps, at the gas pump."

Which, thinking globally and acting locally, is precisely what I've decided to do with mine.

Though I don't consider myself an automotive fashionista, I must admit I followed the thundering herd of protective parents unable to resist the allure of what is basically a comfy Sherman tank. My SUV, a Lincoln Navigator, was, I was told, the safest way to transport my kids. And, as a bonus, I could haul around a decent-size Girl Scout troop.

But now we're at war, right? A new war. Everything has changed, hasn't it? Perhaps in rhetoric. In practice, what are we being called to do for the war effort other than shop till we drop, eat out, and visit Disney World? Given that our ability to play hardball with nations that harbor terrorists is going to be seriously compromised by our foreign-oil habit, shouldn't we be doing everything we can to reduce that dependence on oil—starting, say, yesterday?

It's time for Washington to dole out some tough love to the energy and auto-industry lobbies and help put them on the path of reform, starting with increasing fuel-efficiency standards for all cars, light trucks, and SUVs: this is the single biggest step we can take to conserve energy. Raising the standards from the current 27.5 miles per gallon to 36 miles per gallon would save us roughly two million barrels a day—about the same amount we import from the Persian Gulf.

Washington must also push Detroit to radically increase its production of hybrid cars and must team with corporate America to rapidly accelerate investment in energy efficiency, hydrogen-based technology, and renewable sources of energy like solar and wind. A great model for this is the new Apollo Project (www.apolloalliance.org), a $300 billion program proposed by unions and environmental groups to create three million new jobs while helping America achieve energy independence within a generation.

Because of the corporate takeover of our democracy, Washington has remained firmly stuck in the Dark Ages of energy policy. That's why Bill Clinton came charging into office promising to raise fuel-efficiency standards to 45 miles per gallon but left without having increased them one inch per gallon. And why George W. Bush can try to score points by proposing to raise the ludicrously low SUV mileage standard by an equally ludicrous 1.5 miles per gallon over his second term in office.

It's also why the Big Three, once again, have to play catch-up with Toyota and Honda, which have been putting out hybrid cars since 1997. How ironic that if American car buyers want to do something truly patriotic, they have to buy Japanese to do it.

Detroit has sensed that public opinion is shifting and has taken some baby steps toward meeting the rising demand for more socially responsible cars. Now it's up to all of us to make sure that the pressure and the demand continue to grow. Otherwise, the auto industry will gladly underfund and under-advertise its hybrid models, allowing them to crash and burn—yet more "proof" that American consumers don't really care about anything other than their precious SUVs.

Consider how many loopholes have already been driven through by light trucks and SUVs, which are allowed to average 7 miles per gallon less than regular cars. And the ultimate absurdity is that if an SUV is massive enough, it is entirely exempt from federal fuel-economy standards. That's right, build one with a gross vehicle weight of more than eighty-five hundred pounds—like the Ford Excursion or the new Hummer—and the lousy gas mileage doesn't even have to be reported to the government!

And all the while, oil prices steadily increase. But don't let the skyrocketing numbers on the gas pump fool you: America isn't confronting a shortage of fuel; it's confronting a shortage of leadership.

The public is galvanized for action, just as it was during World War II. Back then, Americans answered their leaders' call for sacrifice in dozens of altruistic ways: they collected scrap metal to be refashioned as guns, planes, and tanks; planted twenty million "victory gardens"; and made do with three gallons of gas a week—just about what the average SUV devours on a few latte-hauling trips to Starbucks.

Of course, when it comes to acting on our patriotism, we don't have to wait for our leaders. If they won't lead, we can just step around them. And when it comes to the vital issue of energy policy, it appears that we'll have to. As well as giving up our SUVs—or, even better, switching to hybrid gas-and-electric cars that currently get up to 64 miles per gallon—we can all make simple adjustments to wean our country from foreign oil, even if our leaders are too beholden to the energy and auto industry lobbies to guide us.

We can, for example, make sure our tires are fully inflated, reducing gas consumption by 2 percent; we can slow down to 65 miles per hour, reducing highway gas consumption by 15 percent; and we can stop idling our cars in drive-through window and school car-pool lanes. At home we can help conserve fuel by turning thermostats down, weather-stripping doors and windows, buying energy-efficient fluorescent light bulbs, and unplugging cell-phone chargers and hair dryers.

Would it be so painful for us to slow down the intravenous drip of oil that keeps hideously anti-American regimes alive? Look at the positive potential of this dilemma: if we were to unleash a new wave of good old American inventiveness, we might be able to regain some of the respect for America that has been lost in recent years. Let's step up to the challenge!

∽◌∾

"As we head to war with Iraq, President Bush wants to make one thing clear: This war is not about oil, it's about gasoline."

—Jay Leno

CONSERVING OUR RESOURCES,
RESISTING WAR

JULIA BUTTERFLY HILL
Eco-activist Julia Butterfly Hill rose to international prominence when she sat in a tree for two years to draw attention to the devastation wrought by the clear-cutting of ancient California redwoods. Her organization, Circle of Life, educates people about making sustainable choices in their daily lives.

Every day, the choices we make are either weapons of mass destruction or tools of mass compassion. Every action we take is an opportunity to create peace or hurt, to end the war on the planet or to perpetuate it.

What do weapons of mass destruction look like? Saws that clear-cut the forests. Plastic cups, plastic bags, plastic silverware, plastic to-go containers. Paper napkins, paper plates. Gas-guzzling cars. Books printed in ecologically unsound ways. But above all, our laissez-faire attitude toward throwing things away. I am also passionate about discouraging anyone with consciousness from using water bottles—the water wasted in *making* that water bottle is more than the water that fills the bottle up.

We need to realize that all these kinds of things are literal weapons of mass destruction. Because of this, sustainable choices, including voluntary simplicity; reducing, then reusing, and finally recycling; spending every penny as a vote; and so on, are all tools of mass compassion.

But there are even larger steps we can take to avoid supporting the war—for me, one is choosing not to pay taxes. There's no constitutional provision mandating that people pay income taxes, because at the time the Constitution was written this new country had just rebelled against taxation without representation. Since 2002, I have not paid my income tax, and now my money cannot go to the war effort. Instead my money is going to projects like native peoples, community gardens, environmental protection, arts and education, and alternatives to incarceration.

Many people prefer to protest on a more symbolic level—for example, by withholding the few pennies or dollars of federal tax on their phone bills every month. This tax began as a war tax in 1914, and although it was supposed to end when the war was over, the people didn't know any better and so the government kept it. But no one can force you to pay it. Today, a big movement supports these kinds of resistance efforts, a movement that's been going on for well over thirty years. Visit www.warresisters.org for more information.

We live in very challenging times. Yet we also live in times of incredible possibility. There's a saying that goes: "When the night sky is at its darkest, that's the time for the stars to shine the brightest." We're in a really dark time right now, which means it is an opportunity for every one of us to dazzle.

We're responsible for cocreating the world we want to see. Where there is love and consciousness in action, there is beauty, and there is peace. It's time for the revolution of the heart.

"There is enough for all. The earth is a generous mother;
she will provide in plentiful abundance food for all her children
if they will but cultivate her soil in justice and in peace."

—Bourke Coekran

OIL ADDICTS
ANONYMOUS

JENNIFER KRILL
Jennifer Krill is the director of the Zero Emissions Campaign at Rainforest Action Network.

Hi, my name is Jennifer, and it's time for us all to admit that we have a problem: we are addicted to oil. The United States represents only 5 percent of the world's population yet consumes 25 percent of the world's oil. From the Middle East to Nigeria to Colombia, more than half of our oil comes from conflict regions. We are willing to topple governments to get more oil. We will risk the principles of democracy itself in order to get our fix.

Today we are fighting for access to oil, but our next war may occur because of our consumption of oil. According to a leaked Pentagon report, global climate change poses a greater threat to our peace and security than international terrorism. Global warming is melting ancient glaciers, warming the world's oceans (thus raising sea levels), and intensifying catastrophic weather events. As frayed resources are pressed to the limit, climate change will provoke increased conflict.

If oil is such a dangerous substance, why do we continue to abuse it? We burn most of our oil for transportation—specifically for automobiles. One out of every seven barrels of oil globally is consumed on America's highways alone. Carmakers that refuse to improve fuel efficiency are like dealers keeping us hooked. The worst culprit is the Ford Motor Company. Ford's fleet has had the lowest average fuel efficiency in America for five years running. Ford's gas-guzzling SUVs, like the Excursion and Expedition, get worse gas mileage than the Model-T did eighty years ago. But Ford is far from alone; think of General Motors selling a military vehicle (the Hummer) as a family car!

DECLARE INDEPENDENCE FROM OIL

Rainforest Action Network and Global Exchange partner to push Ford to increase the efficiency of its fleet, and continue development of environmentally sustainable automobiles.
© Innosanto Nagara

JUMPSTART Ford
www.jumpstartford.com

RAINFOREST ACTION NETWORK

GLOBAL EXCHANGE

DEMAND ZERO EMISSION CARS

It's time for a twelve-step program to break America's oil addiction and halt global climate destruction.

What you can do as an individual:

1. Declare independence from oil. Walk, ride a bike, or take mass transit.
2. If you must drive, carpool and choose the most efficient vehicle you can.
3. Demand zero-emission cars. Tell the Ford Motor Company to stop driving America's oil addiction. Take action now at www.jumpstartford.com.

What we all can do as a movement:

4. Separate oil from state. Get big oil money out of politics and get politicians to stop subsidizing big oil. Visit www.publicintegrity.org.
5. Green the grid. We cannot halt global warming without clean energy. Demand solar and wind alternatives. Find out how at www.seen.org and www.nrel.gov.
6. Support sustainable mobility. Help encourage bike lanes and mass transit and discourage sprawl in your community. Go to www.newrules.org for information.
7. Reform global finance. Get banks to stop making destructive investments in oil and fossil-fuel development. Instead, encourage them to join Citigroup and Bank of America and start supporting sustainable energy and transportation alternatives. Learn more at www.ran.org.

What Ford and the other carmakers must do:

8. Bring today's cars into the twenty-first century. Existing clean-car improvements are sitting on shelves instead of in Ford's engines. If Ford used today's technology to clean up its internal combustion engine, its cars would get an average of 40 miles per gallon, a big improvement over Ford's 2004 average of 18.8 miles per gallon.
9. Develop hybrid electric vehicles. The battery system in hybrids uses energy that most engines waste. But hybrids do still burn some oil, which carmakers could limit further with a "plug-in hybrid" option, allowing consumers to use solar-power electric batteries for short commutes and a gas tank for long trips.
10. Find other alternatives. Use intelligent alternative fuels like biodiesel and vegetable oil, or create solar-charged electric vehicles. With a simple conversion, diesel engines like those used by Mercedes and Volkswagen could run on vegetable oil. Full-electric vehicles plugged in to solar power offer an affordable zero-emission alternative.

11. Stop using hydrogen-fuel cells as an excuse to delay production of the easy alternatives above. To produce hydrogen, we must find an affordable, climate-neutral means such as solar power. Electric vehicles, available and on the road today, are a sustainable shortcut. We don't need to wait a decade to begin our clean-energy revolution.

∽o∾

"While anti-terrorism and traditional national security rhetoric will be employed to explain risky deployments abroad, a growing number of American soldiers and sailors will be committed to the protection of overseas oil fields, pipeline, refineries, and tanker routes. Inevitably, we will pay a higher price in blood for every additional gallon of oil we obtain from abroad."

—Michael Klare

BRING HALLIBURTON
HOME

NAOMI KLEIN

Naomi Klein, award-winning Canadian journalist and activist, is the author of *Fences and Windows*, and *No Logo*. She wrote and coproduced *The Take*, a recent documentary about the worker movement in Argentina, with her husband, Avi Lewis. The following is excerpted from an article published November 24, 2003, in the *Nation*.

Cancel the contracts. Ditch the deals. Rip up the rules.

Those are a few suggestions for slogans that could help unify the growing movement against the occupation of Iraq. So far, activist debates have focused on whether progressives should demand that the United States begin a complete withdrawal of troops, or that it cede power to the United Nations.

But the "troops out" debate overlooks an important fact. If every last soldier pulled out of the Gulf tomorrow and a sovereign government came to power, Iraq would still be occupied: by laws written in the interest of another country, by foreign corporations controlling Iraq's essential services, by 70 percent unemployment sparked by public-sector layoffs.

Any movement serious about Iraqi self-determination must call for an end not only to Iraq's military occupation but to its economic colonization as well. That means reversing the shock-therapy reforms that former U.S. occupation chief Paul Bremer fraudulently passed off as "reconstruction" and canceling all privatization contracts flowing from those reforms.

How can such an ambitious goal be achieved? Easy: by showing that Bremer's reforms were illegal to begin with. They clearly violate the international convention governing the behavior of occupying forces, the Hague Regulations of 1907 (the companion to the 1949 Geneva Conventions, both ratified by the United States), as well as the U.S. Army's own code of war.

The Hague Regulations state that an occupying power must respect "unless absolutely prevented, the laws in force in the country." The Coalition Provisional Authority has shredded that simple rule with gleeful defiance. Iraq's constitution outlaws the privatization of key state assets, and it bars foreigners from owning Iraqi firms. No plausible argument can be made that the CPA was "absolutely prevented" from respecting those laws, and yet the CPA overturned them unilaterally.

On September 19, 2003, Bremer enacted the now-infamous Order 39. It announced that two hundred Iraqi state companies would be privatized; decreed that foreign firms could retain 100 percent ownership of Iraqi banks, mines, and factories; and allowed those firms to move 100 percent of their profits out of Iraq. The *Economist* declared the new rules a "capitalist dream."

Order 39 violated the Hague Regulations in other ways as well. The convention states that occupying powers "shall be regarded only as administrator and usufructuary of public buildings, real estate, forests, and agricultural estates belonging to the hostile State, and situated in the occupied country. It must safeguard the capital of these properties, and administer them in accordance with the rules of usufruct."

Bouvier's Law Dictionary defines *usufruct* (possibly the ugliest word in the English language) as an arrangement that grants one party the right to use and derive benefit from another's property "without altering the substance of the thing." Put more simply, if you are a house sitter, you can eat the food in the fridge, but you can't sell the house and turn it into condos. And yet that is just what Bremer is doing: What could more substantially alter "the substance" of a public asset than to turn it into a private one?

In case the CPA was still unclear on this detail, the U.S. Army's Law of Land Warfare states that "the occupant does not have the right of sale or unqualified use of [nonmilitary] property." This is pretty straightforward: bombing something does not give you the right to sell it. There is every indication that the CPA is well aware of the lawlessness of its privatization scheme. In a leaked memo written on March 26, 2003, British attorney general Lord Peter Goldsmith warned prime minister Tony Blair that "the imposition of major structural economic reforms would not be authorized by international law."

So far, most of the controversy surrounding Iraq's reconstruction has focused on the waste and corruption in the awarding of contracts. This badly misses the scope of the violation: even if the sell-off of Iraq were conducted with full transparency and open bidding, it would still be illegal for the simple reason that Iraq is not America's to sell.

The UN Security Council's recognition of the United States and Britain's occupation authority provides no legal cover. The UN resolution passed in May 2003 specifically required the occupying powers to "comply fully with their obligations under international law including in particular the Geneva Conventions of 1949 and the Hague Regulations of 1907."

According to a growing number of international legal experts, this means that if the next Iraqi government decides it doesn't want to be a wholly owned subsidiary of Bechtel or Halliburton, it will have powerful legal grounds to renationalize assets that were privatized under CPA edicts. Juliet Blanch, global head of energy and international arbitration for the huge international law firm Norton Rose, says that because Bremer's reforms directly contradict Iraq's constitution, they are "in breach of international law and are likely not enforceable." Blanch argues that the CPA "has no authority or ability to sign those [privatization] contracts" and that a sovereign Iraqi government would have "quite a serious argument for renationalization without paying compensation." Firms facing this type of expropriation would, according to Blanch, have "no legal remedy."

The only way out for the administration is to make sure that Iraq's next government is anything but sovereign. It must be pliant enough to ratify the CPA's illegal laws, which will then be celebrated as the happy marriage of free markets and free people. Once that happens, it will be too late: the contracts will be locked in, the deals done, and the occupation of Iraq permanent.

Which is why antiwar forces must use this fast-closing window to demand that the next Iraqi government be free from the shackles of these reforms. It's too late to stop the war, but it's not too late to deny Iraq's invaders the myriad economic prizes they went to war to collect in the first place.

It's not too late to cancel the contracts and ditch the deals.

<small>ॐ</small>

> "There is a revolution under way that will take us toward a distributed energy system based on efficiency and progress in photovoltaics, fuel cells, wind power and microturbines. It can be slowed by shortsightedness driven by greed, but it cannot be stopped."
>
> —David Orr

ENDING POVERTY,
ENDING TERRORISM

BENAZIR BHUTTO

Benazir Bhutto is chairperson of the Pakistan People's Party and a former prime minister of Pakistan. This essay first appeared in the *Guardian*, August 9, 2004.

While the world focuses on the war against terror, the war against poverty slides onto the back burner. Since the attack on the World Trade Center in 2001, the world has seen the political rise of those on the religious margins coupled with a growing gap between the rich and the poor.

There appear to be groups in both the Muslim and non-Muslim worlds who believe that a clash of civilizations is needed. The Christian fundamentalists believe that Christ will be resurrected once the people of the Jewish faith are resettled on the banks of the Euphrates. The Muslim extremists believe that the Mahdi will arrive when the battle between Muslims and non-Muslims intensifies.

Extremist groups are rising in the Muslim world, in India, in America. They spew hatred against Muslims, or Jews, or Christians. The extremists are united in hate, in intolerance, and in sparking religious wars where they can prosper.

This political scenario is threatening to undo the entire global social fabric built since the end of the Second World War—one based on the tolerance between different faiths, races, genders, and cultures. A clash of civilizations can lead to Armageddon, where there will be no winners on earth. But perhaps the religious extremists are not searching for winners on earth.

The challenge for the world community is to emphasize the values of tolerance, moderation, and interfaith understanding, on which rest the pillars of a less violent world. However, the World Trade Center attack and the

Environmentalist Diane Wilson and young Iraqi boy during CODEPINK delegation visit to Iraq before the 2003 U.S. Invasion.
Photo by Medea Benjamin

events in Iraq have made that more difficult. The former led to suspicion against Muslims and a loss of civil liberties; the latter, to a countersuspicion from Muslims as to the real purposes of the war in Iraq. The inability to find weapons of mass destruction and the prison abuses at Abu Ghraib undermined the reasons given for the Iraq war.

We must certainly work together to root out terrorism, and Pakistan has been a frontline state in the war against terrorism. In fact, most of the leading terrorists, such as Khalid Sheikh Mohammed and Ahmed Khalfan Ghailani, have been arrested in Pakistan.

But while global attention is focused on terrorism, the crisis of poverty is effectively disregarded. While most Muslim intellectuals strongly condemn the attack on the World Trade Center, they believe that unaddressed political problems and neglected social injustice provided a petri dish allowing the germs of terrorism and hatred to multiply.

Without a war on poverty, terrorism will never be defeated. Unfortunately, today big business seems to be in the driver's seat, while every hour a thousand children starve to death in the world. One recent report found that while twenty years ago CEOs made an average of forty times what factory workers made, in 2003 they made four hundred times as much, and their incomes are now climbing to a multiple of five hundred.

This staggering rise in the fortunes of those on top, while those below suffer, is a festering sore that has the potential to erupt. The 2004 Indian elections showed that a stock-market economy alone could not make India shine. The Indian electorate went against all predictions, as peasants, laborers, and the middle classes voted for change. Similarly, in Pakistan the talk of stock-market rises and foreign-exchange increases hides a more troubling picture. This is one of increasing poverty, hunger, misery, and frustration. The number of young people killing themselves because of hunger was twelve hundred in a six-month period. That is the officially recorded figure—the real figure is believed to be much higher.

In Pakistan, the average income has been shrinking. The cost of living is rising sharply. It is becoming increasingly difficult for the ordinary citizen to pay fat utility bills and buy the basic necessities of life. The Pakistan Economic Survey admits that poverty has increased since democracy was derailed in 1996. The gap between the rich and the poor is growing at an alarming rate.

The war against terrorism is primarily perceived as a war based on the use of force. However, economics has its own force, as does the desperation of families who cannot feed themselves.

The neglect of rising poverty against the background of religious extremism can only complicate an already difficult world situation. Militancy and greed cannot become the defining images of a new century that began with much hope. We must refocus our energy on promoting the values of democracy, accountability, broad-based government, and institutions that can respond to people's very real and very urgent needs.

THE CRACKED **MIRROR**

WANGARI MAATHAI

Wangari Maathai is Kenya's assistant minister for environment, natural resources, and wildlife. Winner of the 2004 Nobel Peace Prize, she is the founder of Kenya's Green Belt Movement and the author of *The Green Belt Movement*. The following is excerpted from the November/December 2004 issue of *Resurgence* magazine (www.resur gence.org), and from a speech by Professor Maathai on the occasion of receiving the Nobel Peace Prize.

Mount Kenya is a World Heritage site. The equator passes through its top, and it boasts a unique habitat and heritage. Because it is a glacier-topped mountain, it is the source of many of Kenya's rivers. Now, partly because of climate change and partly because of logging and the encroachment of crops, the glaciers are melting. Many of the rivers flowing from Mount Kenya have either dried up or become very low. The mountain's biological diversity is threatened as the forests fall.

"What shall we do to conserve this forest?" I asked myself.

Mount Kenya used to be a holy mountain for my people, the Kikuyus. They believed that their God dwelled on the mountain and that everything good—the rains, clean drinking water—flowed from it. As long as they saw the clouds (the mountain is a very shy mountain, usually hiding behind clouds), they knew they would get rain.

And then the missionaries came. In their wisdom, or lack of it, they said, "God does not dwell on Mount Kenya. God dwells in heaven."

We have been looking for heaven, but we have not found it. Men and women have gone to the moon and back and have not seen heaven. Heaven is not above us: it is right here, right now.

So the Kikuyu people were not wrong when they said that God dwelled on the mountain, because if God is omnipresent, as theology tells us, then God is on Mount Kenya too. If the people still believed this, they would not have allowed illegal logging or clear-cutting of the forests.

The Green Belt Movement (GBM), which I led until joining the new Kenyan government in January 2003, set out to mobilize community consciousness toward self-determination, equity, improved livelihood, security, and environmental conservation—using trees as the entry point. When we began, we believed that all we needed to do was to teach people how to plant trees and make connections between their own problems and their degraded environments. But in the course of our struggles to realize GBM's vision, we discovered that some of the Kenyan communities had lost aspects of their culture that had facilitated the conservation of the beautiful environment the first European explorers and missionaries recorded in their diaries and textbooks.

During the long, dark decades of imperialism and colonialism from the mid-nineteenth century to the mid-twentieth century, the British, Belgian, Italian, French, and German governments told African societies that they were backward. They told us that our religious systems were sinful, our agricultural practices inefficient, our tribal systems of governing irrelevant, and our cultural norms barbaric, irreligious, and savage.

Until the arrival of the Europeans, communities had looked to nature for inspiration, food, beauty, and spirituality. Their habitats were rich with local biological diversity, both plant and animal. Today these are the very habitats most at risk from globalization, commercialization, privatization, and the piracy of biological materials found in them. This global threat is causing communities to lose their rights to the resources they have preserved throughout the ages.

Of course, some of what happened before the Europeans arrived was bad and remains so. Africans were involved in the slave trade; women are still genitally mutilated; Africans are still killing Africans because they belong to different religions or ethnic groups. Nonetheless, I for one am not content to thank God for the arrival of "civilization" from Europe, because I know from what my grandparents told me that much of what went on in Africa before colonialism was good.

African leaders were to some degree accountable for their actions. People were able to feed themselves. They carried their history—their cultural practices, their stories, and their sense of the world around them—in their oral traditions, and that tradition was rich and meaningful. Above all, they lived with other creatures and the natural environment in harmony, and they protected that world.

Cut off from their cultural heritage by colonialism, African communities began to lose their identity, their dignity, and their sense of destiny. Disinherited, they had nothing to pass on. Even those who were not sent into slavery became, in effect, slaves—and the consequences were long lasting. In GBM seminars, as participants put down the mirror that has been showing them their own cracked reflections—the mirror first held up by the missionaries or the colonial authorities—there is enormous relief and great anger and sadness.

Cultural revival might be the only thing that stands between the conservation and destruction of the environment, the only way to perpetuate the knowledge and wisdom inherited from the past. But cultural liberation will come only when the minds of the people are set free and they can protect themselves from colonialism of the mind. Only then will they really appreciate their country and the need to protect its natural beauty and wealth.

The thirty million trees planted by GBM volunteers—mostly rural women—throughout Kenya over the past thirty years are a testament to individuals' ability to change the course of history. Working together, we have proven that sustainable development is possible; that reforestation of degraded land is possible; and that exemplary governance is possible when ordinary citizens are informed, sensitized, mobilized, and involved in direct action for their environment.

Many wars are fought over resources, which are becoming increasingly scarce across the earth. If we did a better job of managing our resources sustainably, conflicts over them would be reduced. So, protecting the global environment is directly related to securing peace.

When we plant trees, we plant the seeds of peace and the seeds of hope. We also secure the future for the generations to come.

For more information, visit www.greenbeltmovement.org and www.wangarimaathai.com.

∽o∾

"Those who contemplate the beauty of the earth find reserves of strength that will endure as long as life lasts."

—Rachel Carson

Chapter 10

CELEBRATE **JOYFUL** REVOLUTION

❧ GRITO DE VIEQUES ❧

AYA DE LEÓN

*Aya de León is an award-winning writer, performer,
and teacher. Her one-woman shows include* Aya de León Is
Running for President *and* Thieves in the Temple:
The Reclaiming of Hip Hop. *She is a coauthor of the book*
How to Get Stupid White Men Out of Office.

Note: Vieques, Puerto Rico, was used by the U.S. Navy for
target practice with live ammunition for more than sixty years.
But in May 2003, after years of struggle, the people of Puerto
Rico forced the navy to leave.

My name is Vieques.
I am a Puerto Rican girl.
My stepfather is the United States.
He comes into my room at night to do his business.

My name is Vieques.
I used to dream that Spain, my real father, would come
    back and rescue me.
But he's gone for good.
I have only the faint and echoing voices
of Africana and Taina ancestors telling me that
I can survive this.

My name is Vieques.
When my body started to change,
my stepfather dressed me in a clingy, itchy dress.
"Smile," he told me. "Smile at the nice foreign military
    man," and pushed me toward him.
The military man was not nice.
His skin was pasty. His breath smelled.
I couldn't understand his language.
He came into my room and did his business.

My name is Vieques.
Sometimes my stepfather sells me to whole groups.
He calls them allied forces.
I fought back the best I could with chains and live bodies
    and fishing boats.
It happened anyway.

My name is Vieques.
I am still fighting back.
I am bigger and stronger now.
I have put a church, an encampment,
a struggle up at my bedroom door.
My stepfather can't get in.
He has not been able to do his business for months now,
    longer than I ever dreamed.

My name is Vieques.
Without the shock of constant bombardment,
the numbness is subsiding.
I look at my body and see the devastation.
Lagoons, like self-esteem, have dried up to nothingness.
My womb is wilting with radiation
from illegally used uranium ammunition.
Where my skin was once lush and soft, I am scarred.
Old tanks, like cigarette burns, dot my flesh.
Unexploded bombs, like memories, may detonate in
    the future
when chosen lovers touch me in the wrong spot
or without warning.

My name is Vieques.
The numbness is subsiding.
Tender shoots of grass push up toward the sky.
A lizard sneaks back to sun itself on a chunk of shrapnel.
A butterfly alights on a rusted-out jet.
Fish slowly make their way back toward my shores,
no longer reverberating with shock waves of violation.

My name is Vieques.
This is *my* body.
It may be worth eighty million dollars a year to you,
    Yanqui,
but it is priceless to me.

My door is barred.
I have burned the clingy, itchy dress.
The encampment grows stronger.
The lizards, the grass, the fish, the butterflies stand
    with me.
I'll never be the same,
but I'll never be yours again to do your dirty business.

My name is Vieques
and I will be free.

SING AND DANCE

IGO ROGOVA

Igo Rogova cofounded the Kosovar women's group Motrat Qiriazi.

When I was working with women and girls in the Chegrane refugee camp in Macedonia, a woman from the office of the United Nations High Commissioner for Refugees (UNHCR) came to the women's tent, where we were singing and dancing, to give us some information. "I have not come here to sing and dance," she told us.

But singing and dancing help many women overcome the traumas they experience. Our meetings in the camps included women who were raped, who had lost their families. We met daily and shared stories. We even had a comedian. A thirteen-year-old girl who had been raped by the Serbian police came with her mother. The girl didn't speak to anyone, not even her mother, but when we sang and danced, she slowly joined in, and her spirit came alive again. There are similar stories of other women who attended our meetings. So when the UNHCR woman came that day, I quoted Emma Goldman: "I don't believe that a cause should demand the denial of life and joy."

LESSONS FROM THE FIELD: IGNITING THE SPIRIT OF JOY

ALLI CHAGI-STARR

Alli Chagi-Starr is a Bay Area cultural organizer, workshop leader, and writer on the power of arts activism. She is a founder of Art and Revolution, Cultural Links, Art in Action Youth Leadership Program, Dancers without Borders, and the annual Radical Performance Fest.

Sustainable movements share a secret—they cultivate the power of joy. The elements in our movements that are vital, innovative, and colorful motivate even the most serious, stalwart activist. Organizing work often suffers from a lack of fun. Yet, we thrive on the moments when we cast off the stress and despair that often accompany change work, and remember to play. If there was ever a time for social-justice organizers to encourage joy-filled practices, it is now.

Following in the tradition of Bread and Puppet, Sweet Honey in the Rock, the Zapatistas, and Augusto Boal's Theater of the Oppressed, I have worked with artists and activists since the late 1980s to develop strategies for getting off our booties and plugging in to the critical struggles of our times. Giant puppets, dance, spoken word, music, and humor draw media attention, build community, and illuminate our humanity. When we prioritize creativity in our efforts, we ignite our power and remember why we are working for justice.

After years of performing in modern dance companies and producing cultural arts benefits, I got a taste of how delicious art in conjunction with street activism could be. I was invited to a San Francisco demonstration protesting nuclear dumping on First Nations' sacred land in Ward Valley, California. The protest was planned to coincide with a visit by President Clinton. The demonstrators were forced to stand in a small fenced-off area out of view. Our group refused to enter their little pen. Instead, we gathered in a circle and each person made a simple dance gesture with a protest placard. In about ten minutes we had a fully choreographed dance. We took the street in front of the Civic Center and began performing. A confused police officer approached us mid-dance. I reassured him that our free theater performance would be done soon. He said, "Well, finish up, then." Television cameras, eager for film-worthy visuals, followed us as we moved from street corner to street corner with our dance number. Our signs reading, "Mr. Prez, Stop Dumping on Native Land" got on network TV, and we left feeling uplifted and ready for more.

This was one of the many moments that catalyzed what would become Art and Revolution, a national movement of arts activists in the United States who revitalized many movements during the turn of the millennium. It has defied the social construct that only some are destined to be artists, while reclaiming the knowledge that every individual has creative potential.

Art can never be separated from the work of cultivating democracy and building a just society. It is often the creative visionaries who are capable of illuminating the passions of the heart and kindling the fires of change. We can make present our humanity and joy without denying the histories and realities of slavery and colonization, racist wars on poor communities at home and abroad, and ecological suicide. Indeed, humor, music, and art have supported communities in surviving the worst travesties and injustices ever perpetrated.

We shift what is expected when we collectively pull down the walls of a two-story cardboard jail and free a twelve-foot puppet to lead the march. We change the tune when we take the microphone at a schmooze-fest of government and industry elites and sing, "Now is the time for democracy—corporate cash, won't you set me free?" Imagination frees us from the confines of the activist box. Why not have fun as we challenge business as usual?

Passing on creative tools to the next generation, Art in Action programs bring together emerging youth leaders from vastly different communities. By the end of ten days, living, learning, and creating art together, profound respect and love grow between people that are typically divided by our oppressive society. Participants recently created a multidisciplinary performance that included a corporate cheerleading squad mocking the current administration with pom-poms, pleated skirts, and funky moves: "We are the corporate thugs, yeah, the corporate thugs, right on! We start all of the wars, yeah, and push the drugs, right on!" President Bush was played by a young woman who calls to her cronies, "We need an excuse to go to war!" and then sings, "We'll find weapons of mass destruction, even if we know that they really don't got none." By the end of the show the audience was on their feet.

At every instant we have an opportunity to spark or dull people's spirits. We are experts at critique and cynicism. How can we as change makers become adept at mobilizing, encouraging, and inspiring? We often criticize ourselves for preaching to the choir. While it is crucial to reach beyond our activist enclaves, the choir still needs encouragement. When we are despairing, there is a need for our spirits to join and be uplifted. When we sing together, we hear what community sounds like.

The giant protest against the WTO meeting in Seattle was several years ago, but I am still approached by unfamiliar people who remember the power of our dance group when we took the center of a major intersection before another impending violent police onslaught that day. Thousands of people sang together through the tear gas and rain. We disarmed the police, who backed off, with the greatest antiweapon we have, the power of our collective creativity.

How many times were people beaten down in the civil rights movement, the labor movement, women's suffrage movement, and others before they were victorious? The songs from those movements still resonate today. Bernice Johnson Reagon's words from "Ella's Song," "We who believe in freedom cannot rest until it comes," are sung time and time again at our demonstrations, to close our meetings, and often alone in our kitchens on the days when we don't know how to go on. These songs help us to get up again and to keep going when we can see no light.

Victory happens in subtle acts, moment by moment. We are building the new world during every conversation, meeting, and action. We are modeling our vision as we tear down the old world—with every urban garden, every car traded in for a bike, every white person who begins to challenge racial privilege, every activist who remembers once loving to sing, every gift made by hand, every stranger who becomes a friend.

It is vital to keep the fires burning in progressive communities in this time in history. Now more than ever we must cultivate our collective passion for justice and keep each other strong for the times ahead. Even if we do not expect to see the change we hope to create in our lifetimes, we must see ourselves as part of a long, courageous struggle. We are the seed planters. Whether or not we will get to see our sprouts become trees, we must keep joyfully planting, even in dry soil. The rains will come—the fruit is for our children's children. May it be sweet.

~ PLANET CALLED HOME ~

HOLLY NEAR

Holly Near is an entertainer, teacher, and activist.

Can you call on your imagination
As if telling a myth to a child
Put in the fantastical, wonderful, magical
Add the romantic, the brave and the wild

Once upon a time there was a power
So great that no one could know its name
People tried to claim it and rule with it
Always such arrogance ended in shame.

Thousands of years would pass in a moment
Hundreds of cultures would come and go
Each generation with a glorious calling
Even when they were too busy to know

Then one day after two millennia
Which after all was a small part of time
Hundreds of souls found their way out of nowhere
To be on earth at the threat of decline

Let's all go, they moved as one being
Even though each would arrive here alone
They promised to work in grace with each other
To brave the beautiful planet called home

There was no promise that they could save it
But how exciting to give it a try
If each one did just one thing beautifully
Complex life on earth might not die

And so they arrive in a spectrum of colors
The population on earth did explode
Some threw themselves in front of disaster

Other slowly carried their load

Some adopted small girls from China
Some lived high in the branches of trees
Some died as martyrs, some lived as healers
Some bravely walked with a dreadful disease

They mingled among each class and culture
Not one of them could be identified
But together they altered just enough moments
To help the lost and the terrified

To step outside our egos and bodies
To know for once that we truly are one
Then quickly we would forget to remember
But that's OK, their job was well done

And earth went on for another millennium
Now it's time for my song to end
This magical story of hope and wonder
Invites you all to wake up and pretend to be

Fabulous creatures sent from the power
Souls that have come with a purpose in mind
To do one thing that will alter the outcome
And maybe together we'll do it in time

Can you call on your imagination
As if telling a myth to a child
Put in the fantastical, wonderful, magical
Add the romantic, the brave and the wild

The Souls are coming back
The Souls are coming back
The Souls are coming back

PICTURE PEACE

JUANA ALICIA

Juana Alicia is a muralist, printmaker, educator, and activist who incorporates issues of social justice, human rights, and environmental health into her art. Her public works can be seen throughout the country—from the San Francisco International Airport to the United Electrical and Machine Workers Union Hall in Erie, Pennsylvania.

"Democratic vigilance has been disproportionately expressed by artists, activists, and intellectuals in American life . . . to be a democratic individual is to speak out on uncomfortable truths."
—CORNELL WEST

I work for peace with pigment, plaster, and clay. With images from dreams and international news reports, with the voices of our ancestors, with insights

Ceasefire/Alto al Fuego. Acrylic on stucco, 10 by 15 feet. Twenty-first and Mission streets, San Francisco. © 1987 and 2002 (restored) by Juana Alicia.
© Juana Alicia

from family and friends, with scenes I witness in the world, and with the private struggles of the heart. All of my work is the product of many peoples, and an intimate experience all my own. The whisper of the charcoal as it brushes across paper; the easy, sensual glide of the paint as I stroke the wall with my brush; the warm, responsive way the clay bends to my touch: these are the physical delights of making my work.

The other satisfactions are harder to describe. I use the process of painting, drawing, and sculpting to resolve problems in my own life, to bear witness to the conflicts we are living through, and to propose resolutions for those struggles in dialogue with many other people facing the same challenges. Painting a mural is a tremendous opportunity and responsibility, no less than trying to create a monumental identity for a community through the skin, muscle, and bones of its architecture.

What interests me is not simply including multicultural faces and traditions in the same social tableaux, but instead expressing the vital, painful collective project in which we are engaged. I am always striving to reveal the hidden, or unofficial, narratives of our lives in the Americas and internationally. The Chicana/o mural, like African American blues or jazz, is a narrative full of the pain and sacrifice of a marginalized people who have played a crucial role in the struggle for democracy, social equality, and civil rights in the United States.

Once preoccupied with issues particular to Chicana/os, Latina/os, and Native Americans in America, our struggles have expanded from the farmworkers' movement and fights for equal education in urban American schools to include international liberation movements in Central America, South America, Africa, Asia, and the Middle East. We have also fought forces inside and outside our own communities, with people of many colors battling to be included in the women's movement or represented in the gay/lesbian/bisexual/transgender community. Through our large-scale murals, we can tell these stories, little-seen histories of women and of people of color that run counter to the mainstream images and stereotypes that advertising and mass media promote. These paintings are our cinema of the streets.

When I am actually making the work, I feel a sureness of purpose, a calling, the knowledge that this is what I came to this life to do. This in itself is an act of peacemaking, claiming a role that feels rich and fulfilling, doing work that feels meaningful. The right to do such work should be the goal of all who struggle for a world without war. So many potential young painters, composers, writers, actors, healers, dancers, and poets are dying in senseless wars, with no way to escape poverty apart from the military.

Our communities often suffer the casualties of these economic disadvantages most deeply, because our children pay with their lives for the affluence of the classes that exploit the lands and peoples where those wars are fought. I do my work in public places as an effort to prevent and heal those casualties.

Murals claim the space of both the public square and the human circle. Whether I am creating a mural that celebrates the flowering of human development in elders or the contributions women have made to the world, or conceiving a work about healing and diversity for an urban medical center, I am striving to bring the interior life of the community to the fabric of the environment, to promote a dialogue between members of diverse communities. I am hoping that this dialogue energizes the people who engage in it to know each other and to act for peace.

∽✺∽

"There is talk in Colombia about an armed revolution. But for us, revolutions are not made with weapons. *Revolution*: what does it mean? To renovate, to create, to invent. War was invented long ago, and so were weapons. There's nothing revolutionary about violence."

—Leonardo Jiménez

MAKING **A SCENE**

KATHRYN BLUME

Kathryn Blume is a cofounder of the Lysistrata Project, the first worldwide theatrical event for peace. She has toured *The Accidental Activist*—her critically acclaimed one-woman show about the Lysistrata Project—to more than twenty-five cities in the United States and Canada. Her new play, *Vanya/Vermont*, a modern adaptation of Anton Chekhov's *Uncle Vanya*, premieres at the Vermont Stage Company in 2005.

On March 3, 2003, hundreds of thousands of people in fifty-nine countries and all fifty U.S. states gathered together to read a play. They gathered in groups of twos and threes and tens and hundreds. They gathered in the streets, on boats and on subways, in parks, living rooms, bars, and restaurants. They gathered in jungles, in theaters, and on the Internet. Some met in secret, and others in the most public manner they could muster. Some of them

Houston CODEPINK women give Bush a "pink slip" while getting folks fired up to vote in Texas.
© 2004 by Scogin Mayo

were world-famous, A-list Hollywood actors, some were Broadway stars, and some had never picked up a script before in their lives.

The play they chose to read was *Lysistrata*, a twenty-five-hundred-year-old comedy about achieving peace by sexual boycott, and this event, the Lysistrata Project, protested the Bush administration's seemingly inexorable march toward war on Iraq.

When I ask myself the big questions—what are the causes of conflict? What are the roots of imperialism? What makes anyone think it's acceptable to hurt, maim, torture, or sacrifice others on the battlefields of war or commerce?—the most basic answers I can come up with, the most universal impediments to living a peaceful existence, are *too much fear* and *not enough compassion*.

Those are easy and understandable imbalances in our makeup. We all know what it's like to be afraid, to feel alone and disconnected, to fear we won't get enough of what we need in our lives. We all know what it's like to fear losing what we've got. And we all know what it's like to think of someone else as the "other," as not like us, not quite as human, not as vulnerable to pain or fear or loss. We know what it's like to see someone as deeply and insurmountably different—and therefore dangerous. We've all fallen into that trap: red states and blue states, radical fundamentalists and secular humanists, terrorists and . . . the rest of us.

The hardest work comes in remembering that while differences between us do exist, we are mostly the same. We share not only basic genetic patterns but also the same needs for food, water, shelter, safety, love, and meaning. Turn to the world's tales of spiritual growth, and they all describe enlightenment as the dissolution of the illusion of separateness.

We grow the roots of peace when people go from being "other" to being "us." I have a photograph, one of my favorite "other"-to-"us" examples, of a *Lysistrata* reading in Nikko, Japan. Look at twenty-five Japanese people sitting around the sanctuary of a Catholic church, reading an ancient Greek antiwar sex comedy, and you know the universality of human experience.

Another *Lysistrata* reading happened at a Kurdish refugee camp in an abandoned factory in Patras, Greece. None of the Greek architecture students who organized the reading had ever met the Kurds before. Nevertheless, in spite of language barriers, and in the face of a massive power outage, the performance generated tremendous intimacy among the participants. As one of the organizers wrote, "We could see our shadows in the white tent, and we could feel more the voices. . . . We talked in ancient Greek (text), Greek (text and dialogues), some English, and Kurdish (through spontaneous translations). We also talked a lot with our eyes, our movement, and our body. We drank tea."

I love how the ritual of theater generates a safe space, a well-bounded sanctuary for the actors and audience to share stories and unguarded, authentic emotional experiences. Many Lysistrata Project participants hadn't felt comfortable writing letters or joining marches, but they were happy to get up in front of their communities and wave a giant balloon or vegetable phallus to protest the war. And the audience members, by their very presence, were active partners in that protest.

The theatrical experience helps us drop our personal defenses to watch live human beings, right there in front of us, trying like hell to connect with one another. And most of the time, we cannot help but identify with what we see. We notice characters who remind us of ourselves and the people in our lives, and we instinctively ask ourselves the question, What would I do if I were in that situation?

In the Lysistrata Project, what inspired us was a fictional tale of strangers coming together with chutzpah and creativity to solve the intractable problem of the (all too real) Peloponnesian War. Therein lies what may be theater's greatest value: the ability to enact what is, but then to stride into the lands of imagination, the realms of the possible—the infinitely possible. Through theater, we can model new worlds. We can dream them up, act them out, make them live and breathe, and render vivid and true ideas that only a moment before were daydreams of maybe-perhaps-someday.

That's the work—what playwright Tony Kushner calls "the great work": coming together, revealing our common humanity, opening hearts, modeling new possibilities. Hopefully, through that work, we can make the world a little less lonely, a little less scared, and a little more prone to peace.

∽o∾

"What struck me was that people all over this country and in England really want peace. And they are very upset—no, it's not upset. What is it? It's like despair: What are we going to do?... And I found CODEPINK women everywhere in my audiences. I would walk in thinking, Gosh, I'm really alone here, but I'd look up and there they were, the CODEPINK women with their boas and their pink shirts!"

—from an interview with Maxine Hong Kingston

THE NEW AMERICA

CYNTHIA MCKINNEY

Georgia's first African American Congresswoman and the only woman serving in the state's congressional delegation, Cynthia McKinney has emerged as an internationally renowned advocate for voting rights, human rights, and the strengthening of business ties between Africa and the United States. This essay is based on a talk at the UC Berkeley's African Studies Department graduation ceremony on May 17, 2003.

Consider the current state of America. Under President Bush, the United States has turned its back on the United Nations and the entire international community and has waged war in Afghanistan and Iraq; more potential conflicts are threatened with nations like Iran, Syria, North Korea, and even China. Here at home, unemployment is rising, our economy is on its knees, and our national debt is threatening to reach unprecedented levels. The word *deflation* is whispered by many economists.

More families than ever before try to relieve the mounting pressure by depleting their savings and falling deeper in debt. Yet, the president advocates more tax cuts, not for poor America, but for the rich.

One million black children now live in poverty, and one million black men and women are in prison. Every night on the streets of America, over a quarter million veterans sleep as our forgotten homeless.

Special interests have taken control of our nation's capital and are perverting it from the noble traditions of Washington, Jefferson, Lincoln, and Kennedy, and instead are using our precious national resources for personal profit and personal needs.

In 1953 Dwight Eisenhower warned of failing to address the pressing social needs of the nation in deference to an uncontrolled arms buildup. He said:

> Every gun that is made, every warship launched, every rocket fired, signifies in the final sense a theft from those who hunger and are not fed, those who are cold and are not clothed. This world in arms is not spending money alone. It is spending the sweat of its laborers, the genius of its scientists, the hopes of its children. This is not a way of life at all in any true sense. Under the clouds of war, it is humanity hanging on a cross of iron.

We cannot plunge our country, which we all love, and the world that we all live in, into a never-ending cycle of war and violence and hate.

The unique American character, the values that we struggled so hard for and won in the civil rights movements of blacks, women, and gays—everything we hold dear to us—are all being threatened today by a small but powerful group who want to silence the people, yet speak and act for them.

Our president tells us that we are now engaged in a war that will last for the rest of my life. He says that for the next generation or more, we Americans must be prepared to fight any foe who is inclined to harm us. And for the Bush administration, that means conflicts with some sixty nations of the world. He says that we must be prepared to invoke this Bush Doctrine of preemptive strike and regime change whenever and wherever we need it. And his secretary of defense, Donald Rumsfeld, tells us that our military must be prepared to seize foreign capitals and occupy them.

To accomplish this, according to the administration, we will need a larger military. That military must have usable nuclear weapons, and the billions it will take to deploy a national missile defense must be spent. In addition, some in the administration insist that our military must control space and cyberspace and that advanced technologies must be utilized for military applications. The Bush administration has a blueprint for the world that will be of its making. But as an American, it will be done with your blessing—and in your name.

For the first time since the founding of our country, our nation's foreign-policy blueprint calls for global military domination—an "American Century." In his speech at American University on June 10, 1963, John F. Kennedy spoke of seeking genuine peace, "not a Pax Americana enforced on the world by American weapons of war, not the peace of the grave or the security of the slave." George Washington, a century earlier, recommended that the United States conduct its foreign policy as "our interest, guided by our justice," directs. He cautioned against passionate attachments to foreign countries and warned against militarism. Yet the very priorities outlined by the current advisers to our current president go against the very cautions and concerns that both George Washington and John F. Kennedy expressed.

What can we do? How can we navigate with conscience a terrain littered with the remains of those who sacrificed themselves before us, but who now seem like a distant memory? We can steep ourselves in the intergenerational dialogue that allows us all to be students in wonderment of how much we can accomplish when we love one another, stand up for one another, defy conventional wisdom with one another. A new possibility can be created. The war machine must stop now.

We've seen it happen before. From the Africans who passed through that portal of no return, to the Maroons who escaped slavery high in the Jamaican mountains, to the workers on the South American *latifundias*. Our story has been written by our resistance.

College students in Greensboro, North Carolina, wrote the page on sit-ins at lunch counters across the South; they all contributed to the passage of the Civil Rights Act. Young black children facing dogs and fire hoses began the chapter on harassment, threats, intimidation, and death; four little girls blown to bits in church don't even end that chapter. Agitation for the right to vote contributed to the passage of the Voting Rights Act. Just imagine what America would have been like if Sojourner Truth hadn't journeyed across America and told the truth! Suppose Fannie Lou Hamer had gotten sick and tired of being sick and tired and just left the movement to someone else?

Who among you will step forward and continue the struggle against injustice? And if no one is willing to do it, what kind of America will our children inherit?

The new America that is being made right now.

∾⦵∾

"The future belongs to those who believe in the beauty of their dreams."
—Eleanor Roosevelt

TO THE
NEXT GENERATION
OF PEACEMAKERS

ADRIENNE MAREE BROWN

Adrienne Maree Brown is a writer, pleasure activist, and singer living in Brooklyn, NY. She is coeditor of *How to Get Stupid White Men Out of Office* (available at www.indy voter.org). During the day she is the program director of the League of Young Voters, a national nonprofit voter-organizer-training organization.

If Churchill was right, and the power of the heart gives in to the cold calculations of the mind with age, then those who are young must beat now, while their hearts still know how. Rarely do young people start wars, but often they must carry the burdens, the shame and guilt of the struggle, long after it is over. But you must understand—war isn't something any of us merely inherit, even if a conflict is well under way when we come of age; we play our own part, either exacerbating or impeding it. We must battle back.

How? Begin by developing a revolutionary analysis. Challenge yourself to imagine the world without superpowers, without profit-driven education and health care, without advertisement-based media. Create your own sacred vision, and make your mind a home for your revolutionary dream.

Next, holding tight to this dream, wake up a realist. Who could you elect into what positions who would help realize your revolutionary dream? Some argue that we can't work within the current political system—that we must

Music vs. Military. Linocut.
© Eric Drooker/www.drooker.com

reject it, wholesale, or otherwise be trapped in a negative, reactive process. But on some level, I think, we must acknowledge when we are backed into a corner and we must learn with our hands the shape and walls of our corner in order to break free from it. You must understand your prison, the system, to change it and escape it. Don't give up on your radical dream; instead, actively promote it with each word, each action, each vote.

Question everything. Trust no one's rhetoric, even mine—we all want to be believed. With a loving heart, be critical of those who would presume to lead you. Make your own voice heard in letters to the editor and on the airwaves.

Don't be active only in election years—the stage for war is set in the years when we're not watching. Involve yourself in the politics of every day. Stand up for human rights today, tomorrow, and the day after that. Don't buy the coffee that builds walls through Palestine. Don't buy the shirts that bear the blood of weary fingers. Don't travel with the oil our brothers died to steal. Don't fund wars. If you truly want peace, you must invest in it. Research where you spend your money and where your schools spend their money, and fight to pull resources out of the war effort.

Remember that war is not only the dropping of bombs, though we do that. War is not only the torturing of prisoners, though we do that. War is also the daily oppression of people through prisons and poverty. If your luxury demands war on other nations or the oppression of people on the other side of the world, live a simpler life. Do everything you can not to be indulgent at the expense of other people's lives.

To generate power for peace, run for office, or donate to community candidates so they can afford to run. Fill some of the less-glamorous roles in your local government—sheriff, school board member, city council representative. Vote in every possible election. Then pay attention to whether your representatives are acting on your community's behalf; organize policy watchdog teams and make your elected officials accountable for their decisions. Seek out alternative media and donate to it. Make peace a constant part of your life and your world. Seek out mentors for living in peace and learn from them. Be completely engaged.

Have a revolutionary dream and then wake up with strategies to stake a claim on the power you need to realize that dream. It is not an option, as a human aware of the beauty and ills of this world of ours, to sleep.

∽o∾

"Life is a tragedy for those who feel, and a comedy for those who think. It is vital to mourn for the victims of this government but not at the expense of losing our sense of humor. Our ability to laugh coincides directly with our ability to fight. If we can make fun of it, we can transcend it."

—Margaret Cho

THE OPPORTUNITY
OF IMPRISONMENT

SHARON SALZBERG

Sharon Salzberg is one of America's leading spiritual teachers and writers. Her latest book is *Faith*. Her work has been included in *Meetings with Remarkable Women, Gifts of the Spirit, A Complete Guide to Buddhist America, Handbook of the Heart, The Best Guide to Meditation*, and most recently, *From the Ashes*. The following piece is adapted from *A Heart as Wide as the World* by Sharon Salzberg.

In 1989 Aung San Suu Kyi, leader of the prodemocracy movement in Burma, was placed under house arrest for her political activities. At the time of her arrest, Suu Kyi's sons were only twelve and sixteen, and it would be years before she was able to see them again. It took more than two years before she was even able to see her husband. By 1991, the same year she received the Nobel Peace Prize, Suu Kyi was still a prisoner.

Describing her years of imprisonment, Suu Kyi wrote, "I refused to accept anything from the military. Sometimes I didn't even have enough money to eat. I became so weak from malnourishment that my hair fell out, and I couldn't get out of bed." Despite the depth of her suffering, this awakened warrior later said, "When I compared notes with my colleagues in the democracy movement in Burma who have suffered long terms of imprisonment, we found that an enhanced appreciation of *metta* (lovingkindness) was a common experience. We had known and felt both the effects of *metta* and the unwholesomeness of natures lacking in *metta*."

How remarkable to be separated from your family, to face hunger and fear, and yet be able to view the ordeal in terms of an enhanced appreciation of lovingkindness. During her imprisonment, Suu Kyi did not have food and money, but she did have *metta*, and she did have her spiritual practice. I have talked both to people imprisoned by their bodies, who are in long-term chronic pain, and to people who have been held hostage in some way by an unsympathetic person or uncaring system. Years ago in South Africa, I talked to people who shockingly asked about the efficacy of the practice of spirituality in facing torture. I've known many people deeply, horribly afraid of someone or something in their lives. I myself have felt completely out of control at times, sitting in a doctor's office, waiting to see how my own life and death could turn on a dime.

It is tremendously inspiring for me to see someone whose situation is frightening and full of personal loss, and who yet remains steadfast in the values of her spiritual practice while accomplishing what she feels needs to be done. Qualities like *metta* allow us to remember what our efforts for freedom are fundamentally about: to remember the light in this life and in this world. Suu Kyi has said, "The spiritual dimension becomes particularly important in a struggle in which deeply held convictions and strength of mind are the chief weapons against armed repression."

About a year after Aung San Suu Kyi's release from house arrest, the State Law and Order Restoration Council, also known as SLORC, made sweeping arrests of members of her political party. Outside her Rangoon home, Suu Kyi told a crowd of about ten thousand that her party would not bend to pressure from the military government but would push ahead toward its goal of democracy for Burma. Rumors rapidly spread of SLORC's intention to re-arrest her. Suu Kyi's response was, "It will be an opportunity to strengthen my spiritual life."

How could the threat of reimprisonment not make her waver from her goal for others or herself? Instead of giving up, returning to her family, and leaving the country, she made this statement: "SLORC doesn't understand how helpful my years of house arrest were to me. If I'm arrested, we'll go forward. If I'm not arrested, we'll go forward." Aung San Suu Kyi remains essentially free, even when she is imprisoned. For she knows this, and we must know it too when we face imprisoning conditions in our own lives: whether we are imprisoned or not, if we follow the tenets of lovingkindness, we will know what it means to be free.

❧❦

"Hope is the dream whose time has come, whose dance is
already real—even if some of us cannot hear the music."

—Sister Joan Chittister

❧ WE ARE THE DECISIVE ELEMENT ❦

I have come to the frightening conclusion that I am the decisive element.
It is my personal approach that creates the climate.
It is my daily mood that makes the weather.
I possess tremendous power to make life miserable or joyous.
I can be a tool of torture or an instrument of inspiration.
I can humiliate or humor, hurt or heal.
In all situations, it is my response that decides whether a crisis is escalated
    or de-escalated, and a person is humanized or dehumanized.
If we treat people as they are, we make them worse.
If we treat people as they ought to be, we help them become what they are
    capable of becoming.

—JOHANN WOLFGANG VON GOETHE, 1749–1832

AFTERWORD:
WHAT YOU CAN DO TO HELP PREVENT THE NEXT WAR

MEDEA BENJAMIN

The world we want to see, one in which nonviolent solutions to conflicts are sought and all people are treated as brothers and sisters, is far from the one we have today. Here are ten actions you can take to move us closer to a world free of terrorism and war:

1. **Educate yourself on the issues.** One key prerequisite for stopping war is to have an educated citizenry. That means you and me. Make a commitment to learning more about a part of the world or a country that has an antagonistic relationship with the U.S. government, such as Cuba, Iran, Iraq, North Korea, or Syria. Learn about the history, culture, language, religion, and values of that society. The more we understand, appreciate, and humanize people we are taught to see as enemies, the harder it is for our government to persuade us to fight them.

2. **Demand truthful media.** The media is the voice of democracy. Without a truthful, diverse media, democracy is squelched. Pressure the mainstream media to cover events fairly and to be an outlet for a true variety of voices. Give your local media a list of peace "experts" they should turn to. Complain, call, write, or organize a protest when the coverage is skewed toward war. Support independent news outlets that provide critical information and alternative viewpoints, and encourage others to do the same.

3. **Communicate!** After you educate yourself, don't be afraid to speak out. Talk with your neighbors, friends, relatives, co-workers, classmates. Talk to people outside the choir and learn from people you disagree with. Call radio and television talk shows, including the conservative ones. Write letters to the editor and opinion articles for your local newspaper. The only way to become an effective communicator is to practice communicating, just as the only way to become an effective writer is to write.

4. **Hold your leaders accountable.** Whether or not you voted for your city council member or your congressperson, elected officials are civil servants who are supposed to represent you—so pressure them to do so. Develop a

relationship with your local representatives, setting up regular meetings between them and your allies in the community. When they take bad positions, like supporting the war in Iraq, make sure they hear from you loud and clear. And if they consistently take bad positions, support alternative candidates.

5. Help the United States kick our oil addiction. U.S. policy in the Middle East and other regions is conditioned by our dependence on foreign oil. It ties us to repressive regimes (Saudi Arabia) and encourages wars for oil (Iraq). A good first step is to cut down on your own oil consumption. Use public transportation, ride a bike, drive fuel-efficient cars, make your home and workplace more energy efficient. Volunteer with a group in your community that's promoting local and statewide initiatives to decrease oil consumption, and join national campaigns like the Apollo Alliance (www.apolloalliance.org).

6. Build the peace movement. The massive outpouring of antiwar sentiment before the U.S. invasion of Iraq showed that there is a wellspring of support for our cause. It just has to be tapped. Join a local group that speaks to you. Go to teach-ins, speak-outs, and marches. Learn from them and help organize new ones that reach out to broader sectors of the community.

Make sure you're connected nationally by joining the Listserve of the largest antiwar coalition in the country, United for Peace and Justice (www.united forpeace.org).

7. Support members of the military who are speaking out. Support military families who are speaking out against the war, and soldiers who are speaking out and refusing to fight. Two excellent groups are Military Families Speak Out (www.mfso.org) and Veterans against the Iraq War (www. vaiw.net). We also need to support counter-recruitment efforts that provide young people with a truthful picture of the risks of joining the military and of their other options. See www.objector.org for a list of counter-recruitment and support groups for soldiers (including a GI rights hotline).

8. Protect our civil liberties and oppose the backlash against immigrants. If we're going to stop new wars, we've got to be able to speak freely and organize without government interference. Unfortunately, after 9/11, some of our basic freedoms enshrined in our Bill of Rights are being eroded. Be a community watchdog ready to speak out against repressive measures, from new INS and Justice Department regulations to local police behavior and cases of bigotry. Oppose bills such as the USA Patriot Act that erode our basic rights. Join civil liberties groups such as the ACLU (www.aclu.org) and the Center for Constitutional Rights (www.ccr-ny.org). Remember, when civil liberties are taken away in an emergency, they're rarely restored afterward; and when constitutional rights are denied to any one group, you could be next.

9. Support the creation of a Department of Peace. We now have a huge, bloated, overactive Department of "Defense," but where is the government body dedicated to preventing war and violence? Thanks to U.S. representative Dennis Kucinich, there is a piece of legislation in Congress that would create a Department of Peace. Domestically, the department would address issues such as domestic violence, child abuse, and mistreatment of the elderly. Internationally, it would advise the president on addressing the root causes of war and interventions that can be taken before violence begins. Go to the Web site www.dopcampaign.org to learn the status of current legislation and how you can support the bill.

10. Teach peace. It is easy to teach children about war; it is much more challenging to teach them how to create peace. Encourage your public schools and libraries to carry peace curricula and create "peace places" in schools. For ideas contact Educators for Social Responsibility (www.esrnational.org), the National Peace Foundation (www.nationalpeace.org), or the Alliance for Childhood (www.allianceforchildhood.net). Help young people find active ways of working for peace and justice through organizations like Kids Can Make a Difference (www.kidscanmakeadifference.org), Free the Children (www.freethechildren.org), or PeaceJam (www.peacejam.org), through which students work directly with Nobel Peace Prize laureates.

The struggle to end war will be the culmination of a global movement that rejects violence on the part of individuals, terrorist groups, and nation-states. That's why your contribution, however big or small, makes a difference. With patience, energy, and determination, keep your eyes on the prize: a world that thrives in peace.

To get involved, contact CODEPINK at info@codepinkalert.org or www.code-pinkalert.org

ACKNOWLEDGMENTS

In putting this book together, we were nurtured by a host of wonderful friends, colleagues, and family members.

CODEPINK cofounder Gael Murphy conducted several of the interviews and gave invaluable feedback, and our awesome coordinator Dana Balicki acted as both drill sergeant and midwife who saw this book through its birthing process.

Many talented volunteers gave freely of their time and energy, including Mary Arno, Sara Bella, Brooke Biggs, Chuck Blitz, Trisha Boreta, Lane Browning, Andrea Buffa, Shelley Buschur, Claire Cooke, Patricia Dowd, Claire Droney, Hoda Fahimi, Dana and Lisa Fredsti, Pat Garrison, Lucie Gikovich, Susan Griffin, Shannon Kindle, Melody Lee, Robyn Lee, Nancy "Hallie" Mancias, Heather McArthur, Eileen McCabe-Olsen, Deena Metzger, Linda Milazzo, Seyoum Michaels, Carol Norris, Kelly Nuxol, Panha Ouch, Pilar Perez, Lindsay Pinkham, Erica Pitkow, Lizzy Sandoval, Cissy Sims, Gail Smallridge, Alice Slater, Whitney Stone, Shana Winokur, and Saria Young. A special godsend was sixteen-year-old intern Max Lavine, who turned out to be a stellar researcher.

We are indebted to Anthony Arnove and Mahnaz Isphahani for helping us communicate with Arundhati Roy and Benazir Bhutto, respectively. Dr. Nayereh Tohidi for her assistance in communicating with Dr. Shirin Ebadi. We owe much to Fred Askew for the amazing photos and his commitment to documenting the peace movement. This book would not have been possible without the support of Connect U.S.

We would have ended up with a thousand-page tome had it not been for our wonderful editors, especially Jan Richman, Julia Scott, and Valerie Sinzdak. At Inner Ocean, Karen Bouris was the most awesome publisher we could have hoped for. Her vision, passion, and thoughtfulness were a constant source of nourishment. And kudos to Alma Bune for always keeping us on track.

Medea's family—Kevin, Maya, Arlen, Alvin, and Debbie—kept her grounded and inspired, as did Kirsten Moller and the rest of Medea's extended family who make up the staff of Global Exchange. As always, Jodie's sons—Matthew and Jasiu—and Max Palevsky gave bountiful love, support, and encouragement.

Finally, we acknowledge our CODEPINK sisters and brothers, whose time, energy, and creativity never cease to astound us. Among those who were particularly supportive of this book are Susan Adelman, Elaine Broadhead, Susan Clark, Paulette Cole, Donna Deitch, Adelaide Gomer, Marion Greene, Nancy Kricorian, Dal LaMagna, Lara Lee, Bokara Legendre, Sara Lovell, Sarah Rath, Bonnie Rubenstein, Nancy Schaub, Anas Shallal, Barbra Streisand, Jade Tree Two, B. Wardlaw, Judy Wicks, and the Women's Foundation. And then there's the heart of CODEPINK, the forty thousand activists around the world who respond to our alerts and hit the streets in their vibrant pink. We are indebted to you all!

COPYRIGHT NOTICES

"Do Turkeys Enjoy Thanksgiving?" by Arundhati Roy. Excerpted with permission from a speech delivered at the World Social Forum in Mumbai, India, January 16, 2004, and published in *An Ordinary Person's Guide to Empire* (Cambridge: South End Press, 2004) 83–94. Copyright © 2004 by Arundhati Roy.

"Colombian Women Create a Path to Peace" produced by the American Friends Service Committee and the Fellowship of Reconciliation. Excerpted with permission from a pamphlet *Building from the Inside Out: Peace Initiatives in War-Torn Colombia.*

"Building a Just and Caring World" by Riane Eisler. A different version of this essay appeared in *Tikkun*, May-June 1998. Copyright © 2005 by Riane Eisler.

"The Challenge of Educating for Peace" by Joan Almon. Copyright © 2005 by the Alliance for Childhood. All rights reserved. Reprinted with permission.

"Dark Enough to See the Stars" by Catherine Ingram. Adapted from *In the Footsteps of Gandhi* by Catherine Ingram (Berkeley, CA: Parallax Press, 1990). Copyright © 1990 by Catherine Ingram. Reprinted by permission of the author and publisher.

"The Mind Can Be a Prison or a Door" by Susan Griffin. Copyright © 2005 by Susan Griffin.

"A Mother's Plea" by Nurit Peled-Elhanan. Adapted with permission from a speech delivered at the Israel-Palestine Day of Engagement at the ICA London in July 2002. The opening and closing paragraphs come from a speech delivered at the European Social Forum Convention in London in October 2004.

"What We Expect from America" by Mary Robinson. This essay appeared in slightly different form in *The American Prospect*, Volume 15, Number 10: October 1, 2004. Copyright © 2005 by The American Prospect, Inc. Reprinted by permission of the author.

"Heading into the Cave with a Torch" by Katrina vanden Heuvel. Adapted with permission from a talk originally given in New York City, at the New York Town Hall with the Dalai Lama, September 23, 2003. Copyright © 2003 by Katrina vanden Heuvel.

"Ending the Nuclear Crisis: A Prescription for Survival" by Helen Caldicott. Excerpted with permission from an interview transcribed by Julia Scott that took place on Chicago Public Radio's *World View* on October 12, 2004.

"Armies for Peace" by Gar Smith. First published as "Live from Iraq" in *Common Ground* in June 2004. Copyright © 2004 Gar Smith. Reprinted by permission of the author.

"Bring Halliburton Home" by Naomi Klein. First published in the *Nation* magazine, November 24, 2003. Copyright © 2003 by Naomi Klein. Reprinted by permission from the author.

"Ending Poverty, Ending Terrorism" by Benazir Bhutto. First published in the *Guardian*, August 9, 2004. Adapted with permission from "Without a War on Poverty, We Will Never Defeat Terror Dictatorship and Religious Extremism Fueled by Gross Inequality." Copyright © 2004 by Benazir Bhutto.

"The Cracked Mirror" by Wangari Maathai. Excerpted with permission from *Resurgence* magazine, November/December 2004; and from a speech by Professor Maathai on the occasion of receiving the Nobel Peace Prize.

"Planet Called Home" by Holly Near. Copyright © 1999 Hereford Music (ASCAP). Reprinted by permission of the author.

"The New America" by Cynthia McKinney. Based on a talk originally given in Berkeley, California, at the UC Berkeley's African Studies Department graduation ceremony on May 17, 2003. Copyright © 2003 by Cynthia McKinney. Reprinted by permission.

"The Opportunity of Imprisonment" by Sharon Salzberg. Adapted from "Finding Freedom in Imprisonment" in *A Heart as Wide as the World* (Boston, MA: Shambhala Publications, 1997). Copyright ©1997 by Sharon Salzberg. Reprinted by permission of the publisher.

ABOUT THE EDITORS

Medea (right) and Jodie (left) on the Jordan/Iraq border in January 2005.
Photo by Matthew Palevsky

MEDEA BENJAMIN is the founding director of Global Exchange and cofounded CODEPINK with Jodie Evans. She also helped bring together the groups forming United for Peace and Justice.

Medea has traveled several times to Afghanistan and Iraq, where she organized the Occupation Watch Center. At the start of 2005 she accompanied military families whose loved ones had been killed in the war to bring a shipment of humanitarian aid to the Iraqi people.

In 2000, she was the Green Party candidate for the U.S. Senate from California. Her campaign mobilized thousands of Californians around issues such as paying workers a living wage, providing universal health care, and building schools, not prisons.

Medea is a key figure in the anti-sweatshop movement, having spearheaded campaigns against companies such as Nike and Gap. In 1999, Medea helped expose indentured servitude among garment workers in the U.S. territory of Saipan, which led to a billion-dollar lawsuit against seventeen retailers.

She is the author or coauthor of eight books, including the award-winning *Don't Be Afraid, Gringo*, and helped produce TV documentaries such as *Sweating for a T-Shirt*.

With master's degrees in public health and economics, Medea worked for ten years as an economist and nutritionist in Latin America and Africa for various international agencies. She lives in San Francisco with her husband and two daughters.

JODIE EVANS has worked on behalf of community, social-justice, environmental, and political causes for more than thirty years. Her book, *Twilight of*

Empire: Responses to Occupation includes her journal entries from trips to Iraq.

Jodie cocreated the first Dubrovnik Peace Conference in June 2000 and produced Shadow Conventions 2000, held in parallel to the Republican and Democratic national conventions. Every three years she coproduces the World Festival of Sacred Music, and in 1998 she produced the documentary *Stripped and Teased: Tales of Las Vegas Women*.

From 1973 to 1982, Jodie worked on the campaigns of California governor Jerry Brown and served as his director of administration. She also oversaw the Office of Appropriate Technology, ushering in breakthroughs in wind and solar energy. Between 1985 and 1990, she supported women candidates for federal office as a board member of the Women's Campaign Fund and Women's Political Committee. She ran Jerry Brown's campaign for president in 1991.

In the early 1990s Jodie opened the first environmental department store, Terra Verde, along with Tom Hayden and Cathryn Tiddens.

Jodie serves on the boards of Rainforest Action Network, Dads and Daughters, Drug Policy Alliance, Bioneers, the Garden Project, Community Self-Determination Institute, 826 LA, and the Circle of Life Foundation.

A mother of three, Jodie is a harpist, gardener, and potter when not working to end war.

ABOUT CODEPINK:
WOMEN FOR PEACE

We call on women around the world to rise up and oppose war. We call on mothers, grandmothers, sisters, and daughters, on workers, students, teachers, healers, artists, writers, singers, poets, and every ordinary outraged woman willing to be outrageous for peace. Women have been the guardians of life—not because we are better or purer or more innately nurturing than men, but because the men have busied themselves making war. Because of our responsibility to the next generation, because of our own love for our families and communities and this country that we are a part of, we call on all peace loving women—and men—to join us in building an outrageous, unreasonable, unstoppable movement for peace.

CODEPINK: Women for Peace is a dynamic women-led grassroots peace and social-justice movement where political savvy meets creative protest and nonviolent direct action. Medea Benjamin, Jodie Evans, Starhawk, Diane Wilson, and approximately one hundred other women kicked off CODEPINK on November 17, 2002. They marched through the streets of Washington, D.C., and set up a four-month vigil in front of the White House. Every day through March 8, 2003, International Women's Day, CODEPINK held a day-long peace vigil in front of the White House, inspiring people from all walks of life and from all over the country to stand for peace. Beginning March 8, CODEPINK celebrated women as global peacemakers with a week of activities, concluding with a rally and march with ten thousand people encircling the White House in pink.

CODEPINK can be found at presidential speeches and in the halls of Congress, in the neighborhoods of Baghdad and the streets of Manhattan—vigiling, chanting, protesting, and making peace wherever peace needs making. In addition to conducting these peaceful protest activities, CODEPINK was one of the only international groups getting humanitarian aid to the war-terrorized people of Iraq in 2004 and 2005, and it raised more than $600,000 for victims of the 2004 assault on Fallujah. CODEPINK has also traveled to Iraq and Afghanistan, bringing together families who have lost sons and daughters, husbands and wives, to share their grief. In 2005, CODEPINK will be working on ending the occupation of Iraq and preventing wars in Iran, Syria, or anywhere else.

CODEPINK now has over one hundred local chapters all over the country—and several overseas. We send out weekly action ideas to a list of some fifty thousand supporters.

> We call on all outraged women to join us in taking a stand now. And we call upon our brothers to join and support us. Engage in outrageous acts of dissent. Get active and get effective. Throw on your most powerful pink clothes and join us for the most fun you'll ever have working to make our world a more just, peaceful place. Check our site often at www.codepinkalert.org for updated actions and events to see how you can get active with CODEPINK in the days, weeks, and months ahead. Peace.

CODEPINK
2010 Linden Ave
Venice, CA 90291
310-827-4320
info@codepinkalert.org
www.codepinkalert.org

ALSO AVAILABLE FROM INNER OCEAN PUBLISHING

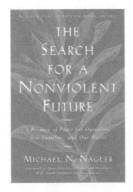

THE SEARCH FOR A
NONVIOLENT FUTURE
A Promise of Peace for Ourselves
Our Families and Our World
Michael N. Nagler

MoveOn's
50 WAYS TO LOVE
LOVE YOUR COUNTRY
How to Find Your Political Voice
and Become a Catalyst for Change
MoveOn.org

50 WAYS TO SUPPORT
LESBIAN & GAY EQUALITY
The Complete Guide to Supporting
Family, Neighbors—or Yourself
Meredith Maran with
Angela Watrous

50 WAYS TO IMPROVE
WOMEN'S LIVES
The Essential Women's Guide
for Achieving Health,
Equality, and Success
National Council of
Women's Organizations

To order call toll-free at 866.731.2216 or email: sales@innerocean.com.
For more information on our books and to sign up for Inner Ocean's
monthly e-newsletter, *Making Waves,* visit **www.innerocean.com**.